HOPE

To Craig MacBean –
with a deep sense
of community –

Richard Meryn

RICHARD MERYMAN

HOPE
A Loss Survived

Little, Brown and Company   Boston Toronto

FIRST EDITION

LIBRARY OF CONGRESS CATALOGING IN PUBLICATION DATA

Meryman, Richard, 1926–
  Hope: a loss survived.

  1. Melanoma — Patients — Biography. 2. Meryman, Hope.
I. Title.
RC280.S5M43   362.1'96994   80–18440
ISBN 0–316–56786–8

MV
Designed by Susan Windheim
Published simultaneously in Canada
by Little, Brown & Company (Canada) Limited
PRINTED IN THE UNITED STATES OF AMERICA

To Meredith and Helena

Acknowledgments

Writing this book was an awesome undertaking. The faith and guidance of Robert Ginna and Fredrica Friedman were essential, and I am deeply grateful for the support of my friends, who were unhesitatingly generous with their time and feelings, resurrecting even the most painful memories.

HOPE

Prologue

There is a train of thought that keeps returning to my mind. I look at my two daughters — they are now twelve and fourteen — and I think about all the living that lies ahead of them. I wonder how I can possibly nudge them toward a capacity for joy, or even the experience of joy, so they will always recognize it. Then I wonder about love. That's even harder. Will they have it in their lives, or just hunt for it? Tricky things, love and joy — massive, subtle, and tenuous all at once. Next, my mind takes me into sorrow. I reflect that I will never have to instruct those girls about pain.

Then there comes that familiar clenching in my chest. I am assaulted by my feelings — simultaneous and tumbled, awful and wonderful. One particular set of memories is almost always there, flashbacks that mark both an end and the beginning.

From the start of our twenty-one-year marriage, Hope and I had fed our romantic fantasies with talk of renting a house in France. Finally in 1973 it was possible. My twenty-three years on *Life* magazine as a reporter, writer, editor, had ended abruptly with the suspension of publication in 1972. I began writing a biography of Herman Mankiewicz, an Algonquin Round Table wit and rambunctious Hollywood screenwriter whose best-known credit was *Citizen Kane*. Research aside, it was a movable labor. So with our two little girls, Meredith and Helena, and Hope's younger sister, Whitney, and her family, we rented a house for July in the tiny hamlet of La Honce, near Biarritz on the Atlantic Ocean. Rising at six in the morning, I worked until noon and then joined the two families for the afternoon's outing. On the twenty-sixth of July I broke away for a full day. Whitney took care of Meredith and Helena while Hope and I drove alone into nearby Spain for our self-promised idyll.

As excited as truants, we slipped early from the sleeping house, reveling in the prospect of an utterly indulgent day ahead of us. Thirty miles into Spain at San Sebastián we stopped for breakfast at a snack bar beside a long swimming beach. We were the first customers, and sat unhurried, eating little ham sandwiches and sipping cups of *café negro*. The view from our table was as gala as our mood, a festive canvas city of triangular, blue-and-white-striped changing tents. Hope smiled full at me, and suddenly I was moved by this moment, perhaps because after twenty-one years of marriage we often tended to face out from each other toward the world. Looking across the table at Hope, the coffee sweet and strong on my tongue, I felt my heart lift toward her. I thought how dear and beautiful she was — at forty-three a freckled Katharine Hepburn look-alike — prodigal, red-auburn hair bunched above her slender neck, responsive hazel eyes behind oval, tortoiseshell glasses forever sliding down her nose. And that smile — an explosion of teeth. She called them *les dentelles de perle;* I called them "the keyboard."

Smiling back into her eyes, I reached out in a familiar signal of tenderness, and gently touched the oval of her cheek with the back of my hand. I felt passing between us the binding sum of two decades of intimacy, the tacit agreement that though we had at times failed each other, and would do so again, our affection was far deeper than any disappointment. Hope took off her eyeglasses. She always felt they spoiled her looks. "I love you," I said — and then, "God, these sandwiches are tiny. I'm going to have another."

Driving south toward Zarauz our mood of the snack bar continued. Hope and I laughed at the sooty ugliness of the industrial suburbs of San Sebastián, but then were thrilled by the open countryside — plowed brown fields prickly with sinuous rows of bean poles — a frieze of delicate trees on a high ridge, feathery against towering clouds. All our travels together were painting trips for Hope, a watercolorist and printmaker, and in Zarauz she decided to paint a medieval church belfry. Soon she was seated on the curb across from the church, her feet in the gutter, her old peanut jar of water and her plastic paint tray on the sidewalk. A large sheet of paper rested on the portfolio across her hunched knees. I watched her familiar routine. She would swoosh the brush in the water, twirl the bristles into a fine point between her lips, roll them in the paint, look up at the subject — unconsciously wrinkling her nose under her glasses — and make a brushstroke on the paper. I adored the little grimace — the intensity was classic Hope — but I often begged her to keep the brushes out of her mouth. She always ignored me.

On an excursion like this, I was relieved when Hope had her first picture under way. Until that moment I suffered a vague feeling of suspense, an unease, because I knew that our day, no matter how pleasurable and affectionate, would be a disappointment to her unless there were pictures to show for it. Hope's work, her talent, were at the center of her life. In the past fifteen years, through sheer commitment, she had evolved from a crude amateur to a successful professional, selling her work in shows and galleries.

I was very proud of her, and fascinated that this creator of strong realistic images was also a bemusingly impractical woman full of idiosyncrasies. For good luck she left the price tags on all her sweaters. She spoke a personal vocabulary — "flange" meant limp and relaxed; earth colors were "beasly"; something distasteful was "plutty" or "crippingy." A Collier brother of keepsakes, she accumulated boxes and bundles of recipes and souvenirs: the Sienese box on her bureau contained Meredith's ivory teething rattle, earrings I bought her in Mexico during our courtship, a Polaroid test picture for a *Life* cover of Mae West, and British National Theatre ticket stubs for *Long Day's Journey into Night*. Convinced she was saving money, she bought the shortest tube of toothpaste, the smallest bottle of aspirin, the littlest jar of mayonnaise. Anything at all to do with mechanics bored her: when her wooden paint box split at the hinge, she cinched a strap around it and never bought a new one, though the box came apart every time she opened it. Inside the box was always a chocolate bar, which she insisted, eyes twinkling, was good for headaches.

After she had painted for an hour while I strolled about Zarauz, we poked on down the coast to Quétaria, an ancient fishing village built on the steep slopes of a point into the Atlantic. We ate lunch: a bottle of *vino tinto* and fresh caught sardines, sweet as sugar, broiled outdoors in front of us. We wandered along the harbor edge, watched brown boys, shiny and quick as trout, diving into the blue water, and visited the twelfth-century church. Above an ornate altar was a life-sized, sorrowing Madonna, eerily realistic and dressed in black velvet, on her breast a solid-silver heart. She was faith made as tangible and daily as bread — Roman Catholicism cloaked in a veil of tears, a religion full of pain and by implication fear. This, I always felt, was Hope's own version of Catholicism. She was, as she put it, an RC, educated through high school by nuns. Hope was past thirty before she dared miss her first Sunday Mass.

I preferred my ethical code and my conviction that punishments for transgressions came on earth. But I knew Hope enjoyed a certainty I lacked. I wondered there in front of that Madonna how I, full of religious uncertainty, would someday handle the coming of death. Suddenly uncomfortable, I broke the silence. I said, "Spooky," and Hope nodded in agreement. But she slipped some coins into the metal offering box, and with the long taper lit one of the candles that were banked at the Madonna's feet. I knew the candle was for our first baby, Little Whitney, who had died in 1965, a month and a half old. Hope stood at the metal railing, head bowed, praying. I stepped forward beside her and closed my eyes, and tried to send my thoughts and sorrow upward. I had no sense that they ever left my head. But this sharing of our grief was its own kind of devotion. Leaving the church, I took Hope's hand. Outside in the sun, we could hear the shouts of the boys still diving in the harbor.

Toward the end of that meandering day, Hope painted a fourth watercolor. The scene was a breakwater for the small, open fishing boats that ranged far out into the Atlantic. In the impending dusk, while she worked on the brightly painted boats, I wandered away from her and noticed a young couple on the parapet kissing—what Hope in her private vocabulary called "mooshing." Did I envy them? I wondered. I looked across the breakwater at Hope, her red kerchief a spot of color against the stone, and I could summon up again our own heartsick hunger, the romantic haze that fogs reality, the intimate excitement. That was indeed rapture. I looked again at the two lovers and found myself considering the complications brought on by time—the muddling of feelings, the dimming of ecstasy. After our years of marriage I was no longer able to analyze my irrevocable attachment to Hope. I knew we needed each other. I knew that fundamentally she was my favorite companion on earth. I made believe she was gone from my life—from the earth. My stomach knotted in sudden trauma. I put the idea out of my mind and walked back to Hope in the failing light.

The thought of losing Hope was not an accidental abstraction. The previous day at the house in La Honce I had found Hope sitting on the edge of our bed holding a child's pink, heart-shaped mirror awkwardly behind her bare back. She was studying what looked like a large, dark freckle in the field of freckles covering her skin. She said, "Dick, look at this. Do you think it's cancer?"

I stared at the blackish spot. It was oozing blood. Exasperation rose inside me. During all our years of marriage, Hope had often called out those words, asking me to inspect a succession of bumps, discolorations, sore spots. Always I felt ignorant and helpless. I thought this time it was again a figment of Hope's fear. I recoiled from the terrifying possibility of cancer. Below the level of thought I felt that checking with a doctor would be asking for trouble. Through my head passed the vision of us speaking our tourist French in a doctor's office in Biarritz. I told Hope that I had no idea what the spot was but we would certainly cancel our outing the next day and go to a doctor if she wished — thus passing the responsibility back to her. Hope had her own rationalizations and the more we talked, the more we slipped out from under our alarm. She said the spot had been there for years and this bleeding had happened before; her bra strap had been chafing it. She said she hated the idea of running to a doctor all the time like some hypochondriac — which I took as a dig at me, who swallowed vitamin pills, got tired, and worried about my diet. I told her to stop picking at the sore; it might get infected. We buried the problem and its question. Instead of consulting a doctor, we went ahead with this day trip into Spain — the last serene and unclouded time Hope and I were ever to have together.

One

In August Hope and I and the children returned to our brownstone in New York City, and to the tugging and hauling of career and parenthood. The spot on Hope's back had subsided and we thought no more about it. Early one October morning, as I was leaving to catch a plane for Washington, D.C., and an interview, I suddenly discovered that the furnace had stopped and my wallet was misplaced. At the peak of my frenzy Hope came out of the bathroom, her hand under her right arm. "What do you think this means?" she asked. I could see the fright in her eyes. Irritation coursed through me. I was going to miss my plane! I put my hand into her armpit. I could feel two soft, round lumps. My impatience turned to fear. Could it be cancer? Surely not. But this time she should go immediately to a doctor, if only to put our fears at rest.

I did catch my plane and in the Washington airport telephoned my older brother, Harry, a research biophysicist with an M.D. The lumps, he explained, were probably swollen lymph glands whose function was to halt and contain all kinds of infection. I seized on this to stifle my fear, to believe this was yet another false alarm, and when Harry asked me to stay over that night, I laughed and said facetiously, "I have to get home to my wife who has cancer." Back in New York I found Hope very subdued. She had ended up seeing Dr. Thomas Nealon, a cancer expert and chief of surgery at nearby St. Vincent's Hospital. He had identified the "freckle" on her back as the peculiarly black mole that can signal cancer, and had taken a sample of it for a biopsy. Questioned by Hope, he had voiced his suspicions: the mole and the lumps were very possibly connected. Then, speaking to me casually, almost as an afterthought, but with fear in her eyes, Hope exploded the bomb. She told me, "He said it could be melanoma."

Malignant melanoma. That was its full name, even more menacing in the lilt of its alliteration. One of the most fatal and wildfire cancers. Gazing appalled at Hope seated on the bed, I felt every vein and capillary pump up with terror. In her ragged blue-plaid dressing gown, shabby espadrilles on her feet, a cup of coffee teetering on the bedspread—so usual—Hope sat with her hand under her arm, endlessly rolling the bumps, like worry beads, beneath her fingertips.

On the day I first heard the word "melanoma," I stopped work on my book. Waiting for the results of Dr. Nealon's biopsy of the mole, Hope and I clung together for comfort. The next two mornings we walked an area new to me—SoHo, a warehouse district dotted with galleries showing "off–Madison Avenue" art.

As I was to notice many times, pleasure and panic can exist simultaneously. On those days we had a sense of justified holiday. Torn between children, housework, and career, Hope rarely allowed herself the fun of a morning off, of an unhurried indulgence of our whims and shared interests. Fear amplified all our emotions, especially tenderness. Dread pushed aside our normal irritations and competitions, and centered us. From time to time, out of a silence, Hope would say, "But I feel wonderful. I feel really well."

I remember, as we walked, I moved my arm inside Hope's and

laced my fingers through hers. I drew a kind of reassurance from the feel of life in her hand, her strength—and tried to pour that comfort back into Hope. Bending down toward her, I said, urgently, that we must not borrow trouble. The odds were that it was nothing. Harry had said the lymph nodes could be caused by any sort of infection. And even if it was cancer, we had caught it early and this was certainly not the end. My words did not fit my awful feeling inside.

When we passed a Catholic church we went inside to pray. In our minds, until we were told the answer, God could still change the outcome. I tried to talk to God. I strained to project single words—"please," "live," "Hopie." I bargained away my religious doubts: okay, there is a God, now he's got to save Hopie.

Three days after the biopsy, our family and Hope's sister Whitney, her husband Peter, and their two children plus assorted friends gathered for our annual early October weekend in the huge, white Victorian house in Dublin, New Hampshire, where I grew up and my mother still spends the summer. I drove with our close friend Gene Boe through the fall foliage to nearby Keene to do an errand. As we returned, he asked me about Hope—and uncorked my worst terrors, the opposite extreme of my optimism. I was a gusher of despair. With my knuckles white on the steering wheel, I cried out to Gene, "Hopie's going to die! She's going to die!"

As I stepped from the car onto the circular, dirt driveway, the setting sun struck only the summits of the maple trees beyond the lawn, orange lighting orange, the waterline of darkness moving imperceptibly up their trunks. Free and separate stood a single spreading maple. Each fall for a day or two it was perfection, every flaming leaf red-orange and undisturbed. It had reached this consummation the day my father died in 1963. Now, again, it was at that moment. Gazing at that tree on that 1973 weekend, I thought about my father's full life and Hope's youth, and the terrible sadness in the gap between our expectations and reality.

Dr. Nealon telephoned us on Sunday morning when we had gone for a walk to a nearby pond. Hope wanted to take some color pictures, notes for future woodcut prints — fields of dead flowers, weeds and grasses like vast dried bouquets; fall leaves floating on dark water like Monet pond lilies. Whitney took the call from Nealon. There were still no results, and we should not worry. "Let me do the worrying," he said.

When she repeated this, I was incensed. "Let me do the worrying!" Idiotic. What the hell did he have to worry about. Was *he* going to live with his stomach half sick from anxiety? Would he take over the disease too? "He was very nice," reported Whitney, as though that should make me feel better. No, I wanted to be angry.

Hope, typically, was worried that her troubles would spoil everybody's weekend. She struggled to be cheerful, and her grip slipped only once. On Sunday, as we closed the house for the winter, there was a discussion about taking the liquor with us. Whitney said, "Leave it here. We'll want it in the spring."

Suddenly Hope called out from the next room, "What for? A wake?"

On Monday in New York there was still no news. On Tuesday, I did a tape-recorded interview for *Playboy* in Providence — then cleared up loose ends by telephone and taped my conversations. At *Life* and afterwards on free-lance magazine assignments, taping had become as automatic as note-taking. In my private life it was a way of preserving fleeting moments — the journalist's version of home movies. I was never a diarist, particularly after Hope was ill, when the process would have accentuated my reporter's tendency toward mental notes and detachment, intruding between me and Hope and the sharing of our ordeal. So occasionally on impulse I would record conversations with the girls and sometimes jotted down their memorable remarks, knowing they would love to hear it all in later years. And that day in the Providence airport, with my equipment already hitched up, I compulsively stabbed the record button when I made my fateful call to Hope at home. Her voice when she answered was cheery. "Hi. How are you?"

"Have you heard?" I asked.

"No." Then she wanted to know how my interview was going.

I told her that there had been problems, but I was finished. On an impulse, I asked again, incredulously, "You haven't had any word from Nealon?"

Her tone hardened. "Well," she said, "I have. But I wasn't going to say anything unless you'd finished your interview."

The grim tone of her voice was all the answer I needed. I said matter-of-factly, "Then it's bad news."

"Yes, indeed it is."

When I got the details, I was furious for her sake. She had been telephoned by a nurse who had no information, just an order to tell Hope to check into the hospital for tests. According to the nurse, Dr. Nealon was in Chicago and his associate, Dr. Alvarez, had the answer to the biopsy. But Hope had been paging him all day with no success, and he would not be reachable until four o'clock at his office. The frustration, confusion, and terror in Hope's voice was heartrending. "I'm going to ask Alvarez some questions," she said, "but I don't know what to ask him."

We did, by implication, have our answer on the biopsy. If it had been negative, there would be no need for tests. Did Hope understand that? I wasn't sure, but she should face reality so she could prepare herself for the official news. I said, "Ask Alvarez what the tests are, but I guess the answer on the mole is going to be yes." I was immediately sorry.

Her voice was high with near hysteria: "I just feel this is the end! I do! I really . . ."

I interrupted her. My reflex was to calm her panic for her sake — and for mine. "It doesn't have to be the end," I said with spirit. "We have to believe the doctors when they say that if we get it soon enough, there should be no problem. You've got to know it's not necessarily the end." Then, empty of genuine optimism, I fell back on a cliché: "We've just got to be terribly brave, Hopie. Terribly brave. That's all I can say, I guess." As I heard my own words I knew, without crystallizing it into thought, that talk of courage was simplistic.

Hope's anxiety, searching, swerved onto Meredith and Helena—"I guess I'll have to tell them, won't I!" I knew she was imagining their solemn faces, so vulnerable, so dependent. She broke down, sobbing. "I don't want to have to tell them. I don't want to do that." Sitting in the telephone booth, listening helplessly to her tears, feeling the enormity of her misery, unable to hold her—I was frantic. Keeping my voice strong, I told her a second time, "This is not necessarily the end."

"Well, I don't feel that way," said Hope, now resentful, angry.

I said, "I love you *very* much."

Her voice was cold. "I'll see you later."

My impatience to reach Hope was almost a frenzy. She needed me. I visualized her wandering through the house, angrily, pathetically despondent. I also needed her. My anxiety was physically painful, and only her presence, her vitality, could ease it. When at last I rushed into the house, I was dumbfounded. Hope was lying relaxed across the foot of our huge bed, her face happy with her special, fond grin. Six-year-old Helena was standing in the middle of the bedroom imitating a man they had watched on Fourteenth Street hawking five-dollar bedspreads. "Fi' dolla, fi' dolla," chanted Helena. An hour later, coming out of the bathroom, grinning, Hope asked, "Is it fair to get cancer and the curse on the same day?"

That evening Dr. Nealon's associate confirmed that the mole was malignant. Hope would enter the hospital tomorrow. We could not bear to talk about Hope's plight. We could not think about anything else. On that first night of our life with cancer, we needed drastic distraction. As we sat at the dining-room table late into the night watching television, which we almost never did, Hope suddenly said, "Where is that marijuana cigarette you brought home?"

I felt an illicit thrill. I had tried marijuana at a friend's house, and it was an experience I wanted to share with Hope, but she had unbendingly refused. She disliked losing control; she did not want to risk a hangover. We smoked, slipping into that floating state which oddly combines fuzziness and heightened sensibility. Flicking from one TV show to another, we giggled at our sarcasms — Hope ridiculing the "fluff-a-duff" actress with the "bee-sting eyes" and the actor with shiny lips "who looked as though he had been eating bacon."

There was a subtle loosening in Hope and it was intensely exciting. Our half-suppressed hysteria fed the abandoned mood. We led each other to bed, and made fierce and voluptuous love. That was the beginning of our search for ways to flee incapacitating anxiety.

During the two years that followed, I came to understand that illness and death and mourning — and emergence into the light of a new beginning — are a ritual as formalized as the Catholic Mass or the crowning of an English queen. I thought of it as the Ritual and gave myself up to it. That meant standing with Hope on the same square of ground. That meant sharing all the terrible moments of calamity, outlasting all the throes of terror and grief. That meant ushering our two little girls through their version of our slow-motion catastrophe. That meant understanding that Hope's last years must be approached as a continuation of life, not as a dismal preliminary to death.

Hope and I focused our energies and stratagems on that goal — but our passage was not "beautiful." The day we faced cancer our relationship did not soar into a higher purity of love. Our marriage was still our marriage. Our familiar contentions and clashes remained. We continued in the grip of human nature. We were heroic and craven, devoted and selfish. We embraced whatever denials and fantasies could keep us intact. Then, in time, Meredith and Helena and I were restored by the mourning process. We lived through its three classic phases of recovery — the numbness of shock, the long unraveling of pain and loss, and the diminuendo of grief—before the Ritual delivered us to our new beginning. This, then, is a book about surviving.

A year after Hope died, I was summoned by Sheila Harris, a wonderful friend from our past who was dying of cancer in Memorial Hospital in New York. Her husband, George, sat beside me. Sheila was weak, her voice slow. But she was herself. A delivery boy arrived with a Chinese meal, and Sheila, the hostess, distributed our shares. Then she lay back and quizzed me—how had Hope and I handled our ordeal, how had the children reacted to Hope's illness and death, and what advice did I have for George and her.

It was the first time I had talked about those two years. Full of pain, I poured out the story of what we had thought and felt and done. At the end I said unconsciously, ". . . and that was how we survived."

There was a startled silence. Sheila asked, "Do you realize what you just said?"

Then I did. I had blurted out, "*We* survived." I was very moved. Yes, on the deepest level that is what had happened. Hope and I had managed that.

Two

The day after the mole was diagnosed as malignant melanoma, Hope dutifully entered the hospital for her tests—and the ceremonies of illness began. That morning, before Meredith and Helena left for school, Hope sat with them on the living-room sofa. As we had agreed, she did not mention cancer. Cheerfully, reassuringly, she told them that there was something the matter with a mole on her back and she was going to the hospital for a few days to find out what it was so the doctors could make it well. When she came home, we would all enjoy some special treat together.

The girls were startled and practical. Eight-year-old Meredith asked, "Who's going to take care of us?"

"Daddy and Gertie will be here," said Hope. Gertrude was our wonderful, loyal, baby nurse who still came two days a week and freed Hope for painting. Helena asked, "Will I be able to visit you?"

"No. Children can't visit hospitals, but the first thing I'll do is give you my telephone number, and I want you to call me all the time."

On the way to the hospital we passed a derelict sprawled on the sidewalk, his skin shiny with dirt. "I'd gladly change places with him," Hope said. One minute later, shaking her head and looking down, she said, "Why me? I've always tried to live a good life and do what's right. So why me?"

Begun that afternoon, the tests lasted three days. They were in themselves mini-illnesses. There was the angiogram. A dye was pumped under pressure — like liquid fire said Hope afterwards — through every vein and capillary. One of the tests was a brain scan. When Hope told me it was scheduled her eyes were filled with fright. "They don't think it's in my head, do they?" I instantly pooh-poohed the idea. Clearly there was nothing affecting Hope's mind.

But, alone in the house the next morning after the children had gone, I stood in our kitchen–dining room and went to pieces. Within the Ritual, it was the moment when the trusted fabric of my existence unraveled. Until then I had somehow soothed the terror by ransacking my fantasy for anything that offered optimism. I had found a broken roll of quarters in the gutter and was superstitiously elated by this good-luck omen. I had called my brother, Harry, and his brother-in-law, a top Washington doctor, and beseeched them to find the miracle that medical science must have ready, the new treatment that would save Hope. They told me that if the melanoma had reached her liver, nothing could save her, but if we had caught it in time, she had a good chance of living.

Now, in the silent house, staring at the backyard covered by the brown deadness of city leaves, the words "malignant melanoma" played over and over in my mind. I knew in the honesty of my heart that we had *not* caught it early. For the first time in my life, death was a palpable force. Not one assumption about the future seemed solid. I felt isolated in a cell of air, seeing familiar objects from a great distance. My stomach and chest physically hurt, as though my body believed that Hope was already dead.

I began to cry. The detached part of me noticed that the shaking of my shoulders was uncontrollable and that my sobs sounded strangely like laughter. I went half blindly to the telephone and called my dear friend Edward Kern, a cohort during the years I wrote at *Life*. Ed, a somewhat lonely man who used a veneer of Germanic formality to conceal his feelings, knew nothing of our trouble as I blurted out, "Hopie's dying. Ed, please come — please!"

While I waited, I mechanically cleaned up the kitchen. My hands seemed like somebody else's. When Ed rang, I pressed the buzzer opening the front door. He hurried to me and put a comforting hand on my shoulder, and the tenderness shattered me. Wracked by sobs, I convulsively clutched him around the back. I felt his tweed jacket rough against my cheek, and I thought, "This is a strange and theatrical thing to be doing."

During those days, doing the laundry, going to the supermarket, frying hot dogs, policing homework, I felt excruciatingly lonely, tears always just below the surface. When people asked me, "How is Hopie?" I would hurry my answer, knowing I would soon be overwhelmed by choked, mid-sentence pauses. Like a sophomore in the agonies of first love, the only place I could find relief was beside Hope and I hurried to her at odd hours when she might be back in her room.

She told me about each test with humor, but analyzed the technician's expression and his goodbye for clues to the result. Otherwise we talked about everything *but* cancer and kept up a kind of cheer. I remember Hope, glowing with good health, saying, "I know this is serious, but it's so hard to get it through your head when you feel so great."

I think we had already begun to practice the syllogism I called the mañana syndrome — Hope is so alive today she will not die tomorrow, and since tomorrow never comes, she will never die. It was a key to our survival. We focused our lives down into the present minute, the exigencies of the hour, and we blocked out the frightful possibilities that lay ahead next week, next year. Seen in its entirety, the calamity overwhelmed us with terror. Broken down into small steps, taken one at a time, the ordeal became manageable and endurable.

On Friday in the late afternoon the verdict from the tests was due. I focused my tension on getting through those hours. Since the day of the mole biopsy, I considered ourselves in a perpetual red-alert emergency, and therefore permitted to make demands on our friends. I asked a group to keep our vigil with us. The rear of Hope's bed was cranked steeply up, and Hope, wearing a hospital robe and the ever-present espadrilles, sat erect on top of the covers. Not getting under the covers means you are not sick. Hope had discouraged flowers. They are for sick people. My stratagem was working. Hope on the dais of her bed, facing the semicircle of admirers, was rising to the occasion, charming the group and distracting herself. If she was relaxed, I could be relaxed.

Suddenly a young doctor called me from the room. My eyes met Hope's with a quick exchange of fear. A private medical preview meant news too terrible for Hope's ears — a metastasis to her liver — and that meant certain death. I was physically nauseated as I accompanied the white-coated doctor to a tiny lounge area. I blurted out, "It's in her liver, isn't it!"

The doctor looked startled. "No," he said, "the liver scan was negative." Joy can be just as jolting as disaster. There was that same sense of the body convulsing. My face must have radiated my euphoria. The doctor, with an odd look, continued, "But there was a spot on your wife's spleen."

Hope's liver was clean! She still had a chance! So it was in the spleen. I asked confidently, "That's operable, isn't it?"

"Yes, it is. But that decision will be up to Dr. Nealon."

I thanked him profusely, this bearer of glad tidings, and floated back to Hope's room. My face must have been radiant. I was confident that she would live. Our friends smilingly slipped away. I sat beside Hope on the bed and hugged her. "Oh, Hopie," I said. "It's such good news. Your liver is fine; everything is fine except for a tiny spot on your spleen. You can have your spleen taken out and never miss it." I laughed. "And your disposition will improve." Hope was smiling. We snuggled on the bed.

Dr. Nealon released Hope that Friday evening, after explaining that the next step was a biopsy of the lymph nodes. The biopsy took place the following Monday. In the surgeon's dressing room, I waited with Whitney, a small, dark-haired version of Hope. Together we sneaked out to spy through the window of the minor-surgery operating room. A relaxed Hope lay on the operating table, her mouth talking away like a silent movie, while Nealon in his sterile green suit, a white mask across his face, worked under her arm. Laughing at Hope's expansiveness, we returned to the dressing room. Talk was one of the ways Hope reached out to everybody — words tumbling out of her, eagerness and a grin sounding in her voice. I described to Whitney the routine in Hope's studio when the telephone rang. She would irritably curse the interruption and then speak nonstop for twenty minutes. Finally hanging up, she would make a face and say, "God, that woman talks a lot."

Dr. Nealon came into the room, pulling off his rubber gloves — a tall, well-built, classically handsome man with a casual but in-charge manner — a central-casting surgeon. He asked Whitney to step outside. He might as well have used skywriting: Bad News! Undressing in front of a metal locker, wiping under his arms with a towel — very much man-to-man — he said, "This could get nasty before it's finished."

Nealon explained that he had found dark tissue which looked like melanoma. The mole and the nodes were almost certainly connected, and if the spleen was cancerous, then chemotherapy would be her last recourse and Hope's chances would be small. But I hardly heard him. He had said "finished." Finished meant all over. Dead. I was back in shock, another roller-coaster plunge.

Hope, bandaged under her dress, joined us. Nealon praised Hope extravagantly for her fortitude. She beamed, pleased. I stood dazed, silent, trying to arrange a pleasant expression on my face. Nealon suggested we talk in his office downstairs. There my gloom deepened as I watched Nealon "handle" Hope. At such moments doctors who deal daily with fatal diseases become, in a sense, actors. He had told me the facts. After that, says Nealon, "I do not hesitate to delude a patient when I'm sure I can get away with it. If you write off something as not very important, they'll assume it mustn't be. You talk about the good points, and that really does make people feel better. I've often said, 'The best chemotherapeutic agent is tincture of blarney.' "

Speaking to Hope, Nealon's tone was casual. The next step depended on the biopsy of the lymph nodes. He said this was a fascinating problem — it was an unlikely sequence of metastases to have a spot on the back, a couple of lumps under the arm, and a spot on the spleen. He said he was a perennial optimist.

Hope was not deceived. "Am I going to die?" she asked.

I held my breath. I could not have asked that question.

"We all have to die someday," Nealon said. Hope was expressionless.

Leaving the hospital, Hope headed for her two temples. The first was the Baskin-Robbins ice cream parlor a block away. For Hope, a teenage fat girl, now an everlasting dieter, ice cream cones were climactic indulgences. A new "BR" flavor was an event. But I think at this moment ice cream meant a double dollop of normality — the evidence that she was still the same person. I myself found a symmetry in this pilgrimage. On a deeply happy day of our marriage, the morning we picked up one-month-old Helena from a Los Angeles adoption agency, we stopped to celebrate at a Baskin-Robbins on the way to the airport. Hope cradled her baby at the stainless-steel drinking fountain and tenderly sprinkled a few drops of water on the blond head. She whispered, "I baptize thee Helena in the name of the Father, the Son, and the Holy Ghost." Now Helena was safe; her soul would go to heaven. Every time Hope flew she was sure the plane was going to crash. The only equivalent to her fear of flying was her terror of getting cancer.

Hope's second destination was the Spanish church on Four-teenth Street. We climbed the steep steps up from the sidewalk.

The church was empty. As she headed down the aisle past the font, where Meredith and Helena had been formally baptized, Hope called out ruefully in the silence, "Is there anybody home?"

Now, in my fear, I began wondering whether Hope had the best care I could command. Utterly ignorant of the disease and of the medical profession, haunted by horror stories of medical mismanagement, I was putting Hope's chance for life into the hands of a total stranger. Propinquity, not a systematic search, had settled us on Dr. Nealon, chosen by our convenient GP, himself on the staff of St. Vincent's. I was determined that Hope must *not* be a routine patient. The attention to her case must be special because we were special. When life is at stake, everybody feels unique.

This quandary had to be kept secret from Hope. She strongly wanted to be cared for at St. Vincent's. It was her neighborhood hospital, a landmark in her normal life. She hated the idea of a cancer hospital. Once, driving by Sloan-Kettering, she said, "If you go there, you never come out alive." Also, she had a crush on Dr. Nealon. Flicking one eyebrow, only half joking, she raved about his looks. "He's the man who's going to get me out of this mess," she said.

I thought these reasons were understandable and silly, but in the delicate balance of Hope's morale, important. I checked on Nealon with the chief of surgery at the Columbia-Presbyterian. He told me that Hope was in excellent hands. But I knew in my heart that doctors do not criticize each other to laymen. I decided that to make a judgment, I should know Dr. Nealon's plans and rationale. Whitney and I went to his office without Hope's knowledge. The straight-on analysis of her predicament must have been horrendous: I have blanked out everything Nealon said except that he had decided to operate. He would remove the mole, channel through the flesh to the lymph nodes to pick up cancer cells in transit, clean out the armpit area, take out the spleen. He would also check the abdominal area for other lesions. I was left with no specific reason to change doctors, nothing to warrant an awful, upsetting battle with Hope. I decided that it is almost impossible for a layman to distinguish in advance between good medicine and the best.

Nealon commissioned me to tell Hope his plans for the operation. Since the meeting with him had been clandestine, I pretended that Nealon had telephoned me. I am a poor liar and Hope's suspicions were honed raw. She whirled on me, all her rage at her plight boiling over onto me. "You've seen Nealon, haven't you!"

I confessed, arguing foolishly that it was for her sake, to spare her the ordeal. Her eyes narrowed. "Listen, you're not in charge of me. You're always trying to run my life. Well, not this time. Butt out, see! From now on, Goddam it, I always want to know the truth! Always!"

I promised Hope I would never deceive her. But I promised myself that henceforth I would know only what she knew. If there were delusions and denials, we would share them.

Throughout her illness, our most dire convictions were like a tide, sweeping over us and then receding back into repression and denial. But Hope always faced her danger with more resolution than I could find. In those early weeks she told her friend Joyce Berman, "I have this thing coursing through me that can kill me and it's so hard to believe because I feel so well and I'm so happy and yet it's there." And then Hope said matter-of-factly that she must plan how she was going to live with it, how she was going to behave. My role was to insist that Hope could be saved, saying it to her with such certainty that I induced in myself a strange kind of belief. But many mornings in those first seconds of half-consciousness I would think, "There is something terrible in my life. What is it?" Then I would remember. "Hopie has cancer."

I worried that anxiety and hysteria might immobilize me now, when my duty to Hope and the children was to keep our daily lives together and in gear, to stay calm and strong. So in moments of extremity, when the fear was almost crippling, no thoughts seemed too disloyal if they consoled and saved me. I even told myself, "Better her than me." I dwelt on the black side of our marriage, resurrected my feelings during bitter clashes when I wished I was free of Hope forever. I titillated my imagination with images of future bachelorhood, turning my mind loose into sexual fantasies.

For Hope, that period of transition out of health and into illness may have been the hardest time of all. Our minds were not adjusted to mortality. Hope's sickness was not yet our normality. Alone with me, Hope was in control, but often jittery, irritable, monosyllabic, huddled back into herself. She told me, "I have nothing to hold on to; nothing means anything to me." Her ordinary angers frequently became tirades. Another of my roles was dumping ground for Hope's anxiety, the unconditionally sympathetic person with whom she could safely be petulant, be self-centered, be bitter — be human.

I had expected Hope's Catholicism to be a special solace; she had always kept her side of the bargain with God. But once the mole biopsy was positive, the visits to the churches stopped. Sunday Mass and Communion continued, but she did not begin praying at home.

The children, however, could always pull her out of herself. I remember Hope's smile when Helena, stocky and blond, leaving for school, kissed her four times and said, "That should do it." And there was Hope's grin when thin and brown-haired Meredith, unknowingly summing up human relations, pointed to a bent blade in a fan and said, "This one brings trouble to all the rest."

Hope's specialty — as a woman and as an artist — was children. She made them laugh. She remembered the small importances in their lives. She let them know her fascination with the way they thought and moved, and that her world and theirs were not so very distant. She poured her delight in children into her woodcut prints — boys and girls contemplative or joyously playing, awkwardly graceful. Her keepsake containers were heavy with scraps about children which touched her — a Rembrandt Madonna and Child, a few lines ripped from *Time* telling of a child "listening to the sound of flowers."

But Hope, and perhaps this was the artist in her, followed her strong emotions far more than the policies of her head. In Helena she had her idealized child — a loving person full of wry humor and sudden adult wisdoms. But while Helena was butter, Meredith was wire, hot with energy and impatience. Hope and I ached for Meredith, at center vulnerable and sweet. As Hope once said, "Mere's so prickly and I love her so much." Though Meredith remained the child she drew and printed, Hope allowed uncomplicated, affectionate Helena to become her constant companion. One day Helena said to me, "It seems like I sort of belong to Mommy and Mere belongs to you."

To spare the children our anguish of suspense, Hope was casual and confident about her illness. To spare outsiders and herself the painfulness of pity, she rarely spoke of her condition. When the subject was unavoidable, her tone was rueful, incredulous, humorous. On the sidewalk one day Hope met her friend Jill Robinson, the writer, who was ignorant of her troubles. Jill said in greeting, "How are you?"

Hope grinned and said, "Never again will you ask that question. I have cancer."

Dr. Nealon operated on Hope on the fifth of November 1973. I was told that she would certainly be finished at the very latest by two o'clock. At two, expecting to find her there, I hurried into her room. The bed was empty. There was only her residue — the tube of pale lipstick, the hairbrush laced with red strands, the white canvas totebag, the folder of working drawings for the children's book she was illustrating, and on top of it, her horn-rimmed glasses. I felt punched in the chest. It was as if she had died. In that room — waiting — I felt removed into a quiet hiatus between our past together and an unforeseeable future I dared not imagine. I tried to remember our days of courtship. It was like dredging up high school facts on the Medes and the Persians.

I met Hope Brooks in 1951, when I was assigned to the Los Angeles bureau of *Life*, and her father's lemon ranch was near my uncle's up the coast. I was immediately smitten by all four of the Brooks girls — Hope, Palmer (called Blue), Whitney, and Meredith (called Ky). They were so pretty, so responsive, so delightful, so original with their quick, ironic banter. They had so much fun together, and to be allowed even a partial share in that mutual affection was intoxicating.

There was a day at the beach with all her sisters and a rubber boat we towed out beyond the breakers. I remember Hope diving off it, and then surfacing, wet red hair sleek as a seal's. I thought how unusual she was — no fussy girlishness about her hair. Now, remembering, I laughed to myself. After our marriage, at the first sign of any moisture, that head disappeared under a panoply of protective bandannas.

And I remembered a solitary picnic with Hope, a scramble hand in hand down a rock and clay cliff to a shelf of beach sealed off from the world by vast boulders at each end. We swam and held each other in the water, lifting and falling with the ocean swell until we washed ashore and lay on the sand kissing — waves lapping over and around us — Hollywood circa the 1950's.

I thought about the shower of tender letters from Hope, almost one a day, and how deliriously gratifying they were to one who considered girls mysterious territory — alluring, unobtainable, perilous. I kept those letters: "Oh, Dick, Dick, my heart is so full of love for you, I can hardly tell you of it. Please keep loving me. This separation aches so — being half of what I could be." And I remembered trips to Phoenix to visit her newly married sister Blue, and the pain of too much laughter — and the moment by a swimming pool when I passed a note to Hope. It read: "I love Hopie Brooks. Signed: R. Sumner Meryman."

I thought how sad it was that our elementary rapture did not — and probably could not — survive marriage and human nature. Intimacy brings depth, but depth is rarely simple. Needs, disappointments, and compulsions add up and you act in ways you never expected, and the relationship becomes something you never intended.

I thought about our marriage and the problem of two careers and how hard it was for Hope, wrenched by the demands of being wife, mother, artist. Hope's drive to develop her talent and get recognition was the keystone to her identity, her sense of self-worth. There was always an unstoppable quality to her. She put her work in first place — as an artist should. Her dedication was one reason why I loved Hope, and no artist ever had a more devoted fetcher and carrier. But the art was a thorny dilemma for her — and me. Hope was in constant, valiant motion trying to juggle all her roles, each at the expense of the others. When interrupted, as she often was, she was constitutionally unable to say no to anybody — but me.

I once telephoned Hope and she answered in her studio and her voice was sweet. But when she heard me, it turned abrupt and impatient. "What do you want?" Then in the same breath she shouted away from the telephone, "Meredith! Stop that! What did I tell you!"

"Is this a bad time?" I asked.

"Yes it is," she said, her voice still hard. "Meredith is painting and a friend is coming over."

I hung up, feeling like just another maddening interruption to her work.

Sitting there in Hope's hospital room, I remembered the day I asked Hope to read the rough draft of my latest *Life* article, and the hurt I felt when it stayed untouched on her bureau. I said nothing; she got around to it on the third day, too late to be of help.

It was, I found, fruitless to confront Hope with my resentments. She had a similar set of her own — my late hours working at *Life*, my absences on stories for weeks at a time, my fatigue at night. I could not change my work habits. She was unable to redesign her day to mesh with my needs. So we were both overcommitted—driven, ironically, by natures and ambitions we both admired. I once said to Hope, "What we need is a good wife." She did not laugh at that.

I thought how astounding my feelings would be to most people. They found in Hope a beautiful woman instantly responsive—her eyes bright, her soft voice eager, her sympathies quick, her mind mobilizing to welcome them, to put them at ease, to captivate them. Hope was wooing the world—finding the best in everybody, making them feel at their best, remembering details of lives, names of children, never competing, always modest, accessible, caring.

Though Hope the paragon was not always my Hope, that did not make this side of her any less real and true, any less fundamental in her nature. Hope knew she was safe with me. I loved her with or without the charm.

Immediately after our marriage, I was transferred by *Life* to Chicago and into a four-year romantic adventure in a new city, a new group of remarkable people, and the new world of marriage. But by the time I was recalled to New York, in 1956, I had begun to realize the complexities of marriage—that I had taken on far more than an affectionate, beautiful, and accessible companion. I had assumed responsibility for the happiness and welfare of another human being, and an obligation toward a whole glossary of consequential words: sacrifice, adjustment, effort, accommodation. And I knew that Hope, a Roman Catholic, would never marry again as long as I was alive.

I found myself in a low-grade frenzy of second thoughts—picking apart myself, Hope, our marriage. Am I still in love with Hope? What is married love? Is this truly the woman I want "until death us do part"? The quick and brainy girls at the magazine seemed so fascinating. I panicked. Five years into our marriage, without warning, I packed a suitcase, told Hope that I was leaving for an unknown length of time, and departed for Maryland.

At that time I was religion editor and had access to Msgr. John Courtney Murray, an eminent Jesuit theologian who seemed appropriate because of Hope's Catholicism. I visited him at Woodstock College in Maryland, and we sat together on wooden chairs in a bare room flooded with sunlight. Monsignor Murray, a spare man who spoke gently, talked to me about the necessity of making commitments in life. Men and women today, he said, do not give themselves totally and irrevocably to anything. It is, he believed, one of the serious problems of our time. Such people are adrift and unsatisfied. Contentment only comes with commitment. Success in anything — especially marriage — requires dedication. This appealed mightily to my young Calvinist soul. As we parted, Murray said kindly, "Try not to be so hard on her."

I stayed away four days. Perhaps it was then that I genuinely fell in love with Hope. I understood that we were bound together in some fundamental way I could not analyze. We cherished and abhorred the same things, but it was more than that. We admired each other and were physically attracted, but it was more than that. In short, we suited each other, but it was more even than that. I simply knew that away from Hope my life was in ugly pieces. I went home full of resolve and found her at the ironing board, eyes red from weeping. We began again. I worked to reassure and to rewin Hope. But I also knew that our relationship might have been fundamentally damaged.

In Hope's hospital room, as these thoughts were passing rapidly and half formed through my mind, I made another commitment. I promised all my ingenuity and fortitude and strength to Hope. I promised everything in my power to help her through whatever lay ahead.

Some years earlier I had met a man and his wife toward the end of her long fight with cancer. I learned later that, like many spouses, he had been angry at her for having cancer, for mangling their life. She had been furious that he was unable to give help and moral support when she most needed it. She felt deserted in her struggle. This must never happen to Hope and me. I thought wryly about our wedding ceremony in Santa

Barbara, California. After we had kissed at the altar and were poised to hurry down the aisle, the priest bent toward me and said, "Take good care of her."

My reverie was interrupted by our friend John Groth. I was delighted and touched to see him, and glad of the distraction. John, a leanly handsome man with a full head of white hair, had been Hope's teacher at the Art Students League when we first came to New York. Faithful, kind John. I had known for a long time, without dismay, that he was in love with Hope—and she a little with him, a combination of hero worship, affection, and great admiration for his work. He stopped by the house two or three evenings a week. Sitting side by side on the sofa they talked art, John describing some problem in a current painting and Hope telling him, "Oh, John, you're such a turkey. You're one of the finest draftsmen in America."

Waiting for Hope to return from the operation, John and I talked about sports, my book on Herman Mankiewicz, John's own youthful friendship with Heywood Broun. He entertained me with stories of his career as a war artist: the liberation of Paris; looking up Picasso in the telephone book, going to the address, being the first American to find him. Finally, at five o'clock, an orderly opened the door. John and I hurried into the hall. Hope, still as death, eyes closed, her face the color of gray cement, lay on a wheeled litter. It was the corpse I had imagined in my most morbid daydreams. John turned toward me. I could see the question in his face: Is she alive? She opened her eyes, saw him, and said in the tiniest of voices, "Hello, John."

"Hi there, doll baby," said John.

Dr. Nealon came by later and told us that the spleen had indeed been diseased, but he had checked everything else "while I was in there" and found no other malignancy: "The liver was the healthiest I've ever seen." It was, he said, "hopeful surgery."

During Hope's stay in the hospital, her room was never, in

Hope's word, "uncheered." There were constant visitors and telephone calls. One friend said, "I know we'll all be happy again, the way we were when we didn't know we were happy."

The mail brought an outpouring of attention: "I cannot think of anything but you." "I admire tremendously what a good soldier you are." "You are like my little sister, but dearer, really, and better because I could choose." "For one thing, you are too nice to get sick." Andrew Wyeth, with whom I had done a *Life* interview and a book, wrote from his own hospital room where, coincidentally, he was enduring tests for what could have been, but was not, cancer. He drew a cartoon of himself in bed and wrote, "I feel as if I have been turned inside out so I can understand your feelings. I think it's worse for the artist, who likes to keep secrets."

Dr. Nealon had said there would be chemotherapy "to clean up whatever cells might still be loose in the bloodstream." Having been crucially ignorant and indecisive about the mole, I was compulsively meticulous about the next step in Hope's treatment. I telephoned my brother, Harry. As an established name in research, he had access to the most advanced melanoma authorities in America. I asked him to do a survey and see if there was a consensus on treatment.

While bad medical news had been traveling west, the same had been coming east. Hope's father, after a series of strokes and a stay in the hospital, had lapsed into a coma. He died on the sixth of November at the age of eighty-three.

Hope arranged for a priest to say a Mass for her father in her room. I attended. The priest bustled in carrying a little black case — "like a salesman," I thought, "for eternal life." He spread a white altar cloth on the wheeled bed table from which Hope ate her meals. I wondered what was in Hope's mind. Was she thinking that she might soon be joining her father?

The priest said the Mass and Hope participated — a bedridden altar boy. Afterwards he stayed and talked. When Hope said how eager she was to go home, the priest spoke indignantly of the many patients held in the hospital unnecessarily. Instead of caring for them at home, their families preferred to keep them shut away, out of sight and out of mind. Hope was outraged. I resolved then that if Hope had to die, by God she would die at home.

Meredith and Helena were stoic, but they missed Hope, asking me daily when Mom was coming home. They must also have sensed my state of emotional siege and known intuitively that there was cause for alarm. Meredith, typically, said little. Helena, responding to some minor reprimand from Gertrude, said, "How would you feel if you didn't have a mother?"

Gertrude said, "I don't have a mother."

"Neither do I," said Helena.

"All you have to do," said Gertrude, "is pick up the phone and talk to your mother. I can't do that."

So, in her tortured printing, Helena scrawled the hospital-room telephone number, pinned it beside our telephone, and called her mother right after school and at bedtime.

Both girls were irate that hospital rules forbade them to visit their mother. While playing with my empty suitcase, they found that singly they could curl up and fit inside. I closed it on each in turn and lugged the suitcase around the room — the world's first giggling two-suiter. They demanded that I carry them in to see Hope. I almost did. I am sorry now that I said no. They would have had that memory all their lives.

Instead, we stood across the street from St. Vincent's while, by prearrangement, Hope came to the window of the lounge and waved down at us. First Helena, then Meredith, sat on my shoulders. Everybody waved. They called out, "Hi, Mom. Hi, Mommy." We could see her red hair and her smile. Helena, as she told me later, was thinking how wonderful it was just to see her mother — and find her so happy-looking, not sick. Helena was sure she would get well.

Then Meredith said, "Let's go." That was typical Meredith. Never still. She was ten days old when we adopted her in San Francisco. Her hands moved constantly in front of her. We nicknamed her "the director." Crawling was too earthbound for her. Soon, like a small, agile pet, she began racing across the floor on her hands and feet, her diapered bottom high in the air. She walked at eight months. By then Hope's name for her was Fluffernutter, and describing Meredith in a letter to her sister Ky, Hope wrote, "Little Fluffer has four teeth to help block out the gummy smile, and she is very very very busy — very. She has a milk truck that has chocolate milk and orange drink and she delivers them in the waste can, the toilet, underneath all the furniture. Maybe Arden Milk will hire her in the future. She is sickeningly cute, and says '*hiiiiiiiiii*' to everyone on the street."

I can also remember Meredith in a rare moment of quiet — on her back on her mother's knees, and Hope softly smiling as she studied the piquant little face with its huge brown eyes. Then Hope with one finger rubbed the tiny shoulder and said, "Hello, bright eyes in the acorn."

A week after Hope's return from the hospital, Harry came to the house to report on his investigations. He had talked by telephone or seen in person virtually all the top melanoma researchers. He found them to be men under tremendous pressure to *do* something. When they talked about their studies, they were optimistic. But when Harry asked, "If this was *your* sister-in-law, what would *you* do?" their frustrations and uncertainties surfaced.

Melanoma is an uncommon form of cancer. The odds that Hope would get it were four in a hundred thousand. Often a doctor can assemble less than a dozen patients for a research program. The results from experiments on so few patients do not add up to broad and reliable patterns. Moreover, melanoma is extremely capricious. An untreated patient may die within weeks, live for years, or very occasionally have a total and permanent remission. Therefore, any improvement under experimental therapy may have little meaning. Each researcher Harry consulted urged the particular treatment he was investigating.

The newest experimental approach was immunotherapy. A doctor at Memorial Hospital argued in favor of a combination of immunotherapy—injections of a chemical extract of TB "vaccine" which mobilizes the body's immunity mechanisms against the cancer—and chemotherapy—treatment by a poisonous chemical to which the cancer cells are more vulnerable than normal cells. Harry met with Dr. Nealon and the oncologist of St. Vincent's Hospital. Both of them felt that immunotherapy was unproved, and in some cases actually stimulated the disease. Harry and the two doctors also knew the truth: the chances of curing Hope completely were virtually zero. They agreed that considering the disagreement among the authorities, the unknowns and pros and cons of the treatments, the miserable side effects, the unpredictability of melanoma, the fact that Hope appeared currently clear of cancer—no treatment at all was a genuine alternative and would give her a period of entirely normal life.

When I involved Harry, Hope was instantly angry: "Harry doesn't know anything about cancer. Dr. Nealon's my doctor and this is an insult to him." When I told her about the possibility of immunotherapy injections, she was even madder: "Damn it, you're butting in again! *Nealon* is in charge of my case, not you or Harry. How could you do this to me when you know how much I hate needles!"

I got mad. What the hell was she doing worrying about needles and Nealon's feelings when her life might be at stake! Anyway, nothing would be done against her will. But I did not think it was smart to put blind faith in one man, even if he was God (getting in my dig). I said, "It's your decision," and silently to myself, "It's your life." But I was actually relieved to have her take charge, even partially. There was justice in Hope's attack. Bringing Harry in on the decision, perhaps influencing Dr. Nealon's judgment, was a responsibility that was beginning to frighten me. Part of me wished I had chosen to live with my feelings of ignorance and helplessness, and had simply let fate take its course.

But that day, when Harry made his report, Hope was all smiles. He stood in the living room and outlined his survey — the lack of consensus, his talk with Nealon and the oncologist. He described the various treatments. Then he offered the serious possibility of no treatment. Hope seized on it. So did I. In our sublime state of denial, treatment meant "You are still sick." No chemicals, no needles meant "You will probably live." When Harry left, Hope and I kissed. The black weight had lifted. We could take up our lives again.

Three

Christmas was a happy time. In our minds the melanoma was gone, and Hope's next checkup tests were not until March, a century away.

Recuperating from the operation and from the battle fatigue of her anxiety, Hope allowed herself to relax a little. Instead of charging into her day as though from a starting gate, she would turn off the alarm and curl back under the covers saying, "Heaven." There were times when I moved across the bed and we lay facing each other, arms and legs entwined — quiet talk, small kisses, replays of silly bed games — unsentimental testimonials of tenderness.

Sometimes as we held each other, Hope would say, "I've got to get up." "All right," I would answer. "On the count of three. One. Two. Three!" Neither of us moved.

"Now really," Hope would say. "This is scandalous, lolling around like this. I mean it! Ready? One. Two. Three. *Up!*" We snuggled closer.

"Honestly now, this time . . ."

The start of her daily rituals always snapped Hope's energy into gear. She was a person of routines, a nester really happiest in her own home — husband, children, paintings, furniture, the morning *Times* on the stoop, her studio—the settled scene for the happy grooves of her day.

Her first morning move in the kitchen was running water into a battered, soot-encrusted tin saucepan, long ago appropriated from my camping equipment. I think to Hope it was an old friend and also an underdog, an object of sympathy compared to her ritzy copper pots, Christmas presents she rarely used. As the water heated, Hope plopped the sandwich bread down in neat rows to be painted with peanut butter and jelly while the boiling water dripped through grounds in the hour-glass coffee maker. Then, steaming mug in hand, she banged into the children's rooms, snapping on the lights and calling out above their cries of protest, "Hop-up time! Hop-up time!" Helena got her revenge when we slept late on weekends. She would wake her mother by peeling back Hope's eyelid and saying, "Is anybody in there?"

I was writing full-time again in my workroom in an office building on Fourteenth Street, four blocks distant. On my way I usually biked Helena, the dawdler, to school at the last minute. When I hurried in search of Hope to say goodbye, I felt slightly guilty. Part of me saw her as a reminder of the anguish that could lie ahead, and I was glad to get away. Starting up the stairs to the bedroom, I usually encountered another of Hope's rituals—the pile of dirty clothes tossed down for the morning machine load—and usually I found Hope, dressed in that tattered blue-plaid bathrobe, bent close to the bathroom mirror, nearsightedly giving herself the daily checkup. A beautiful woman who did not consider herself beautiful, she was far more worried than she was vain. But she did admit to herself that her hair was glorious, and if there were gray hairs among the red, they had to be pulled out. If I caught her ministering to a blemish, she would grin and say with mock insistence, "It's just going."

From behind I often laid my cheek against hers, and Hope, seeing us in the mirror, would say, "Sweet!"

Then we faced each other, embracing—the tightness of our

holding the admission of our thoughts. I said, "Call me any time. I can be home in two minutes."

"I'm all right," she said. "I really am." It was a duet of enormous understatements.

Then to lighten the mood I snapped her bra strap and said, "Abyssinia."

"Ethiopia."

We often met for lunch at a neighborhood coffee shop that Hope and Helena had christened the Hot Bowl of Soup after a picture crudely drawn on the window. I was trying to continue the private, tender times begun during those morning gallery expeditions to SoHo, but I was also like the passenger in a speeding automobile who compulsively keeps his eyes on the road to be sure nothing goes wrong. Over our tuna sandwiches we talked about plans for the weekend, our work, the children —the continuing carpentry of our lives. I see in retrospect that our partnership against Hope's illness was an extension of our common front against the ordinary mini-calamities of daily life.

I was extremely nervous about the Mankiewicz biography I was writing—uncertain whether I could make its subject sufficiently impressive and sympathetic to justify a book. At lunch Hope would tell me that I had never yet failed, that I *always* had terrible misgivings, that once again I would find a way.

Hope was illustrating a children's book called *Akimba and the Magic Cow*, which was about a cow that magically spewed out gold coins. She found the idea dumb and uninspiring. I insisted that her pictures would be good enough to carry anything and we laughed together about the story. At one lunch she had just come from showing the editors the first proofs of the illustrations. "They didn't exactly go 'Ooo Ooo,' " said Hope. "And we had to discuss whether the cow extrudes the money from his mouth or his rear end—plop, plop."

Sometimes we talked art and artists, and I jotted down Hope's statement of her own ambition: "I dream that someday in my painting I can say it the way a writer finds a phrase or an exact word to express some wonderful experience or sight or sound. I think of the tide going out at Almuñécar in Spain, hissing over those pebbles, and it's so hard to find what would express that for me."

Often we talked about Meredith and Helena, our most profound point of contact. We could not possibly have loved any children of our own blood more than we loved those two little girls—all the more true because they had healed an excruciating sorrow, the death of our baby girl, Little Whitney. On a visit to a friend in Chadds Ford, Pennsylvania, she was left alone to sleep. She vomited her milk, inhaled it, and suffocated. Hope found her. As we rushed to the hospital, I forced my breath in and out of the little body, feeling her narrow chest rise and fall, testing frantically under the baby blanket to see if her flesh was still warm. I can still summon up the feel of those two tiny, exquisitely soft lips under mine. And I can remember the combination of tearless shock and wonder on Hope's face as I told her that our child was dead—and then the force in her voice as she said, "I want to see my baby." And I remember Hope's strange look of thoughtfulness as she gazed down at Little Whitney, and gently drew the baby blanket up to the tiny chin, kissed her on the forehead, and tucked her in.

That night, after a long, nearly silent drive through the darkness, we arrived home, unloaded the useless, now cruelly ironic baby paraphernalia, and lugged it toward the rear of the apartment and the deep recesses of a closet. We saw inside the bathroom, hanging on the shower-curtain rod, the three tiny jump suits Hope had put up to dry just before our happy departure. Her iron calm shattered, and, weeping, she gathered them in against her face. She cried out, "I can smell her! I can smell her!"

Night after night I lay holding Hope in my arms. Sometimes she wept. In my own despair I felt I had little to give except physical contact. During the day a permanent shadow lay across her. But though she was saturated with grief, she picked up her former, childless routines with an air of resolution, as though, unlike me, she already knew that tragedy was an ordinary part of life. The morning after our return from Pennsylvania we encountered Josie Davis's husband, Peter, who was unaware of the baby's death. In the midst of his cheery greeting, Hope moved decisively toward him, put both her hands on his arm and said, "You know, Little Whitney died."

"She said it," remembers Peter, "not as though describing a great shock, but as though something terrible and possibly inevitable had happened. You could see in Hope's painting that she understood pain, a sense of mortality. When things went wrong, it was not a shock. It was the carrying out of a promise."

I managed surcease by ransacking the country for another baby. A friend in California had adopted two children through a San Francisco lawyer. She called him. Yes, there was an unmarried, pregnant girl whose baby a couple had agreed to adopt — but that very morning they had changed their minds. I have always insisted to myself that this miracle was an act of God. When the hospital nurse placed our perfect little Meredith in Hope's arms, the shadow vanished.

Sometimes during Hope's convalescence we met for lunch at home. I would come in the front door and climb the stairs past rows of art-show posters to Hope's studio, a converted, third-floor rear bedroom. Often I found her cutting a wood block, chiseling out curling ringlets of wood and leaving in relief, like a typeface, the image she would ink and print on rice paper. As many as five or six blocks, one for each color, were usually combined in a single picture. Watching her deftly wield the large U-shaped gouges and tiny V tools, I marveled at the dexterity in her short, puffy, roughened hands, which I teasingly described as work gloves filled with sand. Once, when Hope was bewailing their condition, Helena said, "Well, you could cheer them up with some rings."

Sometimes in the studio Hope showed me her work in progress, always a ticklish moment between us. Whenever I mixed with her work, she was a thicket of conflicting emotions.

She simultaneously cared about my reaction and considered me not qualified to give advice. In addition, despite her success she was vulnerable about her pictures and sometimes called herself a "baby artist." And I, like flint against steel, was the knee-jerk perfectionist, quick to spot weaknesses, unable to stay silent. When Hope was defensive, I would foolishly say, "Don't get so upset," and Hope would shout, "I am *not* upset!"

"You're just one big ON button," I would say, walking away. I feared the explosive side of Hope that paralleled her sweetness, and I detested conflict. I grew up in a family where harmony was prized, and when there was critical introspection it was kept secret. Emotions in general were downplayed; sentiment was embarrassing. But though rarely voiced, the feel of caring in the family was intense.

Hope grew up in a minefield of ambivalence, the product at home of a charming but authoritarian father who, after his heart attack in the 1940's, became reclusive and angry. Mrs. Brooks was an original and loving woman but she used guilt as her management weapon. Hope was educated at a convent school by sweet nuns brandishing threats of damnation—teaching that sin turned her soul black and confession turned it white again. She emerged from those years with great strengths and happy memories. But I think there was a deeply hidden vein of self-dislike that made her shrink from self-scrutiny.

So Hope and I were well matched. We made a natural accommodation, a tacit agreement that we would not spread out for study every gear and bolt of our marriage. Moreover, I think there was in both of us a core of solitude that preferred this judicious distance. Writing and painting require a willingness to be alone. And there is a need to have, behind the emotion, an inviolate you, detached, recording.

After Hope's operation, I half believed our surface calm and confidence—until six-year-old Helena held up her plump little wrist and showed me a bump just under the skin. With our fear now on hair trigger and the scene of the mole in France passing before our eyes, Hope and I were frantic, certain that Helena also had cancer. "My God, is it catching?" I wondered.

I realized then that a wife's illness is one order of trauma, a child's another. Hope and I could be considered separate entities; half our pasts did not include each other. We were partners who had joined forces, literally for better or worse, in health and now in sickness. But to me my daughters were extensions of myself. To them I was still the personification of help, a surrogate God dispensing calamine lotion for mosquito bites, dollars for sneakers, and back rubs for sleeplessness. If that lump on Helena's wrist should be a tumor, I was not certain I could endure the combination of her trustfulness and my helplessness. We rushed Helena to our pediatrician. It was, of course, nothing. He told us to stop borrowing trouble; we had enough of it already.

In February, Hope noticed that her right eyelid was slightly swollen. Remembering our foolishness over Helena's wrist, we cautioned each other not to panic, and soothed ourselves with explanations. I thought a nasal spray for a recent head cold had caused sinus inflammation and swelling. Hope told everybody she had a "cold" in her eye. The children blamed a bad bump on the head — Hope had run into an air conditioner that projected over a narrow sidewalk. Meredith, frustrated, angry, demanded that we report the machine to the police.

The eyelid gradually became more and more enlarged. But the tests in March were negative, and the doctors thought the growth was not cancerous. The interior of Hope's eyeball was normal. Melanoma locates in pigmented tissues, and is common inside the eye but virtually unheard of in the eye socket.

We waited, pathetically eager to believe the encouraging experts. I lectured myself and our worried friends that one *had* to trust one's chosen doctors. The alternative would be a perpetual, unendurable frenzy of second-guessing. I was right — except this time Hope and I, paralyzed by our fear of another malignancy, were still refusing to face up to what we knew was so: given the virulence and unpredictability of melanoma, any mysterious and persistent symptom was almost certainly a tumor. All winter, mired down in wishful thinking, I failed to search out the best and wisest eye surgeon I could find in New York.

As the warmth of May arrived, sudden slugging headaches brought a sense of crisis. Dr. Nealon sent Hope to a cancer specialist at Memorial Hospital. Passing anxiously through the hospital lobby, Hope typically extended herself to somebody else. She noticed a woman sobbing in a telephone booth and offered help. The woman, sure she had cancer, was hysterically afraid to call her doctor for the result of her biopsy. Knowing so well the woman's feelings, Hope counseled and encouraged her like a best friend. The woman agreed to make the call if Hope stayed with her. She dialed. The biopsy was negative. The woman shrieked with relief. Suddenly they were strangers. She quickly thanked Hope and sailed happily in the opposite direction out the door.

Hope made her way to the specialist's waiting room. He concluded that indeed she must have a melanoma behind her eye. A session under an ultrasophisticated X-ray scanner was arranged and ominous shadows were there on the film. Her ophthalmologist arranged a test by another type of scanner. More shadows. I remember thinking that, yes, the word was so appropriate — "shadows," which echoed childhood fears of lurking things and darkness. And I marveled that even with their electronic machines that filled a room with wires and burnished steel and blinking lights and humming sounds — the doctors ended up guessing at shadows.

Dr. Nealon called me at my office with his recommendation for the next step. He had consulted a specialist in head surgery, a charming, older doctor whom Nealon admired enormously and whose distinguished reputation stretched over many years. This surgeon felt he should operate immediately — with the assistance of an eye surgeon named Ira Jones. Dr. Nealon, obedient to his obligation to keep me fully informed, told me his friend predicted that Hope's eye would probably be removed.

Through my mind flashed a vision of the scalpel slicing into the flesh around Hope's hazel eye. First the lymph nodes, then the spleen, now the eye. I hung up feeling bombarded by siege guns. No sooner did we absorb one calamity, than another detonated just ahead of us.

The telephone rang again. It was Elizabeth Hauser, one of the inner group of friends, ready at any moment to help and support and cheer. She checked in regularly for news of Hope, but was the one person who also seemed concerned about *my* condition. As each new development engulfed me, I dumped on her every monstrous ramification, every hideous alternative — and she listened with tireless concern.

That day the topic was Hope and the loss of her eye. How will she react? She once said, "My life is my eyes." Can she draw without depth perception? (I had been covering one eye to see what that was like.) If she can't work, what will happen to her? Can she endure an empty eye socket? If she goes to pieces, will I fall apart? I was wallowing in my forebodings, but that was my dismal process of acclimatization: replacing the present reality with each new — and worse — reality.

I decided, for now, to spare Hope this dreadful prospect. I wondered if I could counterfeit optimism while burdened with secret knowledge — my promise to myself already broken. Going home that night from my office, I tried to close and guard my mind against emotion — switch off my imagination, fasten the sluice gates against dread. To a degree I succeeded, and as we went to bed that night I found myself glancing dispassionately at her eye and wondering what it was going to look like. But I felt as though an enormous black sheet had been flung over my life.

Before the two surgeons could get together on a date for the operation, Hope's eye went berserk. The swelling seemed to explode. The darkened lid puffed out beyond her brow, and the red-veined eye protruded; she had double vision and the Valium and aspirin no longer dented the pain. She lay crucified on the bed. An ice pack leaked across her face and soaked the pillow while I massaged her head and neck. She asked me over and over, "What do you think is the matter?" I told her I had no idea—a lie.

It was an early June weekend—all her crises seemed to come on weekends—and none of our doctors were available. I was very disturbed, but in that weird split existence of the human emotions I was also bored by constant calamity. I was sick of the queasy clenching of my stomach, sick of Hope's pain, sick of her demands for answers I did not want to say or hear. Through a psychiatrist friend, I got Demerol for Hope's pain. It worked and made her high. I immediately cheered up. Then it made her vomit and she was even more miserable, and my terrible restlessness came back redoubled.

On Monday, short-cutting all the other doctors, I took Hope to Dr. Ira Jones, the "assistant" requested by Nealon's head surgeon. He was a small, dapper man, southern, in a diamond-patterned suit and two-toned shoes—exactly the sort of outfit Hope loved to ridicule. But he radiated kindness, competence, and best of all, action. While he examined her, Hope breathlessly recited her history—the mole, lymph nodes, and spleen —saying, "We went to the doctor *right away* and we caught everything *very* early."

Jones answered reassuringly, "That's a good girl. You did everything just right." He told me much later he was confident the eye was a new metastasis, but at the time he merely said that tomorrow he would make an incision above her eye "and have a look."

Told by the secretary that she would have to enter the hospital right after lunch, Hope's level-headed calm suddenly collapsed. Her face, alarming with its eyeglass lens blanked out by tape, was halfway between fury and tears. "Mere and Henny won't be out of school; I can't go to the hospital without saying goodbye to them. I've got work I want to do. Can't we wait a few days? Why does Jones have to do this right away? Shouldn't we talk to Nealon? I'm *not* going to have an anesthetic! It makes me sick. I won't have to, will I?"

I knew Hope was flailing out at fate. I knew that she was

focusing on the solvable, sidebar problems, anything but cancer. But I was still dumbfounded. She was putting daily routines ahead of treatment. However, I now realize that interrupting her daily patterns, the momentum of her life, meant entering the unknown and giving in to the disease.

I told Hope it was impossible to postpone the operation. But we did get Dr. Jones's permission to enter late in the afternoon. We decided to take the children out of school for a family picnic at the Cloisters, high in Fort Tryon Park, the medieval art museum built to resemble a monastery. In the museum we joined the flow of people through the chapels, burial crypts, and tapestried rooms. But what the girls really wanted to do was run into a cloister garden and play in the fountain marked "Do Not Touch," and then race pell-mell along the colonnade.

We followed, while Hope shouted through their giggling jag, "Meredith! Helena! Stop that! Both of you!!" It was hectic family life. It was blessed normality which surrounded and buoyed us, carrying us forward. Hope and I stood against the parapet overlooking the Hudson River far below and the distant cliffs of the New Jersey Palisades. It was a lovely June day, cool and sunny. The leaves were still fresh, not yet tarnished by city grime and summer heat. I put my arm around Hope. Through the black cloth coat, I felt the vitality in this person I wrestled both in anger and in love. I could not believe that anyone so important, so vital to me, to the children, might disappear. She leaned against me; it was a tremendous, silent exchange of tenderness and anguish. The children charged up to us and climbed hazardously onto the wall. Hope said, "It's time to go."

With Hope back in a hospital bed — no matter how smilingly erect she sat, no matter how thoroughly we planned a painting trip to Maine in August — I was back in my "pit." I was certain that this was the beginning of round two. The second shoe had now dropped. I still hoped that if this tumor was destroyed she could be permanently cured, but my outer cheeriness was fake. I could not tell about Hope's.

In the evening we had a visit from a young New York policeman Hope had met while waiting for her X-ray scan. He too was awaiting an operation by Dr. Jones, and we inundated each other with optimism while subconsciously pooling our panic, a kind of comfort for members of the cancer club. But after he left she said, "I wish I could change places with him."

I was startled. "But he's definitely going to lose his eye."

"Yes," said Hope. "But that's all he's going to lose."

After the exploratory operation, with only a local anesthetic, Hope was high from relief. The back of the bed was cranked up straight and Hope sat against it, the one eye hugely bandaged, the other sparkling as she grinned and gestured and imitated Dr. Jones, his "cupcake shoes" peeking out "like this" from under his green gown while he drank a paper cup of coffee. "Too casual," said Hope, laughing. She was shyly proud, repeating his praise: how sensible she was to have a local anesthetic, how brave, how rare. She took her pink heart-shaped plastic mirror, the one she had used in France, and stared at her bandaged head. She said, "I look like that Minuteman carrying the American flag."

That was Hope at her best — poking affectionate fun, pleased to be admired, joking not lamenting — and very dear. I sat on the edge of the bed. With one hand I held hers and with my other hand I rubbed her arm and I can still see that stream of freckles passing under my fingers. I said, "Hope, the thought that anything might happen to you turns me to jelly inside, turns the whole world gray around me. I truly believe that we'll come through this all right. But I want you to know that there are times like now when I absolutely ache inside with love."

I don't remember Hope's answer, just her incredible smile.

Dr. Jones's report to us at the hospital was brief. He had found nothing conclusive, but had taken samples of a brown material. I remembered Dr. Nealon and the dark tissue in Hope's lymph nodes and his words, "This could get nasty before it's finished." Our ordeal was beginning again. My nervous system, overloaded, turned off. But Hope must have seen through my numbness to my despair. At home that night, when I emptied my pockets, I found a note she had slipped into my jacket: "I love you, Dick, and long to be with you now and hug you and lie next to you and comfort you!"

Four days later in my office the telephone rang and it was Dr. Jones. The chief of pathology at Columbia-Presbyterian had found no evidence of melanoma; the dark material had been brown granules of blood, the product of hemorrhage. There had also been inflammatory cells, so there was a possibility that the problem was only a granuloma — a pseudo tumor caused by inflammation. If this was the case, an anti-inflammation drug, Decadron, would melt down the swelling. He wanted to check the effect of the drug after three weeks. A tiny, interior voice furtively told me that he still thought it was melanoma. I silenced that voice and took his stay of execution to mean a pardon. I immediately telephoned the good news home to Hope, now back from the hospital. She was pleased, but there was no lightness to her voice. She wanted to know what would happen if the drug did not work. I had not thought to ask. Abruptly she changed the subject. "What time are you coming home?"

I said, "As soon as I can buy the pills," and hung up deflated and irritated. In truth, I was simply insensitive. It is impossible for anybody once removed to match the feelings of the patient. No matter how involved I was, I could never share the sense of cancer in one's own body.

I remember in the drugstore looking at the vial in my hand and wondering if it contained Hope's salvation. That was one moment when I thought that medical science, after all, might be miraculous. And of course, Hope gobbled those anti-inflammation pills. Each time I changed her bandage, we studied the eye's position. Was it receding? I would lay a ruler across the socket as a gauge. "Yes, it seems a little better." The headaches were definitely easing.

One day I came home and found Hope in her studio. There

was the familiar room: fireplace, bookcase with hundreds of art and children's books spilling off the shelves, white walls hung floor to ceiling with pictures, shelves of supplies, hanging ranks of ink rollers, leaning stacks of woodcut boards and unsold work, forests of paintbrushes, knives, and mementos—the heart of her nest. Hope sat at the far end of the studio between the two windows, bending over the worktable I had made for her out of plywood and pipes. I could see her ink-stained denim apron fastened behind her Levi's with scraggy lengths of haphazard twine, tied, broken, retied. Twists of hair wandered free from the bone pin that massed her hair above the slender arch of neck. Hearing me, she whirled around, a pencil in her hand. Her face was panicky and pleading. I was startled for an instant by her bandaged eye, white as a scream. "I can't do it," she cried out.

She had now, in essence, lost her eye, and was trying to draw again. It was the moment I had prelived a hundred agitated times. I drew another chair in close and took her hands. She sat stiffly upright, pulling slightly away from me. I talked to her urgently, eloquently, I hoped, about the body's genius for adapting and for managing the impossible. She *would* be able to draw and paint. Then I lost my way—and my mind. I reminded her of the armless cripples who paint with their toes.

She exploded. "I don't want to be some freak getting my picture in the Carpinteria *Herald!* I want to be a good artist! I want to produce a body of work! Suppose you had only one hand and couldn't type!"

I tried to involve myself in her feelings, but I was curiously unmoved by Hope's unhappiness. Perhaps I was too tired emotionally. Also I had already absorbed the fact of Hope's one-eyed future. That was now an old crisis. Moreover, detachment was often my defense—but this time I extended it into a crazy perversity. I made jokes about Hope switching into abstract art. Retaliating, Hope played her black ace. If she could not work, she would kill herself—end this whole damn mess— do everybody a favor. I felt even more distant. I knew it was an empty threat. Hope was too Catholic, too involved with life. But in some dark recess was the thought: yes, it might be a deliverance.

The next weekend in Sag Harbor, Long Island, where Whitney had a house, she and I organized a mass sketching trip. Under Hope's tutelage, Whitney had become an excellent printmaker, and her son Brooks and Helena were both embryonic art students. No matter how afraid Hope was of testing herself, she would not refuse the children. The chosen subject was the soaringly steepled Methodist church, impeccably white against the vivid green of June. I carried Hope's painting stool among the straggling flotilla of family artists laden with pads and paint boxes. To a passerby it must have seemed a charming, sun-drenched expedition.

As Hope drew, I saw that all her years of schooled habit had taken over. Moving rapidly and surely across the paper, her hand knew what to do. Her nose, essential to her creative process, was also back in form, wrinkling upward as her head lifted from paper to subject. I relaxed.

In an hour she showed me the picture, claiming it was lousy and discouraging. Deep inside her, however, there was the familiar quietness that told me she was pleased. I praised the drawing judiciously, agreeing it was not up to her standards, but only because she had trouble with verticle and horizontal lines. From now on she could make guide marks with a T square. In the peace beside that church, she — we — had invisibly managed another terrible hurdle. Ultimately, during her illness she painted some of the best watercolors of her career.

In the first days of July we returned to Jones with the eye virtually unchanged. The next immediate step, he said, was a second, more extensive exploratory operation, this time through the side of her skull. If he found a tumor, he would remove it if possible. Sometimes, he said, tumors were self-contained and could be snipped out.

Otherwise, I wondered, would he remove the eye? Was he just sparing us that fact? I could not bear to know — and had to know. I telephoned him. I asked if the operation would follow the original plan with Nealon's surgeon participating. No, that would not be necessary. What about the judgment that Hope's eye should be taken out? No, it would not be necessary to mutilate her. I felt my face flush. All those images of Hope as a one-eyed grotesque, all those days and weeks of concealed agitation, were needless. I was outraged at those doctors. But I did not protest aloud. It seemed ungrateful.

The children were, of course, out of school, and for the period of the operation Harry and his wife, Lanie, took them on their farm in Maryland. The night before Hope was due to enter the hospital, I was on our bed, a king-sized expanse which had become a sort of landing pad during times of trouble. I was watching Hope at her bedtime rite—tidying (she called it "whirling") our expanse of bedroom and living room, the entire parlor floor of the brownstone. With her Ella Cinders look, as John Groth called it, she was adorably funny-looking—tangled red hair (what she called "bouge") under a bandanna, big glasses slipped to the end of her nose, the shabby espadrilles. She moved like a perpetual motion machine through the rooms, picking up the dead leaves under the *Ficus* tree (but never watering it), fitting the wings back into the slots on the South American wooden bird (knowing they would fall out again by tomorrow), putting her shoes back into their original boxes stacked on the floor of her oak armoire (I called her my wife, the shoe fetishist), shoving odds and ends out of sight into drawers (tidiness was out of sight, out of mind), and all the while she talked.

Listening to the laughter in Hope's voice, watching the energy in her body—so familiar, so threatened—suddenly without warning tears streamed down my face. My feelings knew what my head could block out: the unutterable sadness of Hope and our life without a future, of Helena and Meredith without their mother, of myself alone. Hope held me in her arms. "I'll be all right," she crooned. "I'm going to be all right."

"Oh, Hopie," I sobbed. It was a wail—a rush of love and misery—a cry of longing for a life again together. I clung to her, awkwardly from the side, receiving strength.

That second operation accomplished nothing more than a smidgen of medical history. There was a melanoma and Jones photographed it because of the rare location. But the growth was too enmeshed with the eye and surrounding tissue to remove without taking the eye and unnecessarily disfiguring her. It could still be attacked by radiation, and Jones passed us on to a radiologist, Dr. Pat Trettor. Though Dr. Jones could not have saved Hope's life, I have always believed that if we had found him earlier, he would have moved confidently and decisively long before Hope's eye was out of use.

Our cordial, regretful farewell was full of mutual appreciation. Hope delighted in Jones's southern informality, and something in the way he always talked to Hope made her feel beautiful. For his part, he respected her straight-on desire for the truth, her physical fortitude. He said much later to me, "Every patient like that takes a little of the pleasure out of life for you. If you have too many of them, too sad, in too short a time, it can lead to a depression, even to a loss of faith that what you are doing is worth anything at all."

That same evening at Columbia-Presbyterian, Dr. Trettor, the radiologist, a tall, pleasant, sympathetic woman, came to Hope's room. She explained the procedure: sessions five days a week starting immediately. Hope wanted to know how radiation worked. Dr. Trettor explained that the division process of cancer cells, more disorganized than normal cells, is interrupted by an intensely focused X-ray beam. She made no promises, but said there was a possibility that as the tumor shrank, the eye might be pulled back into position. We hugged that to us. Trettor also said the cancer should be attacked on two fronts and Hope should begin chemotherapy. Dr. Robert DeBellis, an oncologist she particularly admired, would be coming by later.

DeBellis was a surprise: a short man, youthful, slightly jaunty, bearded, a touch of the maverick. We appreciated his no-nonsense, energetic way—a man of action with plans and remedies in reserve, with what we hoped was a bag of magic. He explained that the chemotherapy would be administered every twenty-eight days and there would be side effects resembling a case of flu—nausea, vomiting, fever. The chemotherapy would start in his office as soon as Hope was released from the hospital.

Our mood lightened. Positive action always did that. Whenever there came another lurch downhill, another piece of "big bad news," there was relief when medical science was ready with another remedy.

The first night Hope was home from the hospital, the telephone rang at home at two in the morning. It was Meredith in Maryland, very sisterly, wanting me to know that Helena was unhappy and had an earache. Then Helena came on with the subjects vital to her mind: "When are you coming down? Did the operation help Mommy? Jumper the cat has adopted three gray and white kittens."

In mid-July we drove down to Maryland, with a shopping bag of beautifully wrapped presents in the back seat, to celebrate Meredith's birthday and bring the children home. When we pulled in, the girls made an Olympic dash to fling their arms around their mother's waist and legs and pull her down for kisses, and tell her even more news about Jumper's kittens. Helena thereafter plastered herself to Hope. I can remember Hope like an uncomfortable, pauper Cleopatra, sitting in the middle of the swimming raft while Helena poled her around the small pond. After Hope had admiringly watched Meredith ride bareback on Sam, the Icelandic pony, Helena dragged her mother out into the pasture to make the acquaintance of Brownie, a calf with one blind eye. "This is your cow," Helena told Hope.

Later Hope and Lanie sat on the porch watching the girls swim in the pond, splashing, screeching. Hope said, "Maybe we made a mistake in adopting them because of all this . . . but I would do it all over again." Her voice choked and her lips trembled. "I worry whether the kids are going to be strong enough."

Lanie said, "I'm sure Meredith will be fine, and Helena is one of the sturdiest children I've ever known." Hope's good eye filled with tears.

In New York, with Hope taking her radiation treatments and chemotherapy, we decided to accept Whitney's offer and let the girls stay with her in Sag Harbor. Whitney herself had a new baby, and her other two sisters flew east one at a time from California and Arizona to help. Hope and I came out to Sag Harbor on Wednesdays and weekends.

Other mornings I drove her in our ancient Ford over the potholes of the West Side Drive to Columbia-Presbyterian. Whenever there was a parking place, I kept Hope company on her dismal journey to the radiation facility in the basement of the children's hospital. Joining the other souls in the subterrane-an anteroom below, all of us silently awaiting our individual fates with sealed faces, we felt like Dante and his guide exploring another level of Hades.

After her radiation session, Hope would come briskly through the swinging doors, glad to be done for the day, bright in her Marimekko dress, lovely, her blanked-out lens now in my mind blanked out, vanished into the familiar. She would smile at me and my heart would leap and I would believe once more that surely she was one of the lucky ones. We would flee that place, making black and relieving jokes about, in Hope's words, "geezers and geezettes acking out."

We had a cheerful routine to shake the pall of the radiation. We parked at a fire hydrant two blocks away, and I bought containers of tea and hot glazed doughnuts. We sat conspiratorially in the car, sighing with pleasure at this self-indulgence. Sugar and starch were forbidden to both of us — I with my hypoglyce-mia diet, Hope with her potential weight problem. In the midst of our struggle against despair, our tiny gluttony was heaven.

Nowadays our life was measured out in vigils. Would the radiation return the eye to normal? Had its vision been permanently damaged? I would find Hope, her nose within inches of the bathroom mirror, estimating how far the eyeball bulged beyond the socket. One day I discovered her sitting on the bed reading through the bad eye, holding the magazine where the pupil was pointing—down by her elbow. We both laughed at the ridiculousness of the scene. One day when she checked herself in that little hand mirror, I said, "Beautiful!"

She smiled quickly at me and answered affectionately, "But I don't see you there."

All my aspirations were now concentrated on that eye. I blocked out the possibility of metastases to other organs—a subconscious defense. If the eye problem could be solved, Hope could be saved. I enjoyed an almost holiday mood. I had Hope all to myself four days a week, undistracted. We had our companionable, unchic lunches at the Hot Bowl of Soup, and we luxuriated in the peace and quiet of our evenings. There was a nice, illicit sense—like a weekend in a motel. Moreover, like most writers, I detested the act of writing. Now I had an ironclad, guilt-free excuse for goofing off. It was my sacred duty to minister to Hope.

There were moments, however, when her facade cracked, and I faced unwillingly her far weightier realism. I was aghast when she wondered whether the melanoma might attack the other eye and made bitter jokes about blindness—"There's more to an artist's life than listening to WOR." Then there was the night in Sag Harbor when we stayed in the privacy of John Groth's house. Forcing me to lie passive, Hope made love to me for a long time with startling intensity—as though, in a spasm of dread, she wanted to leave her imprint upon me forever.

Four

The twenty-first of July was an important date, long anticipated with pleasure and relief. On that day our dear friends Josie and Peter Davis were due back from Los Angeles, where Peter had been completing *Hearts and Minds*, his Academy Award–winning documentary on the Vietnam War.

In New York our intimate circle was primarily Hope's circle — her sister Whitney and the people Hope captivated. She regarded my writer and editor friends as intellectuals, and perhaps did not feel entirely relaxed in their company, though they were uniformly fond of her and admiring. Neither one of us had the time or strength to cultivate two sets of intimates, and I ceded our social life to Hope. But we both treasured our friendship with the Davises. I knew Peter as an attractive, amusing, and solicitous man with an unusually fluent and informed mind. Josie (christened Johanna) was a former *Time* writer who had moved on to fiction, and her fine first novel, *Life Signs*, had been published the previous year; her father was the subject of the biography I was writing.

As soon as she was back in New York, I expected Josie to be a primary pillar of strength. Her writing was only a sideline; her real vocation was poulticing everybody's wounds, including her own. For Josie, daily life was a dramatic progression of crises, large and slight, real and created, and she survived, in part, by extracting the absurdity from every misfortune, her humming-bird mind puncturing disaster with sardonic wit and a sidelong glance. When she was told about Hope — "The doctor found a tumor" — Josie said, "Let him keep it." Hope laughed at that and told her friends.

Hope, Whitney, and Josie were virtual sisters. But Hope and Josie had a special bond. They were equally dependent on love. In Hope's sense of self-worth I think there was a fissure of doubt and she required the admiration that flowed from her friend-ships, the assurance that she was lovable. Now that she was ill, she more than ever depended on that nurturing. Living these days off capital in all directions, Hope used the affection of her friends as a sort of nest egg to sustain herself.

In Josie's case, friendship actually held her life together. Josie handled love as if it were a special checking account, depositing among her friends daily sums of concern and laughter. Then she would immediately dip into her account, and draw upon these admirers for their support and distraction. When Peter departed to shoot his documentary in Vietnam, leaving Josie in New York with their two young boys, Timmy and Nicky, she right away telephoned Hope. "Okay, you guys, stand by," she announced. "There's sixteen weekends!" Such was the bond she fashioned — the nakedness of her need, the pleasure of her company — that everybody gladly rallied round. And scores of men and women thought of Josie as their best friend.

The evening after Josie and Peter arrived in New York we had dinner together, along with Betty Suyker, a writer-reporter at *Time* whom Josie had designated as her surrogate helping hand to Hope during the past year. We talked gaily about their year in California. As always, the Davises had been adventure-prone, and we heard the story of their robbery in which were stolen, said Josie, "my famous jewels, including the three Brentanos pins at $2.75 each." The sheriff's name, she reported, was Mason Dixon. She also talked about her new friendship with Candy Bergen but bemoaned her problems with a woman that beautiful: "Candy Bergen's navel is the size of a dime. Mine is the size of a quarter. I am not going shopping with Candy Bergen anymore."

That was on Monday. On the following Thursday evening we were invited to come by the Davis apartment on Charles Street near our house in Greenwich Village. Josie wanted to see Meredith and Helena, her godchild. Hope and I and the girls ate dinner at a McDonald's. The city was softly warm after a hot day, and we ambled slowly up Fourth Street toward Charles, coveting useless possessions in shop windows and enjoying the motley sidewalk humanity. We stopped and bought ice cream cones, and meticulously debated the merits of each flavor. It was a cheerful, easy, family outing, Hope's jeopardy briefly in the background.

Ahead of us at Fourth and Charles we saw the revolving roof lights of police cars raking red across the audience of families sitting on the steps of houses and passersby pausing in curiosity. Clutching our ice cream cones as though at a fair, we hurried forward to see and be excited by somebody else's misfortune. I thought, "Street theater!"

One taxi, in running a stop sign at the intersection, had hit another. We crossed Charles Street, and at the corner as we turned left toward the Davis apartment I noticed fresh, scarlet splatter on the sidewalk beside a mail-storage box. "Blood" flashed into my mind. Helena said, "Look. What's that?" The word "knifing" was on my lips but my impulse was to spare her this clue to city violence. I said, "I don't know."

We crowded into the vestibule of the Davises' small apartment house, the girls arguing about the number of months since they had been there. I rang. There was no answering buzz. I rang again. Silence. We went outside and peered through their ground-floor windows. The familiar apartment, Hope's paintings visible on the living-room wall, was clearly empty. At that moment a policeman approached us, his manner oddly diffident and embarrassed. "Who are you looking for?" he asked.

"Mrs. Peter Davis," I answered, wondering if he thought we might be thieves.

"Are you the people she was expecting?" he asked.

"Yes," said Hope. "Mr. and Mrs. Meryman."

"She was injured in an accident."

"Seriously?" asked Hope, her face startled.

"Is she all right?" I said, concerned, but not alarmed. Josie was an institution; nothing happens to institutions. Hope was the one in jeopardy. I remember thinking, "Josie's going to make a great story out of this."

"She's at St. Vincent's Hospital," the policeman said. "You'd better go there." He refused to tell us anything more. We set off. Down the block we encountered Betty Suyker, coming toward us with a frantic air of urgency. Betty told us what had happened. Josie, on her way to meet Hope, had been with Timmy on the corner next to the mail-storage box. When the taxis collided, the rear of one of them swept across the sidewalk and hit Josie, knocking her head first into the storage box. Timmy leaped out of the way. Josie was barely alive. The neurosurgeons were trying to save her. Peter was at the hospital.

As Betty Suyker finished, I felt a pull of my sleeve. It was Helena. I bent down. "Was that Josie's blood?" she asked. I nodded, saying nothing. "Oh," she said, apparently satisfied. I envied the child's literal world, unburdened by those rushes of association, those streams of mental images that multiply pain. Betty had volunteered to take care of Timmy and Nicky, who were with a neighbor. We left Meredith and Helena with her and hurried to the hospital.

At St. Vincent's — to me the central symbol of Hope's own gradual collision with death — we were directed to a first-floor waiting room. Other friends were there, and in muted voices we shared our shock and incredulity. Peter appeared through a rear door. Drawing deep, gasping breaths, he told us that Josie was dead. Immediately, Hope went to Peter and took his hands. She said without sentiment, "It should have been me."

Peter left for a last moment with Josie. Hope and I walked slowly back to our children through the teeming summer city. I wondered if Hope really would have substituted herself for Josie. Yes, she meant it. She was capable of that ultimate reach of selflessness. Not me. I was shamelessly thankful that I was not yet in Peter's shoes.

I was walking with my arm through Hope's while she hugged it against her side — holding on to each other for comfort. It was one of those times of total silent communication. We knew we had been living our probable future, but felt no need to probe that fact with words. I thought there was a kind of grace in our reticence. Once in an interview, Laurence Olivier told me that he created characters on the stage by assuming their outward mask and mannerisms, and then the required inward emotions rose up inside him. Something of that sort was happening to us. We acted outwardly as though Josie's death held no foreshadowings — and our panic never surfaced.

Speaking with a numb and businesslike composure, we talked about the awful irony of the title of Josie's novel, *Life Signs* — the medical phrase she had heard over and over in the bulletins from Dallas as President Kennedy lay wounded in the head, not really alive, not truly dead. We talked about the fateful freakishness of the accident. Josie had traveled three thousand miles to stand on that particular street corner. It was a rendezvous with death. We were silent for a moment, both looking down as we walked, heads turned slightly toward each other, with Hope's patched eye away from me, out of sight. Her face was tranquil. She said, "If Josie can do it, maybe I can too."

With Betty Suyker we walked the Davis boys and Meredith and Helena to our house. We said nothing of Josie's death. That was for Peter to do. At the dining-room table the children watched television while Timmy and Nicky wondered aloud how long their mother would be in the hospital. They were subdued, but teasing and jousting and fooling as always.

Accompanied by a friend, Bill Smith, Peter arrived. As I let them in the front door upstairs, Peter was stiff with control and determination and dread. He asked where he could be alone with the boys. While he waited in our bedroom, I sent them upstairs. The rest of us stood immobilized in the dining area near the foot of the stairs. From the TV on the table came grotesque bursts of canned laughter. Then, shatteringly from above, came sudden heart-piercing shrieks — primordial cries of pain, indelible. Our false calm was swept away. Turning away from each other with odd modesty, we wept.

I became aware of Meredith and Helena at the table staring with frightened eyes. I went over to them, my face wet, and said, "Josie died." Helena, the little philosopher, was very solemn. Tender-hearted Meredith exploded into tears. I rested her head against me, and said, over and over, my own heart finally aching, "I know; I know, Mere; I know." And still the TV laughter burbled on.

Peter stayed upstairs. The boys returned briefly, and I could hardly bear to look at Nicky Davis, a replica of his mother. It was painful to look at my own daughters, so unaware that they and I might soon be reenacting that horrific scene. I forced those thoughts aside.

At Hope's suggestion, we all walked Peter and the boys back to their apartment, and I stayed there with Peter. He insisted on being the person to telephone the news of Josie's death to her mother and two brothers and while he spoke to each one, his voice infinitely sad and tender, his right hand gripped my wrist with the quivering strength of a seizure.

The next day I performed a melancholy errand. At St. Vincent's I picked up Josie's wedding ring. Returning, I found myself passing the mail-storage box on the corner of Charles and Fourth streets. The blood at its base was now a dark discoloration. I could see rough scratches on the cement made by the police to outline Josie's body. I thought of the inscription on the inside of the wedding ring: "Johanna and Peter 9-13-59 and always." During that moment I think death finally became real to me. Despite all the desperate vigils, the mortal dangers, I believe that I had managed to hold death gingerly at the fringes of my consciousness, a scary word but misty and distant—an eventuality. Beside that tall metal box I came to the point in the Ritual when, with my whole being, I angrily confronted the finality of death—Hope's death, my own death—the end, exit, kaput, nothingness—a stain on a sidewalk.

Meredith never talked about Josie's death. That was her way. Helena brought me a sheet of paper. At the bottom was a recognizable drawing of Josie's face, crying. At the top, printed in capital letters ornate with flowers, was the title, "IT'S LOVE." The words continued underneath: "When Love is Around it's always enough to share. The end. The chapter of Josie. To Josie from all the love in the world."

Hope, I think, now began to regard death as a process, an act you carried out, a rite of passage that Josie had performed ahead of her—"If Josie can do it, maybe I can too." I believe that Hope gathered that iron will of hers and resolved to do it well.

Thereafter, our full attention was centered on Peter. His stepmother came east from California to help find him an apartment uptown. Not only had Josie been killed almost at their door, but also the house had been sold and they were being evicted. After the funeral Peter and the boys settled in with friends in Easthampton, Long Island, near Whitney, the instant surrogate mother to Timmy and Nicky.

Hope's radiation treatment ended in mid-August, and though the chemotherapy continued, we moved into a motel in Sag Harbor for a week. Her eye had receded only a little into its socket, but the pain was gone. We were certain the tumor was dead. Hope was working well with one eye. We began an emotional maneuver that became a familiar part of the Ritual —bargaining with fate: "Okay, we'll settle for one eye, but no cancer anywhere else."

Tests were scheduled in early September. But despite that prospect and Hope's blanked eye and the awful threeness of Peter and the boys, there was a determined festivity—cookouts on the beach, painting excursions with the children, a laughing dinner on our twenty-second wedding anniversary.

The next two weeks we devoted to our normal August routine—a trip to the house in Dublin, New Hampshire, and then on to Maine, Hope's favorite place to paint. Hope's anguish was so painful for me that I took her outward calm during those months at face value and assumed it showed inward equanimity.

But there in Dublin, Hope suffered one of those small blows which were symbolic last straws, shattering her forbearance. She had to be photographed by me for the catalogue of a show of her works in New Jersey in October. She was instantly and extremely agitated. I thought she had made her peace with the eye and the disfigurement. She announced, furiously, that she was not going to be photographed "looking like some one-eyed grandma gruntin'." She finally agreed to a profile picture with her bad eye hidden. I tried to be meticulous about the light meter and camera settings, which drove her wild and so rattled me that I made mistakes and had to reshoot. This drove her even wilder. Over and over she asked, "Are you sure my eye doesn't show?" I sensed that the slightest bruise on the surface of her control would release a scream.

Our trip to Swann's Island, off the coast from Northeast Harbor, Maine, was our third and our second with the children. We stayed as usual in a small housekeeping cabin owned by a lobsterman named Llewellyn Joyce, a dour Down Easter. I once stood with him there on the hillside overlooking the harbor —swaybacked lobster boats at the moorings, the buffer of sea-scoured granite between water and spruce—a scene so conventionally picturesque Hope had pronounced it fake. I said to Llewellyn Joyce that this must be a heavenly place to live. He answered, "When I look down there, I see that my boat needs painting."

In our cabin Hope and I slept in beds in the living area and the two girls had a bunk in a tiny alcove. Early in our stay a saturating, matting fog took over the island. We were housebound, and by midmorning the children were wrangling — their way of entertaining themselves. Hope told them to stop. Full of the righteousness of their silly argument, they ignored her. My outrage exploded, releasing my fury at Hope's illness and its perversion of our lives. It seemed monstrous that our own children would compound our pain.

I ordered Meredith and Helena outside with me. The fog pressed around us like the walls of a tiny, chilly room. In a fierce, intense voice I began talking, not entirely sure from one sentence to the next what I was going to say. I told the two girls there had been something called a tumor growing behind Mommy's eye, but even though the treatments had killed the tumor, she was terribly worried that she would never be able to use her eye again. I told them to imagine what it meant to be an artist and lose an eye — and how would they feel if it happened to them? It was outrageous for them to cause her more unhappiness. I almost struck them with the full facts to punish them with their own remorse. I stopped short of that. The fear in their solemn faces was already draining away my fury.

I was suddenly weary, disgusted with myself. I was taking out my frustration and my helplessness on the children. I was using guilt as a weapon, and was no more adult, no less childish, than they. Life, even around the mortally sick, does not stop and stay as soft and still as cotton batting. Life goes unfeelingly on. Kids are kids; needs are needs. The girls sat silent, cowed, waiting to be dismissed. "Let's go in now," I said sternly.

The fact was that Meredith and Helena did not know their mother had cancer. They thought Hope's operation had solved her mysterious problem, and believed that the eye was a new problem, unconnected and possibly caused that day when she hit her head on the air conditioner. Keeping the girls in ignorance had been a deliberate decision. During the radiation I had begun to worry about sudden questions from them, and having to improvise answers, perhaps in midcrisis when I might be half-hysterical. I wanted a set policy which would guide me in the future. I decided to research the matter much as I would a magazine piece.

Josie Davis's father, Herman Mankiewicz, died when she was fifteen, and she was not told that he was dangerously ill. We had talked about this on tape when I interviewed her for the biography, and I reread that section of the transcript. "I didn't even know how sick he was," she recalled. "When he went into the hospital, they told me it was just for a checkup. So I resented going to visit him. I'd sit on the edge of the bed and say, 'How long are we staying?' These are not your most cherished memories. They were right — I was too young to participate fully in the ritual of death, but I sure as hell could have done a lot better than I did. If I'd known the truth, I would have been a lot nicer to him. I could have prepared myself, steeled myself for the mourning period. Everybody else was allowed to make whatever private deals you make with yourself when you know something terrible is going to happen — you steel yourself, build up what you need to protect yourself, weep when you want to."

But Josie had been fifteen years old then. Meredith was now nine and Helena nearly seven. At Harry's suggestion, I consulted a friend who was a child psychiatrist. I visited him in his office, and he began asking me questions as though I were a patient. I interrupted him to ask my own questions. Should we sit the girls down and tell them about Hope's cancer? If partial knowledge is preferable, how far should we go? What considerations are involved? Is there a known pattern of behavior when a child's parent is dying? Are there symptoms of psychological problems that we should watch for? If he was in my shoes, what would he do? In sum he told me that the children would judge for themselves the emotional load they could carry. What they needed to know, they would ask. What they could not bear to know, they would ignore. They should not be told any lies. As long as Hope's illness was handled at home, they would be participating in the evolution of the disease and emotionally preparing for Hope's death. However, if her symptoms should become so shocking that the girls might be traumatized, they must be separated from her. But I could not get a concrete sense of what symptoms would suddenly be too much.

When I departed, though I was grateful, I almost regretted coming. I was profoundly depressed. For an hour the two of us had been tacitly agreeing that Hope would inevitably decline and die. I tried to remove all such presumptions from my report to Hope, and the two of us agreed that there seemed no useful purpose in telling the girls at this time that their mother might die. We saw a crucial difference between Josie at fifteen and Meredith and Helena. Such frightful knowledge, such suspense, would be a heavy weight for small souls.

But as we made our decision, I could hear Josie's mother saying to me, "I just couldn't bear to break Josie's heart." And I remember saying to Hope, "Can you see yourself looking into those two little faces and saying, 'I have cancer!' " I was never sure what role our emotions played in our judgment. Maybe we had seized on the easy way out and avoided the ultimate confrontation with reality—telling our children that their mother could die. Certainly it was easier to keep up our pretenses of normality if the children believed Hope was well. And I also wondered whether roping children in on your misery could sometimes be a convoluted act of anger. If the parents are going to be locked into that long, dark tunnel, then, damn it, the kids should come along. I know I felt that way briefly in the fog on Swann's Island.

During the rest of that housebound day, Meredith and Helena were delightful. They decided to put on a show. A stage was cleared, the table moved back against the wall. One at a time each girl did a silly, self-conscious, giggling dance—to an obbligato of "Now me. It's my turn." Then Meredith, pliant as a blade of grass, did an encore of backbends, walkovers, and cartwheels.

Hope stood up. She would do her dance. Hope was ordinarily not a person who played. It was my family role to roughhouse on the bed, play hide-and-seek, swim to the raft, bounce basketballs, throw tennis balls, sit at Monopoly boards. Now Hope disappeared into the cabin alcove. I became the announcer: "We proudly present that toast of ten continents, that radiant star of the East, that gorgeous hunk of woman — the ever-popular Hope Brooks Meryman! Here she is, ladies and gentleman. Give the little lady a hand!" The children clapped wildly. Hope sashayed out in her slip — a swivel-hipped, red-haired, one-eyed belly dancer, chanting, "Oh, they don't wear pants in the southern part of France . . ." The girls screamed with pleasure. I stood up cheering, amazed by an abandon and gift for parody I had not seen in Hope before. After a minute she stopped, and I grasped her in my arms and bent her down toward the floor in a burlesque of a Valentino kiss. The children danced around us in delight.

That week we did the Maine things that Hope loved. We took walks to the lighthouse, redolent of past and future storms, and through the spruce woods to granite ledges on tidal inlets, picking wild raspberries along the way. At the abandoned quarry, filled with rainwater, Hope painted its variegated, moss-covered slabs while the children and I swam. We picnicked on a beach of infinitely textured pebbles and built a driftwood fire which Meredith, by superior voice power, won the right to light. There was excited talk about the decaying carcass of a dead dog the children found in the woods, and Hope, utterly at ease, gave them a little talk about dust into dust, nature's way.

I had been asking myself just what joys make life so precious. There is certainly the sense of fulfilling one's potential. Another lies in those moments when a family, despite its rivalries and angers, does jell and senses its intense bonds. So for Hope in particular, who I think felt her family to be an extension of herself, the week on Swann's Island must have been a time of hiatus from the mainland of her dread. Boarding the ferry for home, I was heartsick.

In New York we took up the dismal task of helping Peter Davis dismantle his and Josie's household. A platoon of friends turned out for a country barn raising in reverse, and it was morbidly like packing away Josie herself.

Hope, recovering from another bout with chemotherapy, was not strong enough for such labor. She came to the house with me, saying as she surveyed the wreckage of the familiar home, "This sure takes your mind off cancer." She found Peter and said to him, "Whitney can't face going through Josie's clothes. Would you let me do it?"

During that period I was observing Peter carefully, intensely aware of him as a possible precursor and a role model. His sorrow, deeply contained, was palpable. On the surface he was almost normal, throwing himself into the tasks of resettling his life. I wondered whether in the same way that Hope could treat death as a process, grief could be approached as a process. I thought to myself, deliberately echoing Hope, "If Peter can do it, perhaps I can too."

Five

At the end of September, coincidentally marking one year of illness, Hope had two days of tests: X rays of the liver, lungs, and head — the first since her second eye operation in July. The preceding week was for both of us, as Hope put it, "Sweat City." All ordinary emotions and sensations were cauterized by dread. Nothing but anxiety seemed real. Then Dr. DeBellis telephoned the good news that all the test results were negative. A rush of excitement galvanized my body. Always swelling good news into salvation, I decided I had been wrong. "She's going to make it," I thought. "She's going to be all right." I went to Hope, who was still standing by the bedroom telephone. Deep satisfaction, not exultation, was Hope's way — joy hugged inwardly, filtering out through a small, almost shy smile. I pressed my cheek against hers and felt her skin wet with my tears. "Oh, Hopie," I said, "I'm *so* happy."

But the reprieve, no matter how genuine, was shadowed. Paradoxically, in order to remain healthy, Hope had to be sick. By now there had been two doses of chemotherapy. Because the chemicals were so lethal, they had to be administered in Dr. DeBellis's office in the Atchley Pavilion, a place I irrationally came to loathe. It was a glass and masonry tower, an infinity from those dressing pavilions on that Spanish beach. On the fourth floor the large common waiting room was at once plush and cold — green-blue wallpaper, color-coordinated foam-rubber sofas and chairs, discreet lamps — medical motel modern. Hope and I talked very little. I usually read. Hope, her pen careening across the pages, wrote letters full of news about everything except cancer, admitting only that "I'm going along keeping my fingers crossed." We both covertly studied the other couples, who surreptitiously stared back — all of us stoic, sealed, able to tolerate our own anxiety but not the touch of another's. Soon we recognized DeBellis's patients, and would try to figure out which member of those sad couples had the cancer, which member was sharing my experience. There was one particular woman who always came alone — arrestingly, vibrantly beautiful, as young as Hope. When their glances brushed, there was a silent spark of recognition.

As much as I disliked that place, I appreciated Robert DeBellis. Hope was fortunate in her doctors. But it may be impossible to experience a long illness and a death without hazy negative feelings about the profession. You want doctors to save you, but they become messengers bearing bad news. You want them to be Gods, but you are irked when they put on those airs. You want them to be human, but you are furious when they show frailty. You want them to cure, miraculously if possible, but you resent your utter dependency. DeBellis somehow reconciled these impossible demands. Whenever people talked about him, they used words like "direct," "straightforward." I think that was his solution, which required an extraordinary degree of emotional courage.

In DeBellis's tiny office and examining room, Hope sat on a chrome-legged chair while he faced her, slightly to the left. His first words were always, "Well, how's everything going?" And every time, no matter how debilitated her condition, her answer was "Fine!" Then she would launch into a monologue on how hard she was working, and eagerly describe her plans for a print or painting, the milestone she had passed in her children's book, or her doings on the past weekend and plans for the next—all with a tone of "See, this proves I'm not sick."

While she talked, DeBellis would beam at her. "Hope always made it easy," he told me much later. "No matter how bad things got, she had a sort of composure without any of the craziness and the thrashing about. And I always had a feeling she was the same sick as she was well—the same basic concerns, the same overall view. That's something I admire, something I expect from myself. Dying is a different phase of your life, but it doesn't call for a different behavior."

On our first visit to DeBellis's office Hope said, almost without preamble, "I always want to be told everything and I want to know the truth."

DeBellis said, "Any questions you have will be answered as honestly as I can, and I believe that a patient who is informed about the disease is better able to cope with it and deal with the treatment."

"Can chemotherapy cure me?" asked Hope.

DeBellis said, "The state of the art does not have any cure for melanoma. We will be aiming for an arrest of the disease, holding it in check and then maintaining the arrest."

"Will I always be taking chemotherapy?" asked Hope.

"For the next one to two years, assuming all goes well. Beyond that we don't yet know what the best long-term managements are, but presumably some form of chemotherapy at less-frequent intervals."

"How long do you actually think I have to live."

"Any doctor who prognosticates the future of a cancer patient ends up looking like a jerk. The chances are you'll die before I die—but there's not even a guarantee of that."

DeBellis got out the chemotherapy dosage—startlingly large pills, their colors as gaudy as neon—and Hope grinned over at me, the family pill pusher. "Aren't you jealous?" she said. She noticed on the wall photographs of a sailboat, and asked

DeBellis if it was his. He said, yes, it was a good way to escape the telephones. Hope talked about her own pleasure on the water in Maine, the color of the sea changing with the sky, how beautiful it was, how it drove her crazy when she tried to paint it. I remember thinking that this moment was a portrait of Hope — her body canted forward with energy, her hazel eyes bright with eagerness, her fine-drawn face vivid with smiles and earnest frowns, one eyebrow flicking up — extending herself to another person, almost flirting — body language saying that her words were important to her and so was he.

DeBellis, talking as intimately to her as she did to him, was the one doctor who allowed a personal attachment to build between himself and Hope. He was the rare doctor who had no permanent, self-protective shield between himself and his patients — remarkably brave for a man whose clients, by the time they reached him, were almost all doomed — a desperate fact we did not then know.

DeBellis had spent twenty-one years as a biochemist in medical research, but then deliberately switched to this grueling specialty. "I guess I did it," he told me much later, "out of a sense of warmth and friendship with patients. The concept that I'm trained as a physician to cure, that's nonsense. Yeah, we sometimes cure people. But that's not where it's at. Doctors who cover for me while I'm gone say when I come back, 'How the hell do you stand your patients? They're demanding, they're almost all going to die. How do you even answer the phone when they call? How come you don't tell half of them to go find another doctor?' Well, who else are they going to find? They're going to die and somebody has to take care of them. If they die a little bit happier or a little more composed, then I've succeeded."

Hope and I left DeBellis's office feeling buoyant. He had managed to be honest, as far as he went, without blitzing us with brutal realities. He left us with goals we could hold on to. He once said to me, "I think patients in a very unspoken way know when things are going well and when they're not, and they don't really want to discuss it. It's a rare patient who really wants to know the gory details. As long as there's some hope, they'll continue functioning."

Illness, to Hope, was a sign of weakness, and she was mildly impatient of anybody, like me, who often took noontime naps and went to bed with head colds. She was a person always in motion, walking quickly with brisk steps, leaning slightly forward. There was a time when Whitney lived in Greenwich Village, and Hope would stop for a visit. Coming through the door she would announce, "I can't stay." If she consented to have a cup of coffee, she would keep her coat on. She acted as though cancer was a grand way to lose weight, and claimed to be thrilled when her figure, always good, thinned down to the perfect svelteness that had been her dream. Putting on a skirt that had not fitted for decades, she said delightedly, "I'm a skinny wreck."

Devoted Gertrude begged her to eat more, arguing, "You need something to fight with."

Hope would answer, "I'm all right. There's nothing wrong with me."

"I admired her for that," Gertrude later remembered, "but I didn't admire her for not eating." Sometimes Gertrude would force Hope to take a nap. "But Mrs. Meryman would put her feet on the floor to be sure she would not go to sleep," Gertrude told me. "She'd read a book; say to me, 'I don't have time to sleep.' "

Hope's misery during the chemotherapy "hell weeks," as we called them, made Hope seem sicker than she ever was with a deadly but invisible tumor. During the first two days of treatment she was well enough to go to DeBellis alone by subway, which she insisted on doing so I could work. On the third day I drove her, and by evening she was pathetically ill. The sound of Hope throwing up in the bathroom was now a familiar part of family life. I would rush to help her, and on those days when she was too weak to move, I held a mixing bowl while the vomit poured out the side of her mouth. When she rolled back gasping on the pillows, the freckles on her sweating face were stark against her ashen skin. I wiped her face, kept damp cloths on her forehead. But Hope accepted her immobility and suffering as simply another part of her life—and her only chance for life. She did not complain.

There was one exception—a morning when Hope felt particularly isolated from her family. As usual I was running the house—breakfast, bag lunches, homework, dinner, bedtimes. I liked it. I was close to the children in an entirely new way. In the mornings Meredith was an early riser and I treasured the companionable half hour we had alone together, rummaging in the kitchen. It was a time to talk when nothing was at issue between us. That day we were discussing dreams. Meredith confided, "I tell Charlie, 'No dreams tonight. I'll skip the dreams. You watch other people's dreams.' "

"Who's Charlie?" I asked.

"He's the guy up there who directs the dreams."

Presently I went upstairs to check on Hope. She lay motionless on her side, and I sat down on the narrow margin of the bed and began rubbing her scalp with my fingertips. In a moment, without looking at me, she spoke in a voice full of sorrow and childish resentment. She said, "I could hear you and Mere having a real little conversation in the kitchen. I never have that with Mere!"

One afternoon Hope lay with her sister Whitney on our bed and talked dispassionately about dying. Hope said that she could not figure out what to feel about it, whether to be afraid, or what. "It's so totally unknown," she said, "and there's nothing I can do about it, right?"

The two turned frivolous, as though the intellectual blind alley was also an emotional blank. Whitney wondered, "Do you suppose Josie and Daddy and Jack Kennedy are all walking around up there?" They giggled at the image, and Hope— referring to a red-haired friend who had died suddenly—said,

"Do you suppose when Dick gets there and asks for a fuzzy redheaded witch he'll get Suzy Bernard by mistake?"

That fall Hope and I made our customary trip to Pennsylvania to visit the grave of Little Whitney in Chester Heights. Hope had felt no allegiance to any locale except her home in Manhattan, and it was her decision to bury Little Whitney in Pennsylvania, near where she had died. It was a picturesque, tree-shaded country Catholic church, one of the earliest in the region. The peacefulness of the place was accented by pleasant sounds of living. From our left, out of sight, came the slap-slap of a basketball on pavement. To our right, a lone man was setting up one of the booths for the annual church fair. Hope, stepping over to the woods, broke a branch from a flowering bush and gently laid it on the little grave. Her face was very tender, her blanked-out eyeglass a badge of her own mortality. She said, "This is where I want to be buried."

By now, a year since Hope's mole was diagnosed as malignant melanoma, cancer and emotional survival had become a daily way of life. In retrospect, I realize that we each divided our consciousness into compartments of denial and acceptance, the particular moment dictating which compartment opened up into the mind. I think much of our behavior was managed by this self-protective schizophrenia. Friends have since suggested that Hope and I should have broken down all compartments, exploring and ventilating together her anxieties — that by facing her fate head on and clear-eyed, uncushioned by denial, Hope would have achieved a transcendent peacefulness. And, yes, I can see that in the process of talk, of organizing ideas, finding words and crystallizing feelings, a cleansing of fear could take place.

I remember in a bookstore, out of a sense of duty, picking up a copy of *On Death and Dying* by Kübler-Ross, the evangelist of deathbed talk. I thumbed it and found the book to be mainly case histories, none of them applicable to Hope. They were about the neglected dying, who were full of unanswered needs.

People could lavish love and attention on Hope because she made her dying ritual easy on them. Circularly, she could make the ritual tolerable because she was surrounded by support.

I suspect that for Hope and for most of us our own death is too brilliant a light to be looked at long and hard. I also suspect that we will know instinctively what is best for our particular nature. Hope had never been a person who ruminated, who used talk to clarify or release feelings. She used torrential conversation to charm and entertain, and to be heard. I believe that objectifying our agony in words — irrevocably admitting that Hope's death was inevitable, blasting open our protective compartments — might not have been cleansing and liberating. It might have been damaging, even devastating, to our precarious equilibrium.

"And yet . . . and yet . . ." Then my mind swings back. Perhaps, after all, I was being cowardly. Perhaps Hope wanted to talk, was sparing me the pain while awaiting a signal. Perhaps by appointing myself chief optimist — outwardly refusing to admit defeat, pouring reassurance into Hope — I may have disqualified myself as a confidant for despair. Perhaps in a space of calm we could have probed her predicament together, and in our marriage broken down the deepest barriers between us. I think, "Yes, maybe that was an opportunity we missed."

Whenever Hope's nerve did break, it was at two or three in the morning, the hours of desperation. A sixth sense would rouse me from my own shallow sleep. "Are you all right?" I would ask anxiously.

"Yes," she would say.

There was a temptation to avoid what I knew was ahead. I had her permission to go back to sleep. But in the dark I moved across our wide bed to where her body huddled on its side, facing away from me. Raising myself on my elbow, I would touch her shoulder and find it wet with sweat — sometimes cold, sometimes feverishly hot. "Are you having the horrors?"

Usually she did not answer. As though hoping to press my health and love through her skin, I would fit my body along the length of her back, my knees bent in behind hers, my right arm embracing her, my hand touching a breast, a still caress, "playing spoons." As I held her, I often found that she was crying, but so deep inside I could hardly feel the tremors.

"I'm so scared. I'm so scared," said Hope, her voice small.

I held her tighter. I also was scared.

"I don't want to die."

Speaking firmly and urgently, I answered, "Hopie, it's not necessarily going to happen. It's not inevitable. The odds aren't good, but they're not hopeless. There *are* remissions, particularly with melanoma."

Silence, then, "I want to see Mere and Henny grow up. I want to see what my children turn into."

"You will, Hopie. You will. Nobody says you're going to die tomorrow. You've got a long time. You're very strong. You've got everything going for you. You've got the best doctors. There's all kinds of treatments still to go."

"I want to read your book. I'm never going to read your book."

"Now that's ridiculous! Of course you're going to read it. I'm going to finish that book long before anything happens to you."

"But you can't work on it, and that's my fault. I feel so badly that you have to spend all your time with me. This is such a lousy deal for you."

And sometimes her voice would turn angry, saying, "I want to be a better artist. I want to leave behind a body of work. You'll finish your book and go on. Right now is what I'll always be. I don't have any time left."

I would tell her what I believed: that the work she was doing now was the best of her career. And finally I would hold her even tighter and fervently say, "Hopie, Hopie, my darling, I love you so much. Nothing must ever happen to you."

Often she then turned toward me, and I gathered her into my arms — her damp hair against my face, her sour breath in my nostrils, my sorrow thick in my chest — and we held on to each other like drowning children.

"Do you want a back rub?"

"That's all right."

From Hope, that was a yes. I gently urged her onto her stomach. Kneeling astride her, sliding my hands up under the nightgown, I massaged the soft flesh. My fingers moved over the scar across her back — the channel cut from the mole to her armpit. Was it kinder to avoid it, or pretend it didn't matter? I could feel in the unpleasant moistness of her skin the pall of illness. I could feel in the muscles along her neck and shoulders the terror like an iron bar. I could feel in her body the warm life, the assurance that tomorrow, at least, Hope would be alive.

Presently she would say, "That's enough. That was wonderful."

I always answered, "Do you want a pill?"

She always said, "No."

I always said, "It's better than lying there hour after hour with the horrors." This minuet exasperated me partly because I thought it was silly, partly because I knew what the outcome would be. Hope violently disapproved of sleeping pills. Throughout our marriage, as I stood in the bathroom in the middle of the night taking something to put me to sleep, I would hear her voice accusingly from the bed. "Are you taking a pill?" Usually I lied. Now, dying of cancer, taking poisonous chemotherapy pills that seemed as big as thumbs, Hope still worried that barbiturates were addictive, that using one was "giving in."

One argument swayed her, and I unhesitatingly used it. She owed it to me to get to sleep. Otherwise she was condemning me to hours of wakefulness which would affect my writing tomorrow. I was lying again. Long after Hope's breathing evened out, I would lie staring into the dark and the silence, having my own version of the horrors.

My worries, wild-eyed, overwhelming, tumbled over each other to torment me. "How can I take Hopie's place with Meredith and Helena . . . how can I do that and have time to write . . . my writing career is over, just as I'm moving up out of journalism . . . thank God for the children . . . just the three of us . . . so forlorn without Hopie, so lonely . . . those poor, poor kids . . . poor Hopie . . . poor me . . . I'll have to earn some money and still have time for the children . . . what kind of a job? . . . suppose Hopie ends up in a hospital month after month at maybe $10,000 a month — and me without major medical insurance . . . I wonder how bankruptcy works — maybe I should start hiding money — I'll have to sell my house just to pay a hospital bill . . . maybe Blue Cross–Blue Shield will be enough . . . maybe Hopie will commit suicide . . . mustn't think such thoughts . . . no money to send the kids to decent schools . . . never able to write another book . . . no more dream . . . no Hopie." I had taken a sleeping pill along with Hope. Finally, sweating, I would get up and take another.

There was a daytime brand of horrors that took me, unguarded, by surprise. When I was away from Hope — and usually at my office — I would suddenly flood with grief, as though my subconscious had decided that Hope was already dead. Sometimes I telephoned her. Once when she answered, her antennae hypertuned by her own anxiety, she said, "Are you checking to see if I'm alive?"

Sometimes the feeling was so strong, so unhappy, that I would rush home to Hope's side. I remember one day she was lying, dressed, on top of the bed against a pile of pillows, her glasses on the end of her nose, reading a newspaper. Above her hung an early picture by my father, who had been a professional portrait and landscape painter. Hope smiled, surprised when I hurried in. I told her I couldn't write so I thought I'd come home. I sat beside her on the bed, kissed her, and we read the paper together. Now I was anchored in this hour. With the past months blocked out, there were no poignant ironies. With the future blocked, there was no looming calamity. Hope was alive today. I sometimes thought of Keats's line: "That is all ye know on earth and all ye need to know."

We reveled in discussing the most humdrum family business: what time should we eat dinner, what we thought of Helena's teacher at school, when was I going to fix the squeaky bathroom door, how could we make the kids put their dirty clothes into the hamper. That was exotic survival medicine. I had always thought of daily machinery as an enemy, threatening to overwhelm the creative side of life, but now I realized that a truly shared life means a shared interest in the dribs and drabs of living. The loss of that is loneliness. I thought of the solitary old people I had encountered, and how they drummed my ears with the trivia of their existences—what their lives had finally come down to, and what they hungered to share. For Hope and me, such routine now meant predictability, safety, daily life continuing indefinitely.

The Magic Mother of all routines was Hope's annual orgy of Christmas. That year, 1974, no mere chemotherapy could chill this symbolic time of rebirth and remembrance. Christmas cards reached out to virtually every friend she ever had. Gifts were two-way testimonials of continued affection. For Hope, the giver and believer, it was the quintessential anniversary and the one time she could let go and spoil the children. I had long ago nicknamed her Santa's Helper. She made trays and trays of cookies in animal shapes, cut with dies she made herself. We racked our brains for gift ideas for every friend and relative, and Hope did all the buying. She wrapped everything in hand-decorated paper, made by cutting a motif in an art-gum eraser and stamping it, inked, over and over on the tissue. To-and-from cards were similarly hand-printed. Earlier, during Thanksgiving, on dozens of small cards, she had painted watercolors of single stalks of dried weeds and flowers in the snow—minute works of art, achingly delicate. These went off to special people as Christmas cards, instead of the several hundred little prints she usually made, one by one. That was her one concession to illness.

I adored this Christmas side of Hope and was awed by it. But the blessing was mixed. Inevitably much of the work was done at the last minute, and Hope labored late into the evenings, exhausting herself. This year her strength was less. There was also in both of us that pool of anger at her illness, and it rose closer to the surface as she grew more and more tired.

One of the happiest Christmas rituals was getting the tree —not the Currier and Ives parade into the snowy woods, hatchet in hand, but a trip by car to a stand in lower Manhattan under the elevated highway—an urban woods with trees tied shut with twine. On the appointed Sunday, a bitter-cold day, while Hope and the girls put on their coats, I went out to the curb to warm up the car. It would not start. It was a 1965 Ford, an old friend, but exhausted. I returned inside and broke the news to three crestfallen faces.

Hope was instantly furious: "That Goddam car. I've told you over and over to buy a new one. I'm never going to get into it again." I said there were plenty of other Christmas-tree places in New York and we could easily walk to one. Hope answered, "But I don't want to. We've always gotten our trees at the same place. It's part of Christmas. We can't get a tree home without a car! I can't carry a tree!"

My own disappointment and anger welled up, and I lost control. Suddenly I did not care whether Hope was sick; she had no right to make an unfortunate situation into a disaster. I said, compounding the fiasco, "For Christ's sake, nobody thinks you're going to lug a tree around. Just because of your eye, you think you have to be driven everyplace."

Hope began to cry. The children started crying. It was so awful, I laughed. Meredith yelled at me, "If you want to get a divorce, we can live here with Mommy!"

My present for Hope that year was a five-foot-square projection screen for the slides she used so much in her work. It was not, I knew, a particularly romantic present, but it was my testimonial that ahead of her she had years of art. For the children's Christmas Hope and I decided to give in to Meredith's lust for a ten-speed bicycle. Her bike at that time was a girl's stock model with thick tires. Alas, seven-year-old Helena a year earlier had picked out a shiny red number with a hand brake, a bell, a speedometer, and thin tires. To cap Meredith's jealousy, it was a boy's bike. All of her psychic rivalry with Helena surfaced in endless arguments about bikes—and tantrums in which Meredith lay on her bed sobbing, drumming her feet, screaming that Helena had everything, she had nothing.

For Helena, Hope decided to make a lady and gentleman bear. Helena since babyhood had had a fixation on bears. Her tiny bedroom was a convention hall of stuffed bears—"the gang" as she called them. Each was assigned, along with his name, a fully rounded personality, and once when I teased about Big Teddy reading without moving his lips, Helena answered, "Well, he's not really real, but he is real."

Some years earlier Josie Davis had given Helena her own Hollywood childhood bears, a little husband and wife elaborately dressed, he in a blue cutaway and she in a flowered dress. After Josie's death, Timmy asked for them. Helena was heartbroken, but understood: the bears would help Timmy remember his mother. But they were too precious, too loved, to be merely handed over. As a conveyance, Helena padded and lined a shoe box, and on the cover made a drawing of the two bears dancing. Hope, who hated sewing, set out to make replacements. I can remember her on Christmas eve at her worktable, and the way she cocked her head to make the most of her good eye as she struggled to fit the gold-cuffed frock coat onto the felt shoulders.

I was in the studio assembling Meredith's ten-speed bike, and the scene is a particularly sentimental memory for me: the intense feeling of family—Hope and I, the father and mother, preparing Christmas as our parents once did for us, as Mere and Henny would do someday. In bed on Christmas morning we held each other and kissed. "Merry Christmas."

"Merry Christmas."

We lay side by side, Hope's head on my enfolding arm. I told her the two bears were marvelous, that Helena would be thrilled. Then Hope asked matter-of-factly, "Do you think I'll be alive next Christmas?"

Six

By February of 1975 there had been four symptom-free months, and as each month had passed I told myself that Hope's odds for survival were better and better. I said to a friend, "The anxiety quotient is down."

On March third in the late morning I was writing at my office and the telephone rang. It was Hope, her voice panicky. "Dick, I need you. Something's wrong with my leg. I can't walk."

This was the first time in her illness that Hope had called for help and used that word "need." I said, "I'll be right there," and left at a run. At home the house was silent. No lights on. I rushed into our bedroom. Empty. I called out, "Hopie!"

"I'm here." In the gloom of Meredith's unlit room, she was on the bed, her body very still under the blanket her sister Ky had knitted for Little Whitney.

I sat next to her and asked, "What happened?"

She told me she had been sitting at her table in the studio, drawing. When she got up to start a load of the children's wash, she was instantly dizzy, her head ached, and her left leg went numb, wobbly, and she almost fell down. Her left hand tingled and had no strength. Her left cheek and half her tongue were numb and she could not speak normally, which was why she had not telephoned me immediately. "I didn't want to frighten you," she said, and continued: "On the way downstairs to do the laundry . . ."

Incredulous, I interrupted, "What do you mean, 'do the laundry'? You couldn't walk!"

She said, "Well, one side of my body worked, and I could kind of hop and crawl."

"You mean you still went down three flights of stairs and did the laundry?"

"I had to. Gertrude was coming and it had to be ready for her to iron and fold."

I was dumbfounded and awestruck and almost laughed. That was Hope — keeping the household moving, proving to herself that the mind is still mightier than matter. I asked, wonderingly, "How did you get back up from the basement?"

"I sort of sat on the steps and pulled myself up one at a time. By then I could move my leg a little and that's when I could phone you." She had been speaking with the same persuasive eagerness she used with doctors — emphasizing the good signs — as though the load of laundry proved nothing serious had happened. Now her voice turned frightened. "What do you think it is?"

"I don't know," I said truthfully, shaking my head. "I'm sure it could be a dozen things. I'm going to call DeBellis. Stay right here." His secretary, Marsha, always helpful, promised to locate him immediately. I returned to Hope and we sat together in the kitchen finding simple reasons for her symptoms. Hope decided they were side effects of the chemotherapy, and I suggested a pinched nerve. We ignored the obvious answer — more melanoma. Hope asked me how my writing had gone that morning, and I told her my problems with changing oral wit into written humor. The telephone rang. DeBellis? Like a maniac, I raced up two flights to use the telephone in Hope's studio. There might be questions to ask which Hope at this moment could not bear to hear.

"This is Dr. DeBellis." I told him the details. He asked some questions, and then said, "Get her right up here. Do you want a single room?" I told him she was really fine now, and it would be a big blow to go into the hospital so suddenly. Could she come tomorrow for tests? He said, "She may be sitting on a time bomb. We've got to find out what's going on."

Without the idea ever entering my consciousness, I heard my voice say flatly, "You think it's a brain tumor."

"Probably."

"Is it treatable?"

"There are things we can do."

I also needed another wisp of comfort. "Could it be anything else?"

"Yes, there are other possibilities. But get her up here."

I returned downstairs immobilizing my feelings. Hope had come upstairs and was lying on our bed. She sat up, expectant, frightened.

"He wants you to go right into the hospital for tests."

She looked shocked, "What does he think it is?"

I lied—a snap decision to spare her until the last possible minute—and maybe it was not a brain tumor. I said, "DeBellis didn't want to speculate, and I thought he was probably right and I didn't quiz him."

Her voice was pleading, "Can't I go tomorrow? I'm all right now. I really am. They never do anything until the next day, unless you count taking my temperature. I want to see Mere and Henny."

"Hopie, DeBellis thinks it's important that you start tests right away."

"What tests?"

I rattled off the usual list: liver scan, chest X ray, brain waves . . ." I thought, "Oh, my God."

Hope pounced. "Brain waves! He thinks it's in my head, doesn't he?" She was angry now, sensing that I knew more than I was telling her.

I thought, "I'm supposed to be the Big Protector and I'm

making a God-awful mess of this." I told Hope, "He just wants to check everything. He says there are all sorts of things it could be."

"Why didn't you ask! You're not the one who has to sit here worrying what's going to happen next! You don't have to take all these tests. Goddam it, from now on I'm going to do all the talking to doctors." Her fury was only sad. We both knew it was empty talk, empty anger. We both knew she would leave soon for the hospital, as we both knew she must.

Hope lay back, her hand across her eyes. She said calmly from out of that blackness, "Do you think I'm going to go crazy?"

I sat beside her. "No," I said with a laugh I did not feel. "You're too strong-minded for anything like that." I felt a rush of tenderness. I touched her hair, and said, "Know that I am with you in this every second."

Her eyes still covered, she said bitterly, "Are you going to die with me?"

There was a long silence. Then Hope resignedly, glumly, mechanically, began to pack. There wasn't much: nightgown, slippers, the new *McCall's*, a week of *Women's Wear Dailys*, the picture proofs of her children's book, her bag of "beauty aids" — all in the white canvas tote bag. While she packed, she paused for a moment in the utter silence, holding her nightgown and looking around the room — the bedspread we had bought in Spain, the portraits of Mere and Henny painted by Ky — as though this might be a last look. I put my arms around her and we clung to each other. "I'm so scared," she said.

I got my car from the garage and we drove to the children's school where, miraculously, Helena was playing in the yard. She rushed to Hope's window, all happy surprise. "Hi, Mom."

"How d'ere," said Hope, using their private greeting as she reached out and quietly touched Helena's blond head. I sent Helena to find Meredith, and when the two cheery little faces were crowding the window, Hope gave that dazzling smile and said, almost gaily, "The doctors want me to go into the hospital

· 87 ·

for a few days for some tests. Gertie will take care of you when you get home today and I want you peanuts to be good to Daddy and do what he says."

The two faces were now solemn, eyes large, four hands clutching the bottom of the window. Then Hope said, "Come on, get in the car." Her voice was excitedly conspiratorial, like a naughty friend suggesting hooky. They both piled into the front, Meredith commandeering Hope's lap, Helena right against her, holding one hand. Picking up the brightened mood, I pulled away from the curb and began cruising the neighborhood. Helena, looking up at Hope's blanked-out eye, said, "Hi, Brownie."

"Hello there, Miss Piercing Memory," answered Hope, laughing down at her. With mock exasperation she said to Meredith on her lap, "Princessa, what sharp little buns you have," and then, hugging her tight, "I'd give anything for hips like yours." Mere grinned.

Finally, sadly, but with DeBellis's urgent voice in my ears, I parked again in front of the school. "Kiddos," I said, "I'm always the heavy—but we've got to go."

Hope pulled the two heads in against hers. "I really crunch on you guys," she said. Back on the sidewalk, ignoring my calls of "All right kids, that's enough," they wrestled tirelessly to see who would be the last to kiss their mother through the window. As we pulled away, Hope turned back from waving and she was crying quietly. "They're so sweet," she said.

As always, entering the hospital, Hope and I were miserable. When the processing was finished, a nurse escort was assigned to take us to the room. The woman, glancing at the canvas shopping bag, asked, "Where's your suitcase?"

"I don't have one," said Hope almost belligerently. "I'm not staying long enough for a suitcase."

When she was in her room Hope usually cheered up. I think she felt safer, felt in the very womb of help. Soon she was taken away for a liver scan, and I thought, "If they're rushing her off to that, maybe they're not sure it's in the brain." The telephone rang and it was Dr. DeBellis. He wanted permission to bring in a neurologist, Dr. Margaret Seiden. He described her as a fine doctor, an Englishwoman with a special sympathy for her patients. I said, "Whatever you think best." Fearing the answers, I asked no questions.

The next day, the fourth of March, Hope and I were discussing photographs I had taken of Meredith, and Hope was remarking on Meredith's gift for graceful poses. Suddenly in midsentence her speech fractured into nonsense words. Her mouth opened wide like a scream, but emitted only a guttural gargle. I could see her lolling tongue fighting to mold this awful sound into words. Her good eye, flooding with panic, beseeched me to help her.

I raced to the nurses' station and a nurse came running. She gave Hope an injection and I took Hope's hand; it was cold and clammy. After about five minutes—a century—Hope struggled out, "I can't speak." Now she could form words but half of them made no sense. I knew the term for it—aphasia. I could not tell if Hope knew she was talking gibberish. Looking down at her earnest, scared face, I pretended I understood her, a smile pasted on my face. I felt as though I was babying an idiot. I was very frightened. Was Hope now brain-damaged?

After half an hour she was normal again. I remember the moment when we looked steadily into each other's eyes, and Hope said, "They think it's in my head, don't they."

I nodded, and said, "That's one of the theories." But on his rounds that evening, Dr. DeBellis told us that the brain tests so far had been negative. I was incredulous, elated. Perhaps it was something minor! Hope beamed. When we parted that night we were almost cheerful.

During those days our friends again rallied to keep the mood lighthearted in that hospital room, and I remember thinking one day, surrounded by laughter, that this was the place to be. Whitney came every day, staying hour after hour. She and Hope literally spoke the same language, entertaining each other endlessly with, remembers Whitney, "straight and total trivia." Sometimes they talked about their growing-up years on their father's ranch, listing the names they gave to generations of cats—Pigmy Panther, Bustler Bones, Miss Ball—and laughing at the memory of Hope telling jokes to the cats and then pushing their lips back into grins. Whitney, deflecting dismay with a joke, willing herself like Hope into a facade of cheer, was the catalyst of our survival. She could distract her sister far more than I, who labored in the same morass as Hope. And only Whitney could release me without guilt or worry from Hope's side—the respites from tension I had to have.

On the evening of the sixth, Betty Suyker was a visitor. Spurred by Hope's caustic remarks about hospital food—"This custard tastes like sweat"—Betty, a gourmet cook, brought her a boiled artichoke, its center filled with mustardy mayonnaise.

Much later Hope painted Betty a small watercolor of an artichoke against a background the same color as Betty's apartment. Presenting it to her, Hope said, "This is why you can't ever change the color of your walls." Such gestures were typical of Hope. On a Christmas Eve she once brought John Groth, alone in his studio, a tiny decorated tree and presents. When her friend and baby-sitter Lucille Chasin had blood clots in her leg, Hope put her immediately into our car and drove her to a specialist at Columbia-Presbyterian. For her younger brother, Bobby, in California, she once persuaded the diaper man to give up his T-shirt—ABC Diaper Service—right off his back. Knowing DeBellis's enjoyment of sailing, she painted him a watercolor of boats rounding a buoy on Dublin Lake—it still hangs on the wall opposite his desk.

The night Betty visited the hospital, she gave me a ride home in her car, and, slouching in the front seat, my mood was reflective, removed—an antidote, I suppose, for the suspense. I began musing on marriage—how the accommodations and renunciations tend to merge the two lives into one, and how the mutuality helps make the marriage good—which is one reason why, when death threatens one person, it threatens both, and why part of me would die with Hope.

But I would be saved, I speculated, by the fact that two people can never achieve oneness. The intrinsic singleness of each partner, the built-in isolation, would allow me to survive, even while Hope's death would be devastating. I told Betty, "I only have inklings of how it will happen, but I *will* survive. I *must* survive, if only for the children." I remember thinking that this was perhaps a milestone of sorts, the point in the Ritual when I first felt able to say with confidence that I would come through intact. But I also remember feeling that I was melodramatically posturing the sad and philosophic husband.

To get us through the latest vigil—the long afternoon of March seventh after the tests were finished and before the climactic meeting with DeBellis and Seiden—I summoned the troops into Hope's room. Whitney, John Groth, Liz Hauser, and Peter Davis arrived one by one. Liz Hauser—dark straight hair, striking face, aquiline nose—brought laughter and extraordinary warmth. John Groth brought years of faithful love. Peter Davis, still to arrive, would bring amusement, affection, and the tacit shade of Josie.

Our banter was interrupted by a nurse at the door saying there was a telephone call for me, and in the hall she told me to telephone Dr. DeBellis. I felt the familiar clenching of heart and stomach. Bad news!

At such moments the physical world becomes surreal and indelible—the squeak of the phone-booth door as I pulled it closed, the dim blink of the overhead light, the walls around me covered with penciled numbers, the hieroglyphics of other people's lives. I thought that this was the last moment before the turning of a frightful corner.

"We are now certain," said DeBellis, "based on the EMI scan today and yesterday's electroencephalogram, that there are two metastatic tumors in Hope's head." I think I gasped and my body physically convulsed, the spasm curling my head downward. I remember the sensation of blood draining from my head, the feeling of my brain compressing. I opened my mouth; no words came out. There must have been odd sounds, because I heard DeBellis saying, "That's all right. There's no hurry. Take your time." I realize now that for all my pious talk and my apparent facing of Hope's death, I had actually believed until this moment that somehow she would be saved.

"Will there be brain surgery?"

"No, the tumors would only return. But we can slow down the growth with treatment, and Hope's melanoma seems to be sensitive to radiation." We discussed what to tell her. DeBellis felt she could handle the whole truth.

I pictured the alternative — telling her the problem was minor — the rush of relief, the smile, the quiet euphoria. We could give her that moment. But then there would be inexplicable symptoms, the endless and complicated lies, the fury when she inevitably learned the facts. We would have rewarded her stoicism and her courage with an insult. "Yes," I said, "tell her the truth. That's what she wants." I was too stunned to marshal any searching questions. We hung up.

In Hope's year and a half of illness so far, I had experienced many forms of anguish. But now those months of dread had culminated in one sledgehammer moment, and I felt an emptiness so total it was psychic pain. As I returned down the hall, nothing seemed real. My thoughts drifted: "The brain . . . makes life worth living . . . the seat of the spirit . . . how strange will she become . . . can she stand that . . . traumatize the children . . . none of this will happen today or tomorrow."

Carrying my awful secret, I reentered Hope's crowded room. I was absurdly reassured to find her alive, leaning back against the pillows, smiling. In answer to her look, I said offhandedly, "Just a business call." She moved over and I sat up on the bed beside her. She leaned against me and I put my arm around her shoulders. Peter Davis arrived, and, as he later told me, only just prevented himself from saying, "You two look like the last scene from *Love Story*."

Sitting next to Hope, I was a sort of shadow patient in the focus of that ring of affection in the room. Perhaps, like Hope, I felt it as a force against death, and drawing on it, could be outwardly animated and cheerful. But twice my heart jolted. Hope asked after Peter's "children" and said she planned to watch the "*Mary Terler Moore Show*."

In yet another part of myself, I felt pervaded by my horrendous knowledge. My secret was like the watermelon seed I had swallowed as a very little boy and then imagined it sprouting in my stomach and growing all through my body until it choked me. Peter Davis has always remembered the strange quality in my smile and his sense that there was something terrible inside me.

I remember an amazing phenomenon: I was actually enjoying a perverse sense of power. Perhaps I was redirecting my anger away from fate. Perhaps I had a hidden craving to take Hope's place for a moment in the center of their attention. But I knew that I was about to strike these people in a way that would hammer them with emotion, and bring a rush of sympathy toward me. I dreaded telling them, and I couldn't wait.

Hope was summoned from the room for another test. I asked Whitney to step out with me and we went to the solarium just down the hall. "Whitney," I said, "that wasn't a business call, that was DeBellis. We've come to the end of the line. There are two tumors in Hopie's head."

Whitney's control was complete. All her sorrow poured into her voice as she softly said, "Poor Hopie."

We discussed whether I should tell anybody else. Perhaps Hope would want to keep the tumors a secret so people would treat her more normally. John Groth had left, but we decided that at least Liz and Peter should know the truth. I brought them out to the solarium and we sat in a circle, almost knee to knee. Leaning forward, looking into their shocked faces, I told them the situation quickly, almost dispassionately. I asked them not to tell anybody and told Peter, whose own mother had died of cancer when he was a boy, "Hopie will want to talk to you."

I still felt removed — that my sole concern in life was the delivery of these facts. But announcing the fact of tumors growing in Hope's brain, crystallizing this in words, passing her sealed fate into the public knowledge, was a collision between denial and reality. Those months of fear, those endless vigils converged — the image of Hopie dying, Hopie dead. I felt my face begin to contort with tears. I abruptly fled to a far window and stood, back to the room, eyes closed, hands at my side, sobbing as silently as I could manage. Wiping my face, I turned back toward the room and was aware of a patient in a hospital robe — a man — watching me with curiosity and some irritation. I suppose I was an intimation of his own possible future and I was aware, suddenly, that on this hospital floor there was nothing special about my grief and Hope's eventual death.

Next, worrying that Hope might return to an empty room and her own thoughts, I went there to wait for her. Peter came along to spare me my solitary thoughts. Alone together, I think we felt a curious combination of awkwardness and powerful empathy. We were, in a sense, in the middle of each other's ordeal, and we could not possibly find words to match such enormity. Peter said, "Josie used to call you 'the man.' Well, today it was *really* true. I mean, it was always true, but today you are incredible." That must have embarrassed me, and I remember trying to find a graceful way to say that I was no different from what he had been when Josie died. We were like two soldiers congratulating each other on our courage under fire. Then, very simply and directly, he told me he loved Hopie and all of us. I said, "Peter, I think of you and wonder about you constantly." Giving up on words, we spontaneously embraced. It was unnatural for us and tremendously moving.

Soon Hope returned, and we reassembled in her room, now all but Hope burdened with foreknowledge. The undercurrent of expectancy was strong.

Meanwhile, in an anteroom down the hall, Drs. DeBellis and Seiden were going over Hope's test results, settling on their plans for treatment and mobilizing their own defenses for what lay ahead. Robert DeBellis, by now extremely fond of Hope, felt almost that he was passing a death sentence on a member of his own family. Margaret Seiden saw her own mortality in Hope, a woman her age, also with a career and two children at home. "I felt what she was going to feel," Seiden recalled later. "At such times there is always an anxiety. We have a taboo in our culture that makes it hard to talk about death. Then, too, when you've gone into medicine out of some need to have people say, 'Oh, you've helped me,' and when you come to the point where you can't help somebody, that really drags the rug out from under you. I guess I'm fearful, too — afraid that seeing tremendous psychic pain will be unbearable to me."

In Hope's hospital room, we suddenly saw two, white-coated figures standing in the doorway. I had not met Dr. Seiden, who was unexpectedly small and pretty, with modish light-brown hair. Our three hand-holders hurried out, and I stood by the head of Hope's bed. She sat very erect in her aqua nightgown, a tentative smile on her face. In her lap one hand clutched the other, clenched in a fist.

Without ceremony or small talk, DeBellis made his report. His manner was undramatic, his voice matter-of-fact: "We have the results of the tests. The chest X ray, skull X ray, thermogram, and brain scan were all negative. However, the liver scan was positive, and the CAT scan and the EEG indicated something in the head which is almost certainly a spread of the original tumor to the brain."

Hope's eyes were wide with shock and horror. "You mean I have cancer in my brain?"

DeBellis nodded. As though hit in the face, Hope gave a moaning cry of pain. Her eyes closed, her head sagged, and she wept. In agony I put my hand on her shoulder and felt it quivering. After a minute — an eternity — Hope raised her head. Her face, wet with tears, was very pale, but she had stopped crying. Her voice was very small. "I don't want to die. Am I going to die? How long do I have to live?"

"It's very hard to say," answered DeBellis. "At least six months, but with a little luck it could be much longer."

To me—and I hoped to her—that seemed like the distant future. "She'll have the summer," I thought to myself, "and the luck." Then in one of those millisecond flashes, I noted that the news of the liver, dreaded for so long, was now only an apostrophe.

DeBellis was already telling Hope his plan, and his take-charge, businesslike style calmed her. A new chemotherapy program would be combined with immunotherapy, a treatment so experimental he would have "to steal" the serum for her. Experimental! That was somehow reassuring—the leading edge of cancer research, the latest thing; it must be terrific.

The mood in the room had subtly changed. Now Hope knew the worst. The doctor's bag of tricks was still not empty and she would not die tomorrow. There was a sense of crisis survived, almost relief, as though in our minds the promise of a delay had satisfactorily replaced the dream of a cure. We had a new bargain: okay, we'll settle for even less; she's going to die, but not for a while.

"Will I go crazy?" Hope asked.

"No."

"Will I be able to paint?"

"Yes."

Dr. Seiden, in her English accent, explained the drugs she was prescribing. Phenobarbital and Dilantin would combat seizures, Decadron would relieve the present symptoms by reducing the swelling around the tumors and thereby the pressure on the brain. There was the unfortunate side effect of retaining water in the body. But the drug would also make her slightly euphoric. That appealed to me.

Dr. DeBellis said he would return later for the first of the immunotherapy treatments. Hope would be discharged tomorrow. That news was always a lift, even now. "Dr. DeBellis," I said, "at the very beginning we understood there was always a small chance of a miraculous remission. Is that still true?"

"Yes, it is. Particularly with melanoma. Just when you think you're licked, you aren't."

As the doctors left the room, I felt abandoned, helpless. Tomorrow at home Hope would be in my care. What should I expect? Could I cope? At that terrible moment, I did not want to leave Hope alone, but I darted out of the room and caught the doctors down the hall.

While I talked to them, Hope joined our friends in the solarium. She sat down next to Peter Davis and said quietly, "We've had very bad news just now. The cancer has spread to my liver and my brain." Then she put her head down in her hands and cried briefly. Peter put a comforting arm tight around her. She lifted her head. "The only good thing about this deal," she said, "is I'll get to see Josie."

As she often did with me, she groped in Peter's jacket pocket, found a Kleenex, wiped her eyes and cheeks, and returned it to his pocket. She said, "What's going to happen to all these kids," and began to cry again. Peter took her hand.

"How old were you when your mother died?" Hope asked him.

"Eight."

"Do you remember anything about your mother?"

"Lots. Hundreds of things she said, and hundreds more details."

"We're going to have to talk a lot about this," Hope said. She shook her head wonderingly. "What a year. What's happened to us! We were all so happy and careless!"

At the same time, down the hall, I was asking the two doctors for any facts that they had withheld from Hope, I was no longer just an anguished bystander. Hope had become my responsibility—in the crudest sense, a job of work. I had to know the specifics that DeBellis called "the gory details." Dr. Seiden told me what a seizure would be and how it should be handled. She said it would be like an epileptic fit. As a boy I had seen one—a man thrashing on the ground, awful sounds, face horrifyingly contorted. Seiden told me to jam a wadded hand-kerchief between Hope's teeth to keep her from biting her tongue and to hold her head so the saliva would run out of her mouth and not choke her. Then I asked if Hope might go blind. Seiden said that it was not likely. But she might be paralyzed or lose sensation along one side. Seiden expected that there would be headaches, but pain was one thing doctors knew how to alleviate.

I asked what Hope's death would be like. DeBellis said that she would become increasingly drowsy and finally lapse into a coma. "Actually," added Seiden, "quite a merciful way of dying." Then, while DeBellis looked solemn, Seiden explained that Hope could also die suddenly. She suspected a third tumor at the base of the skull, in back, and one of the three could hemorrhage at any moment.

"You mean," I asked, shocked and incredulous, "she could die . . . tomorrow?"

"It's possible," said DeBellis. "If there's anything that has to be done, she should take care of it right away."

I soberly thanked them, and we separated. I was dumbfound-ed. She could die tomorrow. No! Not Hopie! That would not happen! But what if she did? Well, the ordeal would be over quickly. Like Josie. Maybe that would be merciful. I returned down the hall to Hope's room. It was empty. I was glad not to be alone with her. In the solarium she was sitting between Peter Davis and Whitney, who got up and gave me her place. Hope smiled at me, patted my knee, and said, "Well, old boy, there's twenty-two years down the drain."

"Pretty good years," I said, trying to smile. Instead I began to cry. I turned my head away from her, and she held my hand.

While Hope and I were beginning our adjustment to this new reality, the two doctors were experiencing a desolation of their own. The session with Hope had reached behind their carefully accumulated defenses. In Hope's room, Margaret Seiden had felt for a moment that she herself was going to cry. And now, as they walked down the hall, DeBellis was saying, "Who the hell needs this kind of job! It's really shitty to have to go in and tell somebody — tell Hope — she's going to die." Both as colleagues and as friends the two often discussed the stress of these moments — which, according to DeBellis, are so harrowing that many doctors simply avoid them. "They don't level with the patient," he told me. "They talk to the family and tell the patient, 'There's some inflammation in the head and I'll give you medicine that will get you straightened out.' And when the roof falls in, hopefully somebody else is taking care of the patient."

"It becomes a ridiculous pas de deux," says Dr. Seiden, "with the doctor coming and saying in this bluff, hearty way, 'How do you feel?' and the patient says, 'I'm feeling pretty good.' And they smile and the doctor goes out and they're both lying to each other. So the patient never has a chance to cry a little more, come to terms with his God, make practical decisions — a will — say goodbye to somebody — whatever. I think it is so lonely if you go with that secret locked up in your heart."

Hope and the rest of us returned to her room. While we talked stiltedly among ourselves, she telephoned Gertrude and made her promise to stay with Meredith and Helena until they were grown up. "You're the only one I trust with them," Hope told her, "and if you get too old to make it down the stairs, Dick'll meet you with a wheelchair."

DeBellis came back to give Hope the first of her immunotherapy injections. Peter, Liz, and Whitney departed. I waited in the solarium alone, now exhausted, my mind empty. As DeBellis left, I rejoined Hope. She half shouted, "Well, that's it. That's really *it!*" Then in a soft wail she said, "I can't stand the thought of something growing in my head."

I did not know what to say. There was nothing to say.

She began to cry. I put my cheek against hers with my face buried in the pillow. My arm encircled her chest, as though I were holding her together. When her body stopped shaking, I whispered, "You may have a long time, and we're going to make it terrific." I felt as though I had just thrown a teaspoonful of water onto a forest fire.

We must have said more, but I have forgotten. Hope took my two hands in hers and said, her voice determined, "Dick, I want you to go home now. Mere and Henny need you. You don't have to stay with me any longer. I'm fine. I really am. I'll watch Mary Tyler Moore and Carol Burnett." Then she gave a slight grin. "And I promise I'll take a sleeping pill."

"Okay," I said. I sat down beside her, our hands gripping hard. "I love you so much, Hopie."

"And I certainly love you."

I gently touched her lips with mine. It was tremendous tenderness distilled to the weight of a feather. Soon afterwards I left and I remember how glad I was to go—and how guilty I felt.

At home I took over from the baby-sitter. The sight of Meredith and Helena, so unknowing, was very poignant. But mainly I felt a rush of gratitude for their existence. I could love them with unreserved joy. Loving Hope was pain.

They wanted to know, "How's Mommy?" As though it were an answer, I said, "She's coming home tomorrow. Isn't that terrific?" I suggested they telephone her, and I can remember Helena's deliberate voice saying to Hope, "How d'ere."

Then there was Meredith's sprightly, "Hi, Mom. Guess what . . ." After she had delivered her news bulletins and hung up she turned to me, bewildered. "Why was Mom crying?"

I hugged her to me. "Because she misses you so much." Taking her to bed I slung her over my shoulder and did our joke, saying for the hundredth time, "This is called the fireman's carry because it's the way the firemen . . ."

I always tucked Meredith into bed first because she went to sleep immediately. Bending down to the little face against the white pillow, I gave her what we called the maple-syrup kiss, a kiss on the forehead with the ritual incantation, "It will run very slowly past your eyes, around your nose, over your cheeks like maple syrup until you taste it . . . mmmm . . . on your lips."

Because I had given the fireman's carry to Meredith, I had to do it for Helena, word for word. Then Helena, who had trouble falling asleep, lay on her back, settling in for a long talk. I told her no, not tonight. I was too tired. She reached up and twisted my nose. It hurt. I pulled back, startled, and said, "What are you doing?"

"I'm turning on the TV set," said Helena.

We settled for a back rub instead of a talk. Moving my fingertips over her solid body, I wondered how I could ever tell her and Meredith that their mother was gone from their lives forever. I wondered if I would be able to shepherd them through whatever hurt lay ahead. Yes, I could if I poured out enough love, and I had that to give. And in turn their need would carry me through my ordeal, the rest of the Ritual.

Lying in my own bed, I tried to recall what Hope had written her sister Ky the previous October when Ky's baby was strangled by the umbilical cord. Hope composed the letter in the midst of her own misery: "Here's a line I was just reading in a poetess' obituary: 'Live or die, make up your mind. If you're going to hang around, don't ruin everything.'" Then Hope continued: "What's interesting is, how do you get over the rotten part? We all go on because other people need us badly, and because one really should. For any life to have validity, you must work and show struggle and surmount the impossible tasks, even if you think you can't."

Seven

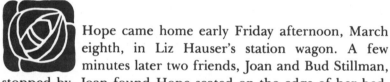Hope came home early Friday afternoon, March eighth, in Liz Hauser's station wagon. A few minutes later two friends, Joan and Bud Stillman, stopped by. Joan found Hope seated on the edge of her bed, looking both lost and utterly astonished. "I'm going to die in six months," Hope said, wonderingly. Then terror took over. "Don't leave me." Joan folded Hope into her arms.

As I watched this moment of transcendent pathos, I realized that Hope and I were now removed from each other by an abyss. I was living. She was dying. Our fates were sealed and my future no longer rode the roller coaster with hers. My loss of Hope was like an advance into an icy lake—gradual immersion and then a shattering final plunge. For a part of me, Hope died during my conversation with DeBellis in the hospital telephone booth—his businesslike voice saying, "two metastatic tumors." In that moment, I began the period in the Ritual known as premourning—grieving for Hope while she was still alive, living in a limbo of last times and too-lates without the finality of death, without the directioning sense of a mourning process under way.

In my case premourning did little to cushion the impact of Hope's eventual death. Enough denial endures so that the shock of death is still all-pervading and strikes as suddenly as the stroke of an ax. But premourning does share many of the mourning symptoms. At home with Hope I was in the state that a death brings — numbness coating the mind and nerves, pain jabbing through the numbness, anguish flooding in until numbness repairs the rupture. Whipsawed between false calm and hysteria, I was not entirely sane.

I flunked the crisis of rewriting Hope's will, that symbol of death as final as coffins and gravestones. I remember as a very small boy the accidental sight of my father's will — "The Last Will and Testament" — and my shock at the realization that he would someday die. Hope's will had long needed updating to include Meredith and Helena, a chore postponed partly because death had always seemed so distant, partly because she had no interest in such pragmatic matters. So now my duty was to get Hope immediately to our lawyer's office and avoid diminishing her legacy by unnecessary income taxes. When I broached the subject of her will, she sensed my tension. Her own mingled fear and anger ignited. "Why do I have to do it now? You think I'm going to die any minute, don't you?" Then she said, "You're only thinking about my money!"

I flushed with annoyance. This was her responsibility, not mine. I said, "Hopie, the money is for Mere and Henny, and you do not want a screwed-up will. I just don't think we dare postpone it."

But Hope came to terms with her will as an instrument of affection. She divided a total of $10,000 — savings from her art income — among six friends. She came downstairs while Gertrude stood folding laundry and said, "Gertie, I've put you in my will, and I want to talk to you about it."

Gertrude walked away. She told me later, "I didn't want to break down in front of her. Mrs. Meryman was the nearest person I've seen like my mother, and I idolized the ground she walked on. Mrs. Meryman never thought about herself; she was always thinking and doing for somebody else."

A few days later, Hope handed Gertrude a check for a thousand dollars, saying, "There is four thousand more for you in my will because I didn't want to go away from here worried about you. But I wanted to have the pleasure of handing you this personally, myself. I promised I'd take you to California someday to see your relatives, but I never made it. Please take this thousand dollars and do it." Gertrude did.

Hope announced to me that she was leaving to each of her sisters and brother twelve prints and watercolors. That meant forty-eight of her best pictures. I reacted badly. I imagined her best work heading west, another loss cutting deeper than money.

I argued unpleasantly, with too much vehemence, that there were not enough first-rank pictures for such a gift, that her first obligation was to her children, that my father still lived for me in his work. I was saying in essence, "Sorry, your dying wish is unacceptable. Would you like to try another?"

Hope said, brusquely, "They're my pictures, and I can do what I want with them. I'm not dead yet. When I'm gone, you can run everything to suit yourself."

Two days later, in the lawyer's office, I told her, "You should do as you wish. I was wrong to say anything." I felt stupid. Being sorry never really mitigates bad behavior, nor does it keep the craziness from happening again. Peter Davis had admired one of her best watercolors, and she decided to give it to him. When he asked me how I felt, I told him the truth—that I wanted her best paintings kept for the girls—and I talked Hope out of her impulse. Then, a week later, impatient with herself, she handed it to him.

Preparing and adjusting for the last lap of Hope's illness, I quietly telephoned the church in Chester Heights and reserved the plot next to Little Whitney's grave. I told Hope, who simply nodded. I rigged an alarm button in her studio that rang a bell in the kitchen. I settled the hospital bills, and Hope said ruefully, "It doesn't seem fair to pay all that money to be told you have brain tumors."

In my premourning state, part of my perception of Hope had slipped into the past tense, and where previously I had often blocked out the future, I now dwelt on it. My hand-wringing sessions with Liz Hauser by telephone concentrated on myself and the children—wondering whether Hope would drop dead in front of them, wondering where I should live after she was gone. In my nighttime "horrors" I would plan a move to Dublin. I could live for under $20,000—work for regional magazines, maybe get a few national assignments . . . what about the girls' education . . . but would I miss the stimulation of New York . . . my friends . . . would my brain go to sleep? Then I would plan a move to Washington, D.C. Maybe I could live in a trailer on my brother's farm . . . my sister-in-law could be a surrogate mother . . . I could do profiles of politicians . . . maybe I didn't have the nervous stamina for that anymore . . . maybe semiretirement would be happier.

To a degree the terror of Hope's melanoma was replaced by my fear that she would be permanently hospitalized. I remembered a newspaper story on a man who divorced his wife to escape her hospital bills. The strategy failed, and he was wiped out—house, property, savings—and still owed $50,000. I secretly investigated nursing homes for the terminally ill in New Hampshire, where costs would be less. I considered the grotesque irony that my bankruptcy would not buy Hope life, just an intravenous tube.

I plotted with a kindly insurance man to slip both Hope and myself into some group major-medical plan—dishonest because Hope was already ill. I was stuck with Blue Cross–Blue Shield, which covered Hope full fare for only three weeks and half fare for ninety days and started fresh every six months. I did take out a major-medical policy for the rest of the family, and ironically the insurance man who came to the house had just lost his wife by cancer. We looked at each other silently for a moment, total strangers knowing an intimate slice of each other's life.

I worried what to tell the girls now about Hope. Wondering whether it was the easy way out, I stayed with our original plan and said the minimum. At breakfast one day, while Hope was in bed, I told the girls that the doctors had found two lumps called tumors in Mommy's head, and if she acted strangely—maybe talked funny or couldn't stand up—they must not be frightened and should call me immediately. I did not explain that the tumors were cancer. The children did not ask. Meredith wanted to know where the lumps were. I said they were on the right side of her head between the brain and the skull. Helena asked if they hurt. I said, "No." I can still remember the word "tumors" sticking in my throat and the effort of pronouncing it to those two trusting, defenseless faces.

Not long afterwards, walking down the street, I encountered my doctor, who inquired after Hope. I told him about the brain tumors. Shaking his head sympathetically, he said, "Well, maybe that's for the best. When it gets into the squash, things go pretty fast."

But as week followed week there were no further episodes. The antiseizure drugs were taking effect—at a price. The drugs, the water retained in Hope's body, the tumors, and the chemotherapy more and more affected Hope's appearance and powers. Saying, "I'm just resting my eyes," she spent hours at a time on the bed. Her once-brisk movements were slowed and subtly uncertain, her mind ever so slightly fuzzy. Her fine-drawn face was puffy, her figure fleshy—taking on the plump-ness she had successfully fought all her adult life. She ignored everything. Holding in her hand a cluster of colored pills, she said to Whitney, "These are my life."

Unrelentingly aware of what was happening, of what might happen, I was more and more of a watcher, vigilant from the corner of my eye, trying not to hover, condescend, humiliate. I found pretexts for preceding Hope down steps, for being in the bedroom while she dressed, for doing chores while she tidied the house. Using one of her chemotherapy hell weeks as a reason, I moved a typewriter table into her studio and began working there. Whitney, Gertrude, other friends, and I formed a conspiracy to order our comings and goings in parallel with hers. I am sure we did not deceive her. I remember my chagrin when Hope announced to me, a little defiantly as though to a nurse, that she was going out with Helena. I was shamed into saying with infinite casualness, "Fine." They went to Lamston's, a five-and-ten, where Helena asked if the shopping bags were free.

"Nothing's free in this life," said Hope.

"Crying's free," said Helena.

In one session with Dr. DeBellis she talked to him about handling her remaining time. When possible, I stayed out of these visits, feeling that it was a way to preserve Hope's independence and dignity—and I was glad to spare myself Hope's reality. That particular meeting impressed Hope, and she repeated to me DeBellis's story of a watershed incident in his own life.

He had had a heart attack and afterwards cut out ice cream, eggs, butter, cheese, beef, driving, stairs, medical literature. At the end of a year his cholesterol count had doubled. One day he was sitting in front of his TV taking his pulse to count the palpitations—"107, 108, 109, oops, there's one; oh, oh, I'd better count some more—257, 258, 259; oops, there's another." Then he thought, "This is ridiculous. Counting palpitations isn't going to make any difference. Nothing I do is going to modify my disease. So to hell with it. If it is going to do me in, it does me in. But I'm going to enjoy myself up to that point." He started racing his car in auto rallies, climbing stairs, eating eggs and ice cream—"doing whatever the hell I wanted to do, and it didn't make any difference. You can't live dreading your disease day by day because, if that's what you're doing, you might as well die."

Remembering his talk with Hope, DeBellis told me, "I said to her that there was nothing she could actively do to affect the disease except lead as normal a life as possible, which would improve her physical well-being, which would modify the disease." So that was Hope's determination, and every person around her collaborated. We went to galleries, to the theater, to dinner parties. John Groth was a judge that April for the American Watercolor Society show and insisted that Hope enter a picture. The judges accepted it unanimously, and Hope, very proud, went to the opening to see it exhibited. With Whitney, she signed up for a one-day-a-week, eight-to-five course in lithography, a print medium she had long wanted to try, and carrying her huge portfolio, refused to let Whitney see her home on the bus — until she took the wrong one and landed in Coney Island. She decided to take on a new children's book, though I thought it too trivial a project for her last months. But, as she told its editor, her friend Bernice Chardiet, "If I don't have a project, what am I going to do, sit around thinking about dying?"

I was never certain of the roots of Hope's fortitude. My guess is that it was a masterpiece of determination and fatalism, assisted by good sense, plenty of support, the Decadron medication — which was an "upper" — and a smattering of denial. And, very important, she had an interest that still absorbed her and a sense that what she was doing had a life of its own.

Whitney and I agreed that her Catholicism did not prove a great strength to her. Hope felt abandoned — still calling out, "Is anybody home?" She once said, "If I am to be deprived of the joy of seeing my children grow up, then I can't make myself believe in a merciful God." Sometimes in the black hours of the night, Hope's "horrors" still poured out, but they focused on her fears of the months ahead, not terrors beyond the grave. She would say, "I can't stand the thought of something growing in my head," and she would remember my beloved Aunt Juliet, demented by senility, cursing us in a wild babble, her face frantic and furious. "Suppose the children saw me like that," Hope would wail. Once, while I held her moist body in the darkness, she said, "I don't know whether I can do it."

I asked, "You mean bear all this?"

"No."

"You mean suicide?"

"Yes." She was quiet for a second and then said, "But I don't think Mere and Henny would ever understand." Beginning to sob, she wailed, "I don't want to leave them."

We decided to visit the Brooks ranch in California after school was finished in June — Hope's last trip home, a fact we ignored. Her sister Blue traveled over from Arizona, and Whitney flew out with us. We all stayed at the family house, occupied now only by Mrs. Brooks and a nurse attendant. After several strokes over a period of years, Mrs. Brooks had sunk passively into her accustomed pocket at one end of a sofa, and her body, her functions, her faculties were gradually deteriorating like an old house abandoned to the weather.

It was a curious visit. I had imagined daily, jolly painting excursions and quiet, happy times with the sisters Hope adored. And those did take place. In the peace of Ky's house in an avocado orchard — an oasis of live oaks and palms and flowers — Hope painted one of her finest watercolors, a nasturtium vine enveloping an oak — a brilliant, joyous expanse of orange blooms. But such interludes were infrequent. Mostly I remember mothers planning days to suit the convenience of children and mob-scene dinners that seemed to be more trouble than they were worth.

This was, in fact, life going on as it must, not coming to a halt for Hope. Perhaps it was also a family form of subconscious distancing, a way of coping with Hope's illness, now so clearly visible. I was no different. One day I left Hope painting a coastal pine in the hot sun and walked along the cliffs overlooking the surf and sea-worn boulders. I was gone too long and knew it. But I was rebelliously reveling in the release — the utter isolation from cancer, from Hope, in a sense from myself. When I returned and found her miserable, I was only mildly guilty. In retrospect the incident was important because it was selfish. It was a gesture of freedom, an act of disengagement and emotional independence — both essential to my survival.

But any disappointments in the visit were mine, in Hope's behalf. She showed no signs of wanting special consideration, and I remember only a smile on her face. I especially remember one happy day together. On the flat reaches of the Carpinteria Valley, acres of commercial flowers were blooming yellow and lavender, with fluffy rows of stock like white dew. The pickers were at work — straw-sombreroed Mexicans snipping and bunching, hands as quick as magicians', the sprays of color fluttering like ceremonial plumes. Hope and I drove from field to field and stood together in the warm sun while she told me what to photograph for a woodcut series on flower pickers. "This is my winter's work," she said.

Inexorably the day of departure arrived. We assembled in the circular gravel driveway, Hope in a cloaking, brilliant Marimekko dress, the sun plumbing all the tints of red and auburn in her hair. She and I went indoors to say goodbye to "Mumma" — into the room where I used to sit courting Hope, where I used to sit pinned and wriggling while Mr. Brooks stood in front of the enormous fireplace, a glass of brandy in his hand, and reminisced about his youth farming the Imperial Valley, and blasted the IRS, the neighbors, the world. The glass-doored cabinet held ranks of graduation and wedding pictures — Hope in her silk wedding dress smiling toward an invisible horizon, the two of us cutting our wedding cake. It was time collapsed.

I bent over the frail figure of Mrs. Brooks, a faint whiff of urine rising from the lap robe over her knees, and kissed a cheek that was too soft but warm under my lips. "Take good care of Hopie," she said haltingly. I was overpowered by the conjunction of time past and present — and by the mother, dying in inches, and the beautiful daughter dying in galloping leaps.

Hope sat down on the sofa and took her mother's thin hand.

"Goodbye, Mumma. Take good care of yourself. I'll be back to see you this winter." Mrs. Brooks began to cry. "Don't, Mumma," said Hope, very cheerful. "I'm going to be all right, and I'll see you in the winter." She smiled radiantly. As we walked out through the hall, she was crying. The second she passed through the front door, she was smiling.

Ky's husband, Duncan, drove us to the Los Angeles airport, the car a jumble of baggage and children. Ky and Hope sat together in back. Suddenly Ky found herself sobbing and saying to Hope, "How can you do it, how are you doing all this?"

Hope answered, "The only thing I can think of that makes any sense is that you build up some kind of platform for your children and you leave behind you a packet of work."

After Hope's next round of treatments we went out to Sag Harbor to be near Whitney and settled in again at the Whaler Motel, this time with the children in the same room on two cots. None of us wished to be separated. Ironically, Hope's illness had in a way returned her to me. With less strength for painting and projects, with fewer commitments, she was willing to be affectionately idle. One afternoon Whitney took the children and gave us time alone. We strolled through a couple of antique stores, and Hope pointed to an old oculist's sign, a giant glass eye, and said, grinning, "This is too, too thrilling. Just what I need." I suggested we go back to Whitney's empty house, and on the way we held hands. We went upstairs without a word and made long, slow love.

With Hope still free of episodes, we existed together in a limbo, holding time itself in suspension. Paradoxically, I was grieving the loss of Hope while simultaneously giving her my total attention. She needed it, but that was also a way of tuning out my own reality. Work on the Mankiewicz book was erratic and going badly—a nightmare. The first payment on the publisher's advance was long since spent; my *Life* severance pay was gone; my *Life* profit sharing was hemorrhaging away. The impact of Hope's death on me and the children, the managing of our life alone together, loomed unknown and enormous. But within the protective compartment of our limbo, my combined fears for myself and Hope were bearable. I was like a child huddling for comfort in his kindergarten cubby.

After the August chemotherapy, we decided to make our annual trip to Maine, stopping first in Dublin. I hungered to get to Dublin, the place where I grew up. It was my one continuity, unconnected to Hope, a spot where she had left no imprint, a place she never completely liked. And at Dublin was Laura Perkins, a girl just out of college helping my eighty-year-old mother that summer. Laura made it possible to leave the children there, and after a week we went on alone to Maine —and there Hope's muse, her skills, short-circuited.

As we departed, the girls clung to Hope, running beside the car, pleading to come too. Hope was in tears. I reminded her of the time she had left Helena with my mother for the day. Helena put on the same performance, weeping, clinging, begging. Finally, Hope broke free and drove away. Helena's brow cleared, and she said, "That was *fun!*"

We spent the night in our accustomed motel in Rockland and the next day took the car ferry to Vinalhaven, an island we had visited before and so knew the inn and the painting possibilities. We were exhilarated, standing together in the bow of the ferry, happy with the press of the wind, the smell of the salt, the sight of the spruce islands outlined by granite shelving like tan waterlines. Decorating the choppy sea to the horizon were boats like the ones Hope's doctors were sailing when we needed them on weekends. "Hi, Dr. DeBellis," called out Hope, waving. "Hi, Dr. Jones."

In the soft warmth of that evening we ambled down the empty street into town. I noticed that Hope kept jostling against me. Her walk was weaving, and her right foot, slightly out of control, slapped against the tar. I glanced into her face. She was serene, apparently unaware. I took her arm and held her close — to show my affection, to keep her from realizing what was happening, to support her if the leg gave way. Sharing a reflective mood of quietude I did not feel — could I charter a plane if anything happened? — we finished our *paseo* uneventfully.

In the morning we drove to a throat of beach and rocks between the ocean and a small inland pond. As Hope looked for a painting subject, her walk was tottery, and I stuck close beside her, carrying the paint box and stool. She was in a frenzy of indecision. Surrounded by the landscape she loved, no composition appealed to her. I made suggestions that only irritated her. In desperation she sat on the ground behind a stone wall overgrown with thistles. Using a pencil, she began drawing the wall, thistles large in the foreground, but the perspective eluded her. She wailed in frustrated anger, "I can't do it. Goddam it, I can't do it!"

In the afternoon she picked a far simpler subject — a dark lobster-storage float like a huge raft in the middle of the pond, spruces reflected in long shadows on the still surface — and she brought off a lovely, loose, semi-abstraction. That evening Hope was cheerful. The next day she began a watercolor of a lighthouse. To my relief her brush moved on the paper with its usual verve and certainty, blocking in the tower and the house. I left her for a half hour to get sandwiches, but when I returned, I could feel her misery flooding toward me. She was almost in tears. "I've been rushing because we have to catch that Goddam ferry," she said, "and now I've ruined it. And there's no time to start over."

Then I saw the painting. I was stunned; my skin crawled in shock. She had jammed the entire scene into the right half of the painting, the trees and ocean weirdly stacked above the house and light. The left side was blank. It was deranged.

"Do another," I said. "We'll go tomorrow morning."

"No, I don't want to." She put her head down in her hands.

"Why do I always have to rush! Why don't I ever have enough time!"

Hope was oblivious to what had happened.

Driving back to Dublin I wondered whether Hope's mind was going, whether the solace of her work was ended, whether there was to be no more fake normality—whether I myself could now endure and survive. I considered the extraordinary defenses that Hope and I had developed automatically and knew I must put my trust literally in my Maker. In fact, a new set of mechanisms was already taking over. From that time forward our relationship fundamentally changed: we were less and less equals. Our areas for sharing were fewer and fewer. Increasingly we had different imperatives. My job was to be Hope's "nurse," seeing circumstances as clearly as possible. Her job was to keep functioning, keep cheerful, and thereby keep her self-respect.

Returning to Dublin I telephoned to Dr. Seiden and reported the new symptoms. I should double the dose of Decadron, she said, and in a few days the symptoms would probably subside. Packing to return to New York, I came across three huge envelopes full of keepsakes from our years in Chicago. I brought them to Hope. She said, "What are you trying to do? Pass my life in front of my eyes?"

In New York DeBellis shifted to a new chemotherapy program. "Don't worry," he said, "I've got some big guns left." That day on her way to see DeBellis, Hope's leg flopped out of control and she fell. Summoned from the car, I found her in one of the leather chairs, agitated and earnest, insisting to a stony-faced nurse that nothing was wrong with her; that she had been knocked down by the revolving door and certainly did not need a wheelchair. Henceforth, Hope found other reasons for her falls and failures, as though admission of frailty might drain her will power. It was again the Olivier theory of acting, that outward actions have an inward effect. Within the limits of her much-depleted strength, ignoring her tottery walk, the slight slap of her right foot against the ground, Hope proceeded with her life.

But somebody, usually me, had to be constantly on duty, nerves stretching into antennae. When Gertrude was there, I could slip away, feeling relieved and fearful. One day I left Hope on the bed reading a book. Her hands suddenly lost their strength, and the book fell to the floor with a crash. Downstairs Meredith said, "That's Mommy," and dashed up to the bedroom. Gertrude, following, found Hope hanging half off the bed and Meredith struggling to heave her back up. Hope, her mind affected, her face angry, was shouting, "I told you to pick up that book." Meredith said, "We can buy a dozen books, Mommy, but we can't buy another you."

Meredith was now almost motherly to Hope, getting damp washcloths for headaches, glasses of water for pills. Once, when Hope fell after a shower, Meredith forbade her to get up till I arrived. Hope thought that was hilarious. Sitting on the floor, stark naked, her bad eye ugly—laughing—she said to me, "Look at this little peanut bossing me around."

I watched the girls closely. There was one tragicomic exchange that seemed to sum up their sense of death in the household—and our family relationships. Hope was asleep upstairs, and I was tucking Meredith in for the night. I kissed her on the forehead, and she said, "I love you, Daddy. I'll be sad when you die."

Helena, standing there waiting for me, said, "But you'll die before Mommy, won't you?"

In general, though, the children treated Hope as though she were still healthy, still beautiful, and, more than anything else, still their mother. Their lives were not changed. Meredith nowadays had a busy after-school social life. Helena continued to pound up the stairs to draw and paint when her mother was in the studio, and they spent hours on the bed together, looking at magazines. Helena still came up in the night, made Hope move over, and went to sleep plastered up against her mother. Once Helena had a cough, and, desperate for rest, I banished her back downstairs. Hope went down with her and spent the night in Helena's tiny bed. We still went on family outings — to the movies, to get ice cream cones, once to the planetarium. When we came out, Helena said to her mother, "I don't think I understand the universe."

"Neither do I," said Hope.

The premourning period was an important preparation for what was to come, if only because the mechanics of the household were gradually altering. Laura Perkins, who was studying art that winter in New York, agreed to come to us on the three non-Gertrude days. Decisions and responsibilities were subtly drifting into my hands, and over Hope's objections I insisted on a cleaning lady, arranging for Whitney's to come one day a week. Often I did the washing on Gertrude days and took the clothes to the cleaners on my way to work. I ran the exchequer, paying the salaries, giving Laura money for groceries. She took the girls to buy clothes and presided over these womanly decisions. I kept track of their after-school lives. But always I tried to be invisible, preserving the fiction that Hope was still mistress of the house. And then suddenly she would reassert herself. I had been sending the children to the dentist with Laura, the newcomer. Now they needed an annual physical, and Hope, thoughtful of Gertrude's feelings, told her, "Gertrude, I made an appointment with Dr. Eiger on your day and you take them. They're your children; you know all about them. Say to him that, if there's anything he wants to tell me about them, he should tell you, and it will be just the same."

Hope still disciplined the children. Meredith misbehaved in front of visitors, and Hope, reprimanding her later, said, "You acted like a brat."

Meredith, looking miserable, said, "That goes right past my heart down to my feet."

Hope's condition continued to deteriorate. She was constantly cold and at home wore ski sweaters and pants. The larger dosage of Decadron had increased the water in her body, and her once-slender ankles were so dropsical she could no longer fit into shoes. Tiny blood blisters dotted her legs and unexplained purple bruises appeared on her body. Sometimes in the morning she had dry heaves, and sometimes she was too weak to rise. Once, to get her to DeBellis I physically carried her to the car and then to a wheelchair; in DeBellis's office she sat slumped, chin on her chest, barely able to speak.

Mercifully, she now went to sleep immediately. I would lie beside her, wakeful, trying to relax my body systematically — feet, legs, chest, neck. Dr. Seiden's words would come into my churning head: "Your wife could die at any time." Despite myself, I would start morbidly imagining what that might be like. I would think about Adlai Stevenson and his sudden death on a London sidewalk — that elegant and subtle intelligence snapping off and the body sprawled in the public grime. I supposed that somebody put a raincoat over Stevenson. Will there be a crowd around Hopie? Will I be trying to pull down her skirts while she dies? Will she die right away — or lie there for a time insisting she's just resting — while everybody stares down at her, watching her smile up at them. When Hopie does die, how will I feel? Will I be grief-stricken — B-movie tears and cries of "Hopie, Hopie, don't leave me"? Will I be relieved?

No matter how far down into her illness Hope sank, her extraordinary constitution would rebound like India rubber, and we began taking it for granted: "That's Hopie!" Because we lived in the moment, even the desperate incidents became our normality. We could believe that the pattern of our lives, including the recoveries, would go on forever. In the morning Hope would whip on her blanked-out glasses to cover her bad eye and then, sitting on the edge of the bed, sip the hot Ovaltine I brought her. While I lurked protectively by the bathroom door, she showered, put on the flower-patterned robe Gertrude had given her, tossed the dirty laundry down the stairs, and descended just behind me, sometimes steadying herself with her hands on my shoulders.

At breakfast she now gave in to what she called her "fat soul," eating "ducks"—sugar cubes she dipped into hot coffee and then sucked dry—and indulging in the most delicious French toast I could make—the egg-soaked bread fried with a huge dollop of butter under each side, then drenched in pure maple syrup. Hope smacked her lips as she ate.

She talked with the children, smiling when Meredith told her last night's dream: ". . . and suddenly the bird was a horse and this man asked if I wanted to ride . . ." There was a morning when the girls showed their art-class paintings to their mother. Hope told Meredith she had a wonderful sense of color. She said Helena's primitive looked like a Brueghel. Helena was upset. "I want my very, very own style," she said.

For Hope the dying process meant a steady contraction of her world. Selling her art, giving dinner parties, housekeeping—all these tasks had virtually ceased. The work and the children remained central. Even the two hours a day in the studio took tremendous determination. Bending over gave her headaches, and she was soon exhausted. She was developing her woodcut "The Swimmers"—boys jumping off a New York pier—and I was in the studio working at my typewriter. Asked for my opinion, I would see a boy's hand that looked like a baseball mitt and say, "The body is wonderful. Maybe those fingers could be a little thinner, but I don't think it matters." These were among my most painful moments—treating with concealed condescension that part of Hope I admired without qualification —treating her like a limited girl doing her best but needing encouragement. I was watching in Hope a version of the possibility that haunted me: the drying up of inspiration when ideas and words stop mysteriously arriving in the mind.

In late September DeBellis recommended radiation treatments in addition to chemotherapy and immunotherapy. I knew that in Hope's case radiation was medicine's last stand, but I thought, "What the hell, shoot the works." There was something comforting about the pinpoint aim of radiation compared to the shotgun assault of chemicals.

"Will I live till Christmas?" Hope asked.

"I would bet on that," said DeBellis. He went on to say in his same informational tone that Hope would lose her hair. Many patients get wigs, and perhaps she could have her hair shaved off and a wig made from it. Hope showed no emotion. There is a sequence in a W. C. Fields movie in which a train, pursued by Indians, is dismantled stick by stick to get wood for the locomotive. Finally, there is nothing left but the iron frames and wheels. Hope's cancer consumed her faculties and talents one by one, but the iron always remained. "How long before my hair starts to fall out?" she asked.

"About three weeks."

"Will it grow back?"

"Yes, about three months after the radiation ends."

As we departed, DeBellis said to Hope, "I wish a quarter of my patients were so well adjusted."

On the way to the car I wondered aloud with some excitement whether a wig really could be made from Hope's hair. She was silent. Our chauffeur that day was Liz Hauser, and in the car Hope said, "I want to go now to Ysugi Suga's" — the well-known hairdresser who cut her hair. As we drove, Hope was composed. At Suga's I sat in the car by a fire hydrant while Liz shepherded Hope inside. Two young Japanese men were seated behind a desk, strangers to Hope. She walked straight to them and said, "I'm dying of cancer, and my hair's going to fall out, and I need a wig."

They gave her names of wigmakers, and at home I telephoned a celebrity friend who might know about wigs — the comedienne Joan Rivers. Hope had gone to college with her sister, and we had met Joan and her husband Edgar through a mutual friend. She immediately took charge; the celebrated Kenneth owed her many favors, and she would have him handle the wig; Hope would go first-class. I talked with Hope, and we decided, yes, we'll trust to Joan.

The radiation trips began again, now with car-parking help from the women who had said, "Any time I can help you . . ." And now a yellow line down the center of the hospital hallway measured the wobble in Hope's uncertain walk. One day her leg gave way, and, while we sat on a bench waiting for sensation to return, I pleaded with her to ride the rest of the way in a wheelchair. She adamantly refused, her pride at stake. It was one of those times when my analgesic, premourning numbness split, and the pain and rage blasted out in all directions — this time at Hope herself. My God, I was sick of living in a miasma of illness, my days and emotions geared to a dying woman. I was sick of walking this tightrope of calm, sick of numbness, sick of exhaustion and sleeplessness, sick of worrying that my wife might fall down, sick of being so alone with my anxieties.

"Don't be so Goddam stubborn," I said to my dying wife. "Do me this one favor. Don't make me lug you down there like a half-full sack of flour. Sure you can get down there without a wheelchair. Who are you proving that to? The nurse down there doesn't give a damn. Jesus, you have the whim of an elephant. How about thinking of . . ."

Hope stood up and tottered alone down the hall toward the elevator. I ran after her in a sweat of remorse. I took her arm, and she tried to pull it away, saying, "Don't touch me." I wished only to placate her. I let go her arm. She almost fell. I gripped her again, and we moved forward, locked together.

Eight

That fall of 1975 our emotional roller coaster picked up speed. Hope was summoned to Kenneth's to have her wig fitted — and her hair cut off. Escorted by Whitney while I waited in the car, she entered Kenneth's town-house salon with eyes straight forward, mouth set. Whitney sat at a distance watching, as she and I had once peered through the operating room door at Hope and Dr. Nealon. Now the sterile white was leopard spots and cabbage roses, antique tables and mirrors, movie-set elegance. Hope took her place in the chair with the dignity of a queen come to be shorn for the guillotine. Draping her in a leopard-patterned cloth, the hairdresser began to cut. Hope began to talk — and talk — entertaining him, charming him, as the last stand of her beauty fell in red handfuls to the floor.

Nowadays Hope was often dizzy, her balance even more precarious. A new and appalling head symptom had been added. During the night Hope would get out of bed and in the dark go toward the bathroom. Instantly awake, I would vault from the bed to reach her side and then wordlessly help her down onto the toilet — and wordlessly she let me. As she strained against chronic constipation, increasing the pressure against some trigger point in her brain, her body would begin to jerk and then thrash uncontrollably—a runaway motor, a broken toy. Kneeling on the tile floor beside the toilet, one arm around her body, the other around her legs, I pitted my strength against the violence of her reflexes and could barely hold her upright. Just before my endurance broke, she would subside. "You're all right now, Hope. You're all right," I said tenderly, still holding her body, damp against my face and arms, soft, repulsive.

I was sweating and cold, both inside and out, a corner of my brain marveling that my feelings could remain so flat, that I did not disintegrate. Suddenly meticulous about Hope's privacy, I waited outside for sounds of toilet paper. I supported her to the bed and tucked her in. Then she sometimes spoke her only words: "Thank you."

After the first of Hope's terrible seizures on the toilet, I telephoned DeBellis, and he told me to double once again the Decadron, which attacked the swelling around the tumors. But Hope's vomit was now chocolate-brown, and on the thirtieth of September, after brushing her teeth, she smiled at me and her mouth was a ghastly half-moon of blood.

The cells that should have clotted her blood—the platelets—were not being produced in sufficient quantity by the bone marrow. DeBellis, worried about internal bleeding, fearful that this was a sign that melanoma had invaded the marrow, ordered her into the hospital for tests. He found no bleeding and the platelet count gradually recovered during the next two weeks. I usually stayed with Hope in her hospital room until after dinner, which was possible only because Liz Hauser often volunteered to be with the children, thereby releasing Gertrude or Laura. Then, when I did get home, I was besieged by the telephone—the sound of my voice reciting the awful realities I desperately wanted to put aside. After the last call I would feel drained and utterly alone—while Meredith and Helena called from their bedrooms, "Come on, Dad, get off the phone." My entry into single parenthood had begun.

Hope's downward slide again dramatically reversed. She had arrived at the hospital in a wheelchair, too weak and wobbly to walk. But the continuing radiation treatments began to shrink the tumors. The pressures on her brain eased. On the sixth of October, waking at five, Hope got up alone and in the tiny bathroom gave herself a sponge bath and washed her stubbly hair. Our perspective had become so narrow that this accomplishment could lift us into gaiety. Whitney came that afternoon. We gobbled apricots and nuts secreted in Hope's bedside-table drawer and reminisced about our month in France. Later, as we were leaving, Hope turned on her television set. There appeared a crowd of African natives, dancing, jouncing up and down, grunting, brandishing spears. "Oh, grow up," Hope said.

The next day DeBellis took a sample of her bone marrow. That evening he again brought good news: there was no sign of melanoma in her blood (the first Hope knew that the cancer might go to the marrow), and she would be discharged tomorrow morning.

Soon Hope's remaining hair began coming out, a plague of red in combs and brushes, on the floor of the shower, in the sink — Hope's hallmark literally going down the drain. But, as her scalp began showing pale and shiny, she only said, "I guess this is the last of the frizzy, redheaded witch." Hope remained as matter-of-fact as Helena, who had always delighted in combing her mother's hair. Now, unperturbed, Helena would finish some wispy hairdo and say, "There," and make her amused mother admire it in the mirror. When Hope was finally bald — a thin rim of hair at her forehead and the back of her head — Helena told me, "I think Mom looks cute, like a puppy."

I have a cruelly stark image of Hope coming out of the shower: bald head, one eye bulging downward under a lid swollen closed, her body heavy, slightly stooped, covered with tiny blood blisters and large bruises, rolls of flesh around her waist. But Helena was right. Hope remained appealing. Her dignity overwhelmed the defacement. Her smile was still glorious. Her beguiling charm — that dear, lovable quality — was still intrinsic. She had kept whatever is the essence of beauty. I was reminded of Mae West's words to me during an interview: "If you want to be sexy on the screen, you've got to think about sex all the time" — the Mae West theory of acting. Well, Hope was thinking about love.

The radiation treatments ended on October fifteenth; more exposure would damage the brain. The chemotherapy, however, would continue. Hope's brother and two sisters had planned to fly east one by one for last visits, and I called them and said the time had come. More than anybody, another Brooks could animate and distract Hope. She needed them now while she still could get to a restaurant, to a gallery, to a store, while she could still be the Hopie they would want to have in their memories.

Her brother Bobby and his wife Kathy flew to Boston and met us in Dublin. It was Indian summer; that solitary maple in front of the house was again like fire. We drove Bobby and Kathy on our customary circuit of nearby, untouched New England towns: Fitzwilliam, Francestown, Hancock, Harrisville. The high point was always Jaffrey Center. The meetinghouse in this tiny cluster of buildings was built during the Revolutionary War, and in the sloping ground of its cemetery are buried a Minuteman, a freed slave, and Willa Cather. It was the place Thornton Wilder had in mind as he wrote *Our Town*. Disturbing the orange and yellow leaves, which lay like bright shadows below each maple, we wandered among the slate markers carved with sad-eyed angels. We read aloud to each other the inscriptions: "Death steady to his purpose from the womb, Pursues till we are driven to the tomb." I led them to Willa Cather's stone: ". . . that is happiness to be dissolved into something complete and great."

Hope and I always felt a kind of comfort in that still place, where death was natural, universal, each of us in our turn, century after century. And to have bypassed it would have insulted Hope, intimating that she could not handle reminders of death. But I was sorry we had come there when Hope, staggering, had yet another "episode," and I quickly helped her to the stone wall. Kathy Brooks thought to herself, "Hopie's thinking, 'I'm going to be next.'"

A few days later Hope's wig was finished, and she wore it home from Kenneth's — every strand in place, smooth as red plastic, dead — to us the symbol of everything that had happened to Hope. We all hypocritically admired it, and Hope joked that this was a dream come true; she had always wanted straight hair.

At home Hope usually wore a ski hat but did use the wig for social occasions. These I ruthlessly screened down to the people who truly mattered to her. Even so, tragicomic contretemps were inevitable. There was the couple who invited us to *Cat on a Hot Tin Roof,* every one of us forgetting that the plot pivoted on Big Daddy's dying of cancer. There was a memorable dinner to which we were invited. One of the other guests was the relative of someone who had recently died of cancer. After dinner she asked Hope about Meredith and Helena. Hope answered that she was trying to fix herself and her beliefs in their minds.

The woman smiled beatifically and said, a little indulgently, "Oh, they won't remember a thing."

In the taxi home we laughed and laughed at the thoughtfulness of our hosts, helping Hope to make new friends and saying to each other, "We'll invite so-and-so; her sister died of cancer so they'll have a lot in common."

As the impressario of Hope's life, I wielded the tremendous power conferred by mortal illness. All Hope's wishes became last wishes. As Hope's representative, my merest murmur was a bugle call summoning attention, sympathy, cheerful visitors, car sitters, companions, casseroles. By extension, I too was handled tenderly. I came to feel that the world would, and should, drop everything to care for us. A few friends announced straightforwardly that they could not face Hope's illness and were bowing out of our lives. I did not fault them. But from all the others I wanted and expected total daily devotion toward Hope and kept a mental list of those who did not meet my exacting standards. For me, every minute took place in the context of Hope's illness. I could not accept that others found the fact of Hope's impending death less important—and infinitely less congenial —than the pursuit of their own lives.

At that time I was incensed at Hope's sisters in Arizona and California. I kept urging them to come east, saying, "The roof can cave in any moment." They did not come. Perhaps they were detached by distance; probably they were shrinking from this farewell. Time kept passing. I was indignant, feeling that they were putting the even tenor of their ways ahead of Hope's needs in her last weeks. In my continuing state of low-grade trauma, all my emotions were simmering just below a boil, and they were convenient targets for my generalized rage. When I expressed disappointment and disgust to Hope, she shrugged her shoulders and changed the subject. Unlike me, she knew the world could not live each day as though it were her last. Nobody, not even she herself, could sustain that fever pitch of reality.

Hope had weekly blood tests, and on the twentieth of October DeBellis said that "nucleated red cells" had been found—a sign of "marrow invasion" by melanoma. Hope, I felt, was like a burning house with flames flaring up in room after room. This time she asked no searching questions. And later at home, when she decided that now was the time to take a trip, there was no admission it would be her last. She said she needed to do some painting for the show of her work that her friend Ann Blodgett was putting on in February. For that reason, we would not take the children. I asked DeBellis for permission, and he said it was a calculated risk but to do it.

We chose the Caribbean island of St. Martin—seven days at a fabulous hotel, La Sammana. I did not dare go without help, and Whitney came with us. On the eighteenth of November, we three gathered early in the morning at the airport. The plane ride was animated, exhilarated. Then in St. Martin's airport Hope collapsed with an eruption of vomiting and diarrhea. We got her into bed at the hotel, and she slept with a deep unnatural consciousness, her breathing rapid and shallow, from time to time vomiting a dark-brown liquid that looked like blood. I was terrified. Would an airline allow her on a plane in this condition? Was she going to die now, so far from the high-powered help she needed? I called a doctor, who gave her injections to quiet her stomach. The next morning, when I returned from delivering a vomit specimen to a laboratory (only traces of blood were found), there was Hope, fresh from a shower, laughing with Whitney about the scene in the St. Martin's airport.

Smiling at her, I thought, "Hopie, my Lazarus." That evening with thickets of tropical flowers nudging our elbows, the sea sounding softly on the sand below, we ate dinner in the hotel like any other tourists.

Hope had a miraculous new lease on energy, and the trip became everything I had wished. Waking each morning at dawn, she did a watercolor study of the voluptuous green vines and orange flowers growing against the brilliant white walls of the hotel. At breakfast with Whitney we planned our days and fed crumbs to the tiny green bird that hopped onto our table. We circled the island in our rented car; Hope and Whitney painted in the tropical, French-feeling towns; we ate elaborate dinners in French restaurants. One day I went snorkling among kindergartens of minute fish, glittering like snow suspended in sunlight.

Whitney, as planned, departed two days ahead of us, and the festive momentum of the trip stalled. I think Whitney, a third person, had forced us to suppress our shared anxiety and anger. Now they were freed. And even under the threat of death, a relationship continues in its familiar pattern but with its highs and lows exaggerated. Returning from the airport we bickered stupidly, Hope with a headache complaining about the jouncing car, me saying defensively that I couldn't help the terrible roads.

Then at dinner in the hotel, Hope was silent. Repeatedly I worked to start a conversation and bring us back in tune, but Hope was unresponsive. I knew that, with anybody else, Hope would be talking and convivial. I wanted some of that effort, some of that warmth. Though aware she could die at any moment, I was swamped by my old anger, by my wish that Hope's wooing of the world was extended to me.

I started a fight saying, "I'm just trying to get a conversation going. Nothing dazzling, just a pleasant exchange between husband and wife so we don't sit here staring at nothing. How about some help?"

"I just don't feel like talking," Hope said.

"Why don't you pretend I'm a stranger?" I said. "That's an idea. Pretend I'm a stranger." The fight went on, recriminatory, ugly, dumb—until we indeed sat silent and now miserable. As usual I was immediately struck by guilt, by the fear that I had said something irreparable, by a need to reconstruct our rapport. I apologized. Hope was silent; the air was not cleared.

But the next morning her mood was sunny. This was our last full day on St. Martin, and I was now glad we had it to ourselves. It was, really, a reprise of that day in Spain: packing the car with painting gear, setting off with the same sense of lift and expectation. I thought about the aeons we had traversed since that tearful Madonna, the two lovers in the dusk, the fishing boats stranded on the tidal beach.

We drove to a tiny beach village, Grand Case, and parked in the weed-grown driveway of a boarded-up, two-story wooden house draped in flowering vines. Behind it, under a tree, was a table on which we spread salami and bread and cheese. I changed into my bathing suit. For protection against the sun, Hope stayed in her uniform of that week—light-blue cotton pants, a loose, light-yellow man's shirt, a cotton hat she had bought, made of squares from flour sacks sewn together. Her face was tanned, relaxed, full of ersatz health. The sounds of bees, birds, miniature waves against the beach, three black children splashing in the water, gently lapped against the quiet.

I was going to paint with Hope, something I had not done since the Bahamas long ago with John Groth. The three of us had stood on a pier painting the Nassau waterfront while a cruise ship tied up and hundreds of tourists streamed past us. Hope, to John's secret delight, wrote in red paint FAMOUS ARTIST on his bare back.

In the same way that I always wanted Hope to love New Hampshire and winter and even skiing, she longed to have me take up painting, for her the ultimate sharing. I wish I had. There would have been many memories as happy as that day. But I lacked skill and always felt compelled to do things well. How silly, how beside the point. In that St. Martin's yard I tried a picture, and Hope was tremendously pleased, maternally squeezing the colored worms of pigment around the edge of a dinner plate, setting me up like a favorite student with a jar of water and a modest pad of watercolor paper. We set to work on the same subject: the side of a house — bleached white wood, with a red door, two green vines — festoons of red and yellow blooms. Hope, enjoying her superiority, coached me on what colors to mix together, but when I tried to paint, one by one, every leaf and flower, we both laughed at the result. Hope, grinning, affectionate, said, "Brutal." The sun was warm. The three children laughed in the distance. The bees toured our subject.

When my paper was soaking wet, like a used paper towel, we took a break. Behind the car Hope changed into her bathing suit, and I supported her down the slope of soft sand into the water. We floated there, moving our arms and legs slowly, our bodies, our past and future, suspended. We marveled together at the deliciousness of the water and the beauty of the moment.

We dressed and walked slowly down the road, the one village street. We leaned against the cement railing of a bridge over a stream. On a pier far out into the sea, small black figures fished, their rods like pencil lines drawn from their hands. Two men placidly rowed a boat sunk to its gunwales under the weight of bright green bananas. We strolled into the town of Grand

Case — sun-bleached houses, faded green, orange, red walls, so French, with their second-story porches on tall stilts. A long-legged, brown-skinned girl in a turquoise dress peered at us from behind the yellow doors of a store. In the shadow of a mud wall, sprawled like a sleeping derelict, lay a dog. "*Voilà le* French *chien,*" Hope said.

As we walked, hand in hand, nudging each other's glance toward what we noticed, we indulged in the ultimate fantasy. We discussed living someday in St. Martin. We wondered whether the permanent tranquillity would be good for us. Like most writers, I considered myself incurably lazy, and I worried about the languid pace. Hope, the dynamo, the painter, reveled in the thought of infinite subject matter. We wondered about the problems of Americans owning real estate, the costs of property, the possible income from renting.

The cliché is true. The heart does swell. I remember it that day — the meshing of emotion, the merging of awareness, the mingling of delight. I have always believed that a deepest need, rarely granted, is contact with another soul. That day we had it — communion founded on confirmed commitment. We had come so far together, through so much, and we had stood by each other. And we knew the final preciousness of this day.

That night in bed, with the warm skin of her scalp against my cheek, I said, "No matter how many times I have spoken to you in anger — said terrible things — I have never wanted to be married to anybody else."

Reflectively, Hope answered, "It's a long way, isn't it, between all the hearts and flowers at the beginning and building a decent marriage." She continued, "I know you hate it when we fight, and maybe you're right when you say I'm willful. But above all I have loved you and will continue to love you." I caressed her body, and my hand touched wartlike tumors on her skin — cancer literally popping out. I felt them, not with horror, but with a kind of tenderness — love heightened by threat. I realized that I could make love to Hope, and this fact alone moved me deeply. "My darling," I said, "I love you so."

"Yes," Hope said. In the faint light through the wooden shutters I could see her secret smile. It was a transcendent moment — making love not to her flesh but to what she meant to me — giving Hope the ultimate proof that she was still a woman. Knowing that this was probably the last time, we joined in a flood of happiness, fear, love, despair. Then, too wet with sweat to want to touch, we lay beside each other on our backs, smiling at the ceiling. I thought to myself that the honeymoon suite had not been wasted. Hope said, "If Dr. DeBellis could see us now, wouldn't he be proud."

The St. Martin idyll was Hope's Indian summer — a gift really. We had a Thanksgiving weekend epilogue in Dublin with the Hansens and Peter Davis, and with Ky, who flew East. On our first morning back in New York, I delivered Hope to the hospital for a blood transfusion and another session of chemotherapy. I returned home to work — and walked into a single moment which for me was the emotional climax of Hope's illness. I telephoned DeBellis to learn the progress of the melanoma in Hope's bone marrow. In the Caribbean, in Dublin, I had managed a cheerful dream state, menace blanked from my mind. Now, alone in the kind of solitude that frightens, I was confronting reality.

Waiting for DeBellis to call back, trying to write at my typewriter, I felt the original, desperate anxiety stringing me tight till I could not sit in my chair, could not squeeze one more word from my mind. It was unendurable. I went to the telephone to have DeBellis paged. I asked my question. He answered, "The blood tests this morning show a very high incidence of nucleated red cells, indicating extensive metastasis in the marrow."

I had steeled myself for this. "How long does she have now?"

"That depends on a number of factors — like the effectiveness of the chemotherapy and the progress of the head tumors. But I would say weeks, not months."

"Couldn't she be kept going with transfusions of platelets?"

"No. It's not practical."

"Not practical!" I shouted to myself. "What does practicality have to do with it? Hope's life is at stake!" But I said nothing as DeBellis continued:

"That's a stopgap measure. The platelets last only twenty-four hours, they're very difficult to get in quantity, and the patient soon rejects them. There's no reason to use them if the patient's going nowhere."

I asked, "What shall I tell Hopie?"

"That's up to you," he said.

"I don't see anything to be gained by the truth. No, we don't tell her."

Our voices had been brisk and businesslike, both of us by now old cohorts. After two years of dreading doctors, I felt close to DeBellis, the other man who had shared Hope's calamity and strained to make it easier. I was in a state of unnatural, almost eerie calm.

Then Dr. DeBellis said, "How do you want to do this?"

I was mystified. "What do you mean?"

"Do you want to do it at home or in the hospital?"

I understood. My insides collapsed. Fire ran through every capillary. My skin shrank on my body. That was the instant when I finally, totally, faced the truth in every compartment of my mind and my subconscious. Every defense was blasted. In the full sense of that ghastly pun, there was no more Hope. "At home," I said. "Anything else is unthinkable."

"Can you handle it?"

"Yes."

DeBellis gave me instructions. He would supply syringes and drugs and pain-killers for emergencies. When she died, I was to call him immediately, day or night, and he would come to the house to write the death certificate. Otherwise there would be painful complications with the city coroner's office. He gave me his home telephone number. I thanked him. We hung up.

I walked back into Hope's studio, a pressure spreading from my head through my body. With the stark clarity of first sight, I stood looking around me — at the birch-bark nest found on a Dublin walk, at Hope's pencil drawing of Meredith asleep, at the photograph of my father in art school in Boston, at the stones collected near Winslow Homer's studio in Maine, at Hope's wood-carving tools, their wooden handles polished by her hands. I began to cry, as though my heaving chest were pumping out the tears. I covered my face with my hands and felt the wetness. I wailed in the silence, "Hopie's going to die."

My anguish and my isolation were intolerable. I telephoned Hope at the hospital and was startled by the normality of her soft voice saying "Hello."

We fell into our almost-ritual exchange. I said, "It's me. How do you feel?"

"Fine."

"That's terrific. Now tell me how you really feel."

"Honestly, I'm fine."

"Yes," I said, "I understand that. But how do you feel?"

"Well, I'm constipated if that's of any interest to you." Hope's voice always had its own vitality, its grin, independent of body ills.

"Oh, I'll call the *Times*."

She laughed. "Have you heard anything from DeBellis?"

"Yes," I said. "Nothing new. He's concerned but not worried." It was strange. Hearing my lie spoken so normally, it gave me comfort.

Hope left the hospital the next day, December second, I knew for the last time. As I look back on her final, swift decline, I think of the stories of Humphrey Bogart's last weeks — painfully dressing each afternoon, riding down on a chair on top of a dumbwaiter, and emerging into his living room, as though onto a stage, to urbanely, genially, receive friends for drinks. Hope managed the same unflinching gallantry, and the lesson in Hope's last weeks was the same: stay connected to those pieces of life that mean you are alive.

Hope woke daily at dawn and sat on the side of the bed

drinking the thermos of hot Ovaltine I made for her each evening. While I lay half awake in bed, she made her way alone downstairs, sitting on the steps and moving herself lower one step at a time. I would hear her in the kitchen — the clatter of dishes and clink of glasses as she organized and reorganized the shelves, putting her house and life in order. I would lie in the dawn light wondering what was going to happen, looking over at Hope's bureau and her childhood statue of the Blessed Virgin Mother — she called it "the BVM." I thought, "I shall bury that with Hope in her coffin."

Deciding, with Whitney, that imprisoning Hope would be far worse than any mishap, I let her go anywhere she wanted — alone by cab to lunch with Ann Blodgett to plan her February show, on Christmas shopping trips with Whitney, to Oscar Chardiet's birthday party for which Hope insisted on baking a cake, to dinner at Peter Davis's apartment with the Hansens and Liz Hauser.

Hope was affectionate to the children, calling them her pet names, "Mereditty" and "Baby Zizzer." She still played little tricks on them — sticking price tags from packages onto their foreheads — still made her jokes: "If your nose went on strike, would you picket?" For Helena's eighth birthday she drew Richard Scarry characters on cardboard and cut them out and Laura hung them from the ceiling over the table. And yet I felt that Hope was growing subtly distanced from Meredith and Helena.

She told Betty Suyker that watching Peter Davis had reassured her that a family did not dissolve and disappear when the mother died. She matter-of-factly told me, after I had finished my morning routines and the children were off to school, "I can see how it's going to be, and that makes me feel better."

I sat on the bed and answered with more confidence than I felt, "Hope, don't ever worry about Meredith and Helena. I am absolutely sure I can bring those little girls up the way you want."

"I know you can," she said. Nothing more was necessary, anything more would underline her fate. We knew wordlessly what we both wanted—two well-adjusted young adults. But Hope was not a person who had long-range plans for others, who would lay out a program of last wishes.

Though now it was little more than puttering, Hope's work had become the pinpoint of her life—the impervious imprint she could leave behind. She climbed daily to her studio, with me one step behind in case she fell. Struggling to finish her "Swimmers" woodcut, she printed the separate figures of leaping boys in queer places on a half-dozen huge sheets of rice paper, and those troubled, troubling images hung henceforth like SOS flags from the rope strung across one side of the room. She did manage a small print of flowering branches, created as a gift to show her gratitude to Elizabeth Hauser, and I agreed to write a thank-you verse she could inscribe.

Hope also began the final prints for *Akimba and the Magic Cow.* As I worked at the opposite end of the room, I could hear her signs of exasperation edge toward tears as she ruined print after print. I sat beside her, and she let me dart my fingers in at the last second to finish the gaps in the inking and the rubbing. The next day I cut pages to size, and she did watercolor wash backgrounds, her hands, puffy on emaciated wrists, moving almost at random. We put the pages in order and wrapped them for delivery. The package lay on the table she had used for twenty years. I bent over and kissed her cheek.

"Do you think it's okay?" Hope asked.

"It's really good, Hopie. They're going to like it. You should be very proud." In my head were images of those pages in all those hospital rooms. Good or bad, that little book was a triumph of spirit. I thought of William Randolph Hearst, who kept building and building his California castle, San Simeon, certain that the day he stopped he would die.

Already launched into grief, I was also embarked on another element of mourning and the Ritual: I felt sealed in isolation. The interlacing of needs and devotion, my unwinking attention, the falling away of conflict, had brought Hope and me supremely close, while paradoxically my loneliness was almost a physical pain. More and more Hope was the most vulnerable of my children, the toddler lurching off in all directions toward disaster, the whole world now a mine field. I lived shadowing Hope to keep her safe, gauging when she boiled water whether she would set her sleeve on fire, whether she would drop the pot and scald herself. It was very lonely behind the scenes, cushioning Hope's agonies—and then ushering her out to center stage, a pulled-together, philosophic Hope starring in her own personal drama.

Once I needed Ed Kern's help in lifting Hope's inert weight out of a pool of diarrhea on the floor. While I washed her, Ed cradled her head against his, murmuring, "My dear, dear Hope, hang on." Always admiring Hope's dignity and almost Victorian propriety, he was intensely embarrassed and very frightened. But my reaction was, "Now somebody else knows what I go through." I must have wanted a little stardom for myself.

Though friends sincerely asked the questions, I felt in my isolation that they were only polite about my problems, that they shrank involuntarily from the ins and outs of Hope's condition. I felt that I was the doomsayer, concentrating only on blackness, that everybody preferred Hope, who would say, "I'm crumping along," and smile and change the subject to Jackie O. More than ever I was orchestrating her good hours, making sure that excursions were brief, that she was home to sleep in the middle of the day, that when she awoke, headachy and morose, friends arrived for whom she would mobilize her spirits.

While Laura or Gertrude guarded Hope, I would stage-manage each tomorrow by telephone, usually from my office five minutes away. That was my refuge, the heart of my own intimate clutter—the home of my book, my tie with the future, the place of release where my self-control could rest. While I sat at my desk, sometimes tears erupted without warning, ungovernable crying almost more physical than mental. As I sobbed, I would think, "Tears *are* hot," and, cooling my face on the smooth, chill metal of my typewriter, I joked to myself, "Don't rust the keys." But I would hear my voice, like somebody else's, calling, "Oh Hopie, Hopie."

Each day I telephoned Whitney. She was crucial to me, but her emotional support went mainly to Hope, and she was a full-time mother to a family. Increasingly I was reaching out by telephone to Liz Hauser to fill blind needs — to ventilate my anguish, to make a contact as myself, not as Hope's nurse — to get reassurance that I was not entirely alone. She and Josie and Hope, kindred, irreverent spirits, had gravitated toward each other at school meetings. Liz, in the process of leaving her husband, feeling very alone, seized on their friendship. So Hope typically became a resource of concern, interest, humor, and when Liz did decide on divorce, Hope was the first person she called. When Liz set up her single life, I counseled her on jobs and living costs. We were attracted to Liz by her innate gaiety (she laughed the loudest when teased), her warmth and quick understanding, her looks: tall, dark-haired, bright eyes that looked straight into yours, a low, melodious voice tuned for sympathy. When Hope fell ill, Liz faithfully brought her cheer to Hope in hospital rooms, to the house. In charge of her own time (by then she was the director of a small art foundation and her two boys lived with their father), she was ready at a moment's notice to drive the car, to baby-sit the girls. Inevitably, she took me on as a patient.

I called her almost every morning. "How's Hopie?" she would say immediately. Then like a tedious old nurse I reported the minutiae of the night, so tremendously important to me. "How are *you?*" Liz would ask. Instantly my private pandemonium was tapped. Despair welled up. Liz told me later, "The quiver was not in your voice, it was in your whole being." I would plunge into my current lament — my exhaustion, my inability to sleep, my worry over the children. The fact that they were adopted obsessed me. Their natural mothers put them up for adoption to give them two parents — that tripled my sense of their tragedy. I would rant about my book: "It's the thing that's going to save me. But, God, I know I'll go broke before I finish it. I feel

· *137* ·

as though I've been half my life in this dark tunnel. My nerves are shot. How can I possibly handle what's ahead for me? What am I going to do?"

"See that pinprick of light up ahead?" she once answered. "It's the end of the tunnel. It may not look like much right now, but it will get bigger."

Finally, I would get to the ostensible reason for the call — the consultation about the next day's arrangements, the Byzantine shufflings of friends and baby-sitters to anticipate every contingency. Usually we ended with humor, often mordant on my part. Once I said, "I've got a foolproof weight-loss program — having a dying wife." Liz did not laugh, but she did not recoil.

One evening I had theater tickets with the Hansens to *The Cherry Orchard* at Lincoln Center. Too weak and sick to go, Hope insisted that I invite Liz Hauser in her place — Laura would stay on duty. After agonizing for an hour, I went with Liz, feeling a mix of disloyalty, escape, and anticipation.

I had never been alone with her.

That evening in the theater I was intensely aware of Whitney on my left as the representative of Hope and of Liz on my right as the essence of health and normal life. I remember the houselights coming on and her striking, aquiline face turning responsively toward me — the curved Roman nose and expressive wrinkles at the eyes framed by the dark hair. I remember the way she stood up, the quick, almost impetuous strength I had already noticed but not till then admired. After two years submerged in illness, ringing every imaginable emotional change, I suddenly ached for an uncomplicated companionship with a well woman. That part of me locked to Hope wrenched my attention away. Had Whitney noticed anything?

On December twelfth, Hope had ten days to live.

We reported to the Atchley Pavilion for another blood test and to DeBellis's office for the results. The last chemotherapy had reversed the melanoma in the marrow. Then, in exactly the same tone as he delivered this good news, DeBellis said matter-of-factly that he was ending the chemotherapy. The compound he was using was not affecting the neurological symptoms. There were no further therapies that crossed over from the body to the brain.

Hope's plug had just been pulled. Presto. The hand is quicker than the heart. The momentum of the moment rushed us past our shock. "What about my liver?" asked Hope.

"When you've got a forest fire burning," said DeBellis, with his usual crisp directness, "you don't worry about a campfire."

Except for a quick, startled look at me, Hope was utterly calm. Though her speech was lucid and her senses sharp, yet nowadays there was an elusive, floating quality about her, as though her buffeted brain were cushioned one short notch from reality. Perhaps this shielded her, but the main emotion she expressed at this instant of crescendo was gratitude toward DeBellis. She told him, "You are a wonderful doctor and a wonderful man."

"You always made it easy for me," DeBellis answered.

It was a bizarre moment, watching them say goodbye forever, knowing that, when they met again, Hope would be dead.

I never did find out what Hope thought that day. But later I saw her press her thumb into her arm till the flesh turned white, and then she watched the blood flow back.

We returned to our routines — the Ovaltine, the shelf tidying, the visitors at five in the afternoon. I drove her on short neighborhood painting trips with a friend, a back-slid watercolorist Hope was encouraging to take up art again. Joan Rivers passed through town and took us to dinner. We discussed everything but the illness, and when the wine came, Hope gave a joke toast — "Here's to the Bicentennial. I'm already sick of it. It hasn't even started, and I feel like it was last year."

A friend from Dublin telephoned and asked if she could pay a call. To our astonishment she arrived with another woman, a stranger, a poet named Elizabeth Atherton, who had recently divorced her businessman husband and was settling into a loft in SoHo — the art-gallery area Hope and I had walked while waiting for the mole biopsy. Hope and she talked about poetry, none of us aware that the Dublin friend had arranged the visit to introduce Elizabeth Atherton to me.

One morning, while Hope was still in bed, I told her that Liz Hauser was stopping by that afternoon. "Why does *she* have to come all the time?" Hope said irritably.

I was astonished. "I thought you liked her a lot," I said. "You're always in a terrific mood when she leaves."

"She's just waiting to take my place," she said, and then, agitated, "No! I mustn't say that or even think it."

I sat on the edge of the bed and took Hope's hand. "You must believe me," I said, my voice intense with sincerity, "Liz is a wonderful friend and a tremendous comfort to both of us. But, as a woman to get involved with, she is truly, truly not my type. She is not a person for me." As I spoke, I wondered what was the truth.

On December fifteenth, Hope had one week to live. Her Christmas presents for California had been mailed, the fudge was made and bundled in little bags left over from Halloween, the stollen was baked and in the freezer. The final sister, Blue, and her husband Don were arriving late that afternoon for dinner, staying the next day, and leaving the following afternoon. In the morning Hope finished her New York shopping in Bloomingdale's with her book editor and friend Bernice Chardiet. For herself Hope bought a sweater on sale like one Bernice had worn to the hospital; she bought me a Joan Baez record and Oscar Chardiet a book. She insisted on buying Bernice an art book on Burchfield, saying, "I want to give you this now. I don't know whether I'll still be alive at Christmas."

At lunch, exhausted, Hope dropped her hamburger in the cole slaw and said, childlike, apologetic, "I didn't do it on purpose." Then she said, "I feel so freaky."

At the curb by a taxi, Hope lost her balance, and Bernice held her and they kissed goodbye. Bernice remembers, "I didn't want to see her go so casually. You think afterward of all the things you wanted to say, but you just keep quiet — and then feel, 'Why was I so cowardly?' "

At home Hope slept and once again revived. Blue and Don came for dinner, and the two sisters spent the next morning alone in Hope's studio, looking at her work and talking about Blue's ambition to learn to paint. That night the three Brooks girls and their husbands had dinner — Hope's Last Hurrah. In a red velvet jacket, new shoes, Hope was beautiful. She spoke little, but at dinner announced she had cut her Christmas-card list by half, saying, "If I didn't get one, I didn't send one. It felt terrific." It was a flash of the old Hopie. We erupted in laughter, so happy. The next morning she went alone in a taxi to meet Blue at Whitney's. After a while Hope went into the living room, lay down on the sofa, and went to sleep. She was still asleep when Blue and Don left to catch their plane.

In a sense, Hope never completely woke again. She was conscious only a few hours of every day. There were jobs to do. She wrote the to-and-from cards for Christmas presents, biting her lower lip as she tried to guide the pencil. She sent me to fetch the print for Liz Hauser, and while I sat beside her on the edge of the bed holding the board on her knees, she struggled to inscribe my verse. That was done, another final piece of business settled.

Early in that week, while I was downstairs getting the children away to school, Hope urinated in the bed, rose from her sleep, collapsed in the bathroom, cut her scalp. She lay on the floor, helpless, too heavy for me to lift, covered with blood. I knew the melanoma was now unchecked in her marrow; her platelet count could be zero. I saw Hope as a honeycomb of blood, and when it had drained away — how long would that take? — she would be dead on the bathroom floor. At that instant, Gertrude arrived. We got Hope back onto the soaking bed, and, as Gertrude held relays of washcloths to the gash, Hope said, "I can't get this umbrella up."

"Mrs. Meryman, you don't need an umbrella," Gertrude said.

"Yes, can't you see it's raining? Everything's all wet."

Gertrude said gently, "I'll fix it in just a minute."

I telephoned all of DeBellis's numbers. The only voice I could raise was an answering service, and I left my name. Who could help us immediately? My doctor was only a few blocks away. I had his home number. Miraculously he was there. Controlling my panic I explained the situation. Could he come? He was sorry, he couldn't, but would see her if I brought her in. "But she may be bleeding to death," I all but shouted. No, he couldn't come. Fighting for control, I asked, "Is there anything you can suggest?"

"Well," he said, "you could try a pressure bandage." He explained about gauze pads against the wound and an Ace bandage wrapped over them. Gertrude did the bandage, tenderly cleaned the blood off Hope's face and body, and began to change the bedding. Hope looked up at her and said, "I'll owe you my life, you take such good care of me."

The bleeding did stop. Hope slept most of the day and was awake when John Groth, as he did almost every evening, came by for a drink. She sat in her usual spot at the end of the long sofa near the tall Federal windows to the street. On the coffee table in front of her were the best cheeses I could find and volumes of Anne Sexton poetry — *The Awful Rowing Toward God, The Death Notebooks*. Helena sat beside her mother, sometimes pulling Hope's head down and whispering in her ear. "Hello, Shirley McDimple," said Hope. She began sewing a new face onto Helena's beloved Big Teddy and asked John about his work, about his health — and teased him about being a he-man war artist who was always half sick. John stuck to the script, now part of the pretense that Hope had no ills, and groaned about his feet. She made him remove his shoes, and taking his stockinged feet one at a time in her lap, she massaged them. "It seemed important to her," John told me afterwards. "Something she could do to help me."

Later, with Big Teddy still not finished, I put Helena to bed. Unable to get to sleep without him, she lay in the dark until Hope brought Big Teddy to her, his face sewn pathetically askew. With a sigh of relief and pleasure, Helena snuggled down on him as her mother kissed her good night. "Thank you, Mommy."

One of Hope's periods of wakefulness I still replay in my mind. As I administered the morning anti-inflammation and seizure pills, she said, "You've always been so good to me. You're the nicest man I know, and you are the dearest person to me. But I'm afraid I haven't given you a very good life."

"Oh, Hopie," I answered. "Don't say that. It breaks my heart. I'm the one who should say he's sorry. I'm the one who started the fights." I sat down beside her. "I've loved being married to you. I'm so proud that you're my wife. Oh, Hopie, I love you so." My eyes were filling with tears. I did not want to break down in front of her. I changed the subject. I was like Bernice. That was the moment to speak my heart, to make Hope see that her life and marriage had been the success she had wanted, even as a romantic girl. But I was daunted by the enormity of my feelings. The split second flashed by, and my farewell to Hope came out in clichés.

I think of Hope's life closing down like the blades of a blind folding downward, slowly shutting out the world, the children, me, the light. Each day Hope was more and more sealed away from us as she slept longer hours and her mind gradually blurred. The aphasia was intermittent but increasingly frequent. No longer able to manage a glass, she drank through a curved glass straw, and when Helena brought her coffee, Hope said, "Is my thermometer ready?" Helena told me much later, "I always knew what Mom meant. And she'd hold my hand to tell me 'It's all right.' "

Now my anxiety was centering on Helena and Meredith. Now the terrible decision was truly confronting me. When should the children be removed from the house? I stood alone in the bedroom looking at Hope, unconscious, her bald head with the fringe she hoped was her hair growing back. Her breathing was shallow. To separate the children from her and me seemed brutal. To risk psychological damage seemed monstrous.

Literally at that moment the telephone rang. It was Marcia Lasswell, a family counselor from California, the subject of one of my *Life* articles who now wrote a column in *McCall's*. Though our contacts were occasional and she knew nothing of Hope's illness, we had remained friends, and she was calling while in New York to say hello. It was a miracle. I hit her with the entire problem of the children now and after Hope's death. We talked for more than an hour. She said the trauma point would be Hope in agony, perhaps crying out in pain—any behavior incomprehensible and terrifying. But only I could make this judgment. As I talked to Marcia, I knew this time had not yet come.

But, if I fell apart, Marcia said, or even showed signs of it, that would be just as devastating as Hope's behavior. "Children of their age," she explained, "are egocentric. They are sad at losing a parent, but their main concern is, Am I going to be all right? They are dependent, and dependency makes them vulnerable. Meredith and Helena are old enough to know they are little children and cannot take care of themselves, so, if anything seems to be happening to their father, it would be extremely threatening and frightening."

That same day Laura Perkins followed me to Hope's studio. I must, she insisted, tell the girls that their mother had cancer and was dying. I was depriving them of the chance to look at their mother closely, to fix her in their minds, to say goodbye. They might feel cheated later. And the most terrifying thing for children, she said, is to have huge questions about what's going on and no answers. Knowing the truth would be more comforting than ignorance. I countered with my instructions from the psychiatrist—that the girls would ask for as much as they could tolerate. To force total reality on them would be to deprive them of their defenses.

"You could tell them, 'She may die,'" Laura suggested.

I answered that Timmy Davis told Peter the worst moment of his life was hearing that his mother *might* die. The uncertainty had been unbearable.

We faced each other across our disagreement, both knowing that we were neither right nor wrong. I followed my instincts, deciding that, if a mistake was to be made, I wanted it to be my own. I did, however, agree that I had to say something to Meredith and Helena and give them a chance to ask questions.

At bedtime that night I sat with the girls in Meredith's room and said, "Mommy is very, very sick. Sometimes she acts queer, saying things you don't understand, but you mustn't be frightened. She's still Mommy, and she still loves you. And you don't ever have to worry what's going to happen to you. I'm right here for you and always will be — until I'm so old you'll have to take care of me."

When I was tucking in Helena, she looked up at me from the pillow and said, "You know I have another mother somewhere."

"Yes, you do, Henny," I said, working to keep my voice ordinary, my face serene while my heart clenched. Like many adoptive parents, I recoiled from the girls' interest in their origins — the bugaboo that perhaps they would like their natural parents better. I asked, resolutely, "Does that thought give you some comfort?"

"Yes, it does."

The next night she wanted to know everything I could tell her about her natural parents, and I repeated to her my few facts, which she already knew. This time she particularly liked hearing that her natural grandmother had been an artist. Helena asked me if she could find her "other mother" someday. I said that when she was older she might want to try — and that would be all right with me. "Okay?" I said.

She nodded, and we kissed good night.

On December nineteenth, Hope had three days to live.

Peter Davis called and asked to come down. Before he arrived, Hope had me remove the last of her head bandage and put on her wig. Peter brought her a huge container of her favorite Baskin-Robbins ice cream, pralines 'n cream, and Hope slowly ate a bowlful while she talked, her voice weak, almost halting. She complained of a headache, and I boosted her upright so she could swallow the pain-killer with water. She sank back exhausted on the pillows, arms and legs pathetically slack. The children bounded in fresh from school, exuberant with the start of Christmas vacation. They leaped onto the bed, jostling and knocking Hope, almost hurting her — and she instantly snapped to life, laughing, face vital, voice almost normal as she hugged and answered them and asked about the Christmas play. I looked at Peter and said in admiration, "Incredible." As he departed through the living room, Hope smiled and waved.

On December twentieth, a Saturday, while I was absent buying a Christmas tree, Hope got dressed with Laura's help. I returned and, surprised, said like a fatuous nurse, "Oh, getting dressed." Hope shot me a withering look. While I put up the tree in the living room, she lay on the bed, wrapping presents with Laura's help. When the tree was up in its accustomed place between the two front windows, I went to the basement to dig out the ornaments. Meredith and Helena sat with Laura on the floor in the living room stringing festoons of cranberries. In the quiet Hope suddenly called out, half crying, half apologetic, "Mere, I don't have any clothes. I don't have any hair."

Meredith came to the bedroom door. "It's okay, Mommy. It's okay," she said, nodding encouragingly.

She returned to the cranberry stringing, the three girls talking and laughing softly. Hope, with Meredith continuing preeminent in her mind, called out again, her voice sharp. "Mere," she shouted, "I won't have you using language like that." Meredith was bewildered and frightened. "It's all right, Mere," Laura said softly. When the ornaments were ready, I helped Hope to the sofa, where she lay watching the trimming ceremony. Helena asked her to decorate with us. "I can't. I don't have any clothes," said Hope. Helena brought ornaments one by one to her mother — the special figures and balls that Hope and I had given each other on every Christmas past. Hope told her where to hang them. "It was almost like she was decorating the tree," Helena remembers.

Late in the afternoon my brother and his family arrived, and I remember my surge of pleasure at this infusion of family from the outside world, this break in the hermetic mood inside the house. Hope was back in bed, sleeping with the doors closed. I woke her, sliding the doors open, and propping her up so she could see into the living room. Mere was on a ladder, leaning out to hang a particular glass ball. Hope, still the eternal, protective mother, called out, "Mere, Mere, look out. You're going to fall."

Helena, on her way downstairs, ran in from the tree, paused by the bed, unself-consciously kissed her mother on the lips, and said, "How d'ere."

Downstairs in the kitchen, making drinks, Harry asked me how I was standing the stress. I told him that with all decisions made I had stopped looking ahead and was simply dealing with Hopie's needs as they arose. We came upstairs, and she looked disapprovingly at my glass. Thinking it was morning, she demanded, "Why are you having that?" As Hope moved herself to the end of the bed with her feet on the floor, the bandanna slipped half off her head. As I replaced it, she said, "I'm getting new hair for Christmas."

Hope asked Harry if he had done his Christmas shopping. He answered, "Of course not. I never do it until Christmas Eve." She told him to go down right away to Canal Street where the stores have bins on the sidewalk full of electrical motors, tools, radio parts, wire — "all the stuff you love, Harry" — and she gave her slow grin and flicked her eyebrow. I realized that Hope thought today was Christmas Eve.

She showed Harry and Lanie the print and verse done as a special present for Liz Hauser and talked with appreciation and approval about this friend and all she had done. Hope said how beautiful my stanza was and then talked about the religious poetry of Anne Sexton, which expressed her own swings between rebellion and faith. Her voice was low, self-possessed, reflective, her mind clear but settled into the past, reviewing. She had me bring her handmade books of poetry illustrated with woodcuts, done for me as Christmas presents—"Little silent Christmas tree you are like a flower . . ." Holding the prized volumes in her lap, she said quietly that her work had never become as good as she had wanted, that there were many pictures she had not finished and Dick had always been after her to finish things and sign them before she went on to something else. "But that was so hard," she said, "because there was always something else I couldn't wait to do."

Hope was tiring; it was time to go. Harry, rarely demonstrative, bent and kissed Hope awkwardly, tenderly, something he had never done before. I turned on the tree lights and turned off the living-room lights. Ed Kern and his wife were coming soon—instead of their customary Christmas Eve call. Hope was still sitting on the end of the bed. She was looking at the tree, her face peaceful. "It's so beautiful," she said.

Nine

 I like to believe that life always ends with peaceful acceptance. And I had a powerful sense of Hope's spirit, of the essence of Hope surviving distinct and entire, semiseparated from her dying body.

As she reached her final calm, my own trauma deepened. Coping each day with Hope's illness, I had hitherto lived a prescribed existence, protected from future realities by an all-consuming concentration on Hope. But now I was at the brink of my liberation and the awesome uncertainties of career, single parenthood, survival. Anxiety was building even higher, and my capacity to take care of Hope was giving out.

In the middle of the night after the tree trimming, I tried to hold Hope's slack body on a bedpan. The task was ludicrous, like balancing her on a golf tee. The pan squirted out, dumping its contents onto her and the bed. Cleaning Hope, changing the bedding, I had to roll her, semiconscious, back and forth, trying to be gentle, but forced to tumble her like an inert carcass. In that moment I broke. The isolation and exhaustion, the help-lessness, were too much. I waited until six and in a muted panic telephoned Whitney and Peter Hansen and said I had to have help. Peter came down immediately. While he boiled water for tea, I stood at the glass sliding door and looked out at the garden emerging in the dawn. I was not thinking, but simply receiving emotions, emanations — Hope, our life, our home. I began to cry. My body shook. Suddenly I felt Peter's arms around my chest from behind, gripping me tight against him. He told me afterwards, "You were shattering, falling apart, so I held you together." We moved upstairs to drink our tea in the living room near Hope. She woke and I went to her and sat on the bed, smelling urine, remembering Mrs. Brooks in California — thinking of the irony of Hope now lying on Helena's babyhood waterproof pad. She looked up at me and said, "Where are the stockings?" She thought today was Christmas. She thought she had achieved her goal. I smiled and said, "Mere and Henny are still asleep."

Peter and I remade the bed, and while I filled the washer in the basement with sheets, he sat alone with Hope on the bed. Now unable to speak, she reached one arm around Peter and gestured with the other. He asked her, "Do you want this? This? This?" He noticed the single rose in a bud vase clamped by a bureau drawer where she could see it. He put the rose in her hand. With clumsy fingers she fumbled it against a buttonhole in his shirt, trying to thread the stem. "It was my goodbye," Peter said to me afterwards, weeping.

When the children awoke I told them their mother believed today was Christmas and we should open our presents with her. They were adamant against the idea — it would not seem like Christmas. I had no strength to control the moment, to tell them now that their mother was dying, that she might not live till Christmas. And, indeed, Hope had made so many comebacks, like a diva on her deathbed reviving again and again to sing another aria, that I half believed she would hold on for four more days.

Whitney arrived. From time to time the children came through the room to visit the tree, but fortunately, sensing our tension and alarm, they stuck close to Laura downstairs. I was glad because during those days, when Hope was awake, her speech would suddenly lapse into gibberish, her words scrambled like a frightening code.

At bedtime Meredith stood nervously in the door and Hope smiled and waved. Soon Helena came up to say good night. Hope had just slipped into gibberish again. I stood paralyzed, fearing the shock to Helena. But Hope knew; she stayed silent. They kissed. "Good night, Mom." Helena took her mother's hand and squeezed it two times—their secret signal, "I love you." Hope answered with that radiant smile—the teeth, the crinkles at the eyes, the love—all of Hopie. It was their last moment together.

That night Meredith lay frightened in her bed, wondering what would happen if both her mother and father died. She told me later, "I prayed to God for Mommy to get well, but he didn't let her."

Peter Hansen had left, and now Liz Hauser joined Whitney and me talking on the huge bed while Hope slipped in and out of sleep. I was terrified of being left alone, and Whitney and Liz agreed that Liz should stay the night. After Whitney left there was another accident with the bedpan, another cleanup. I was very thankful for Liz, but distressed that this outsider was witnessing Hope's intimate agony. Hope, conscious, embarrassed, mustered a joke referring to a time when Liz had held a basin as Hope vomited. "Poor Liz," she said weakly. "If it's not one end of me, it's another."

Now there were no lights lit while Hope slept. Liz sat in the living room in one of the wing chairs looking out at the Christmas tree, impressionistic in the sodium moonlight from the street. I stayed beside Hope, wondering what her loud, labored breathing might mean, overwhelmed again by that crucifying combination of helplessness and loneliness in the night.

I joined Liz in the living room and pulled a bentwood rocker close to her chair so we could talk with lowered voices. Then, impelled by a primal impulse faster and deeper than thought, I leaned forward and placed my head in Liz's lap, clasping her knees with my arms. Through the dress her legs were warm against my cheek. I felt her fingers in my hair slowly stroking, strong, rhythmic, gentle. Eyes closed I listened to my own voice. It was a moment very intimate and strange. Then Hope's breathing quieted. I was silent for a long time, giving myself up to the touch of Liz's fingers, to the stillness of the room, to the easing in my body, to the solace in receiving after so much giving. At last I stood up, conscious of the dim and familiar tree. Downstairs the children slept. In the city twilight of the room there was a sense of waiting. I said mundanely, "We've got to go to bed."

Liz insisted on sleeping on the sofa in her clothes — "Just give me a blanket and a pillow." In bed, waiting for my sleeping pill to take hold, I lay looking at the ceiling, intensely aware of Hope next to me. Her breathing was normal again; perhaps she would live to Christmas. I had a sense then of giving myself up to an infinite, natural order. I felt drained and exquisitely poised between grief and expectation.

I woke at six. Hope was motionless, profoundly unconscious. Downstairs the silence was as deep as Hope's sleep. The sense of waiting persisted from the night before, but was ominous now. Snow was falling, muffling the city sounds, shrouding the brown winter ground. Liz came softly down and made breakfast. We ate, silent in our thoughts. To me the snow was blanketing a grave, making it beautiful, almost warm.

Above us a shattering thump shook the ceiling. Liz said, "Oh, my God." We ran upstairs. It was inconceivable that Hope in her weakness could get out of bed. But, indomitable, beyond strength, she had done it, and now lay on the bathroom floor in a widening pool of urine. We carried her back to the bed. Bathing Hope, dressing her in a man's yellow shirt I took from her bureau, Liz was deeply moved by an almost Biblical sense of preparing her devastated body.

Suddenly Hope surfaced. "Dick," she said.

My heart leaped. I put my head close to hers. "Yes?" No reaction. "Hopie?" She was sleeping again, lying on her back in the middle of the bed. Laura arrived and we woke the children and packed them a suitcase. The moment had come. The decision which had so worried me was hardly a decision at all. Liz was going to take the girls and her own two boys away to her rented house in Syosset, Long Island, for as long as was necessary.

Laura sat by Hope while I moved restlessly about the room. Suddenly Hope's hands rose toward her head, her face contorted, desperate with pain, and she cried out, "My head. Dick. Dick."

I bent close again. "I'm here, Hopie. I'm right here." Her breath rasped shallow in her throat, very loud, as though breathing were her last resource. Frantic at the thought of Hope in pain, I strode to my armoire for DeBellis's syringes and the pain-killer. Liz Hauser appeared at the door. I was distraught that Meredith and Helena might hear that terrible breathing and I half shouted, "Get the children out of here."

Standing beside the bed, trying to keep my hands from shaking, I pushed the needle up through the rubber cork of the inverted bottle of Dilaudid, filled the syringe, pulled the needle out, and forced a few glistening drops from its wicked point. "They are like tears," I thought. I can still feel in my hand Hope's heavy upper arm—the "Brooks arm" I had teased her about—still see in my mind the freckled, ashen skin. With a massive effort of will, I stabbed home the needle. Hope's face was expressionless, but her hands roamed from her head to her chest. The pumping, guttural breathing persisted, deafening to me, a dreadful pulse in the room, each breath striking against my fear that she was sealed away in awful, inexpressible pain. I called Peter Davis on the Upper West Side and he left immediately for DeBellis's office to get morphine.

We began the last vigil. My body was restless beyond my control, my nerves overloaded. Though I could act decisively, my brain was numb, dazed. I both knew and did not know that

· *153* ·

this was a deathwatch. Hope's fearsome breathing was becoming the status quo, and in the normality of the large light room, with the equipment of her life around her, there was an ordinariness that denied the enormity of death. The doorbell rang. It was a priest. He said Hope had telephoned the week before and asked him to come by the house. Now, like a miracle, he was there. Beside the bed he opened his missal and began reading. I realized he was administering Extreme Unction, and I stood sobbing in the middle of the room — and wondering why he thought she was dying.

When Liz Hauser appeared again, her arms full of pillows, and said she was leaving, I followed her into the hall. Confronted by Hope's death, and death itself, and the need to survive, I was no different from my two children, worrying subliminally, "Who's going to take care of me?" I looked intently into Liz's eyes and said, "Will you come to Dublin?"

"Yes, I will," she heard herself answer and was astonished.

Hope died gently, almost prosaically. Without flourish or fanfare, nature vanishes life with simple sleight of hand.

Around noon, her breathing eased slightly and I thought she had returned from her crisis to natural sleep. Peter Davis arrived with the morphine, but I decided not to use it. I told him, "I don't want to wake her." As I reviewed in a hushed voice the past few days for Peter, I glanced casually toward Hope. I saw her good eye turning up into her head, the pupil half disappearing. My hysteria erupted in a giggle — as I realized in the same split second that the room was silent. "Is she breathing?" I exclaimed. I climbed onto the bed beside Hope and asked again, "Is she breathing?" I put my cheek close to her nose and mouth and considered calling for a mirror as in a corny movie. I felt no air against my cheek. Not sure where to find the pulse, I searched her wrist and felt nothing. I was uncertain and yet very sure. I breathed deeply and said, "She's gone."

I was amazed at the matter-of-factness of death — hardly a ripple on the surface of the room — swifter than belief. Like a benediction I extended my forefinger and gently closed the soft lid over Hope's upward-staring eye, a gesture as ancient as human history. It was the most primitive and profound expression of love I can imagine, the ultimate act of farewell.

Then, suffused with tenderness, I started to lay out Hope's body, sprawled awkwardly in the middle of the bed. I slid my hand under her back and lifted her torso. Horror exploded inside me. As though strung together by exhausted rubber bands, her body spilled limply in all directions — head lolling back, arms falling loosely — a terrifying, traumatic hand-to-hand confrontation with the truth of death.

I placed her head on a pillow and crossed her limp hands on her breast. I drew up the sheet — remembering Hope tucking in Little Whitney, knowing this was my final act of comfort for Hope. With a rush of feeling, before covering her face, I kissed her on the forehead. Under my lips the skin was damply warm. I cried briefly, but was self-conscious in front of Laura and Peter, aware that I was showing the emotion expected of me. Now, around me in the room, I acutely felt a new emptiness, a vacancy in the ether, illusive as memory. I checked the living room, half expecting to find the hall door ajar. I turned to Peter and Laura, saying excitedly, "Do you feel it? Do you feel something gone?" Then like a programmed robot I went to the telephone and summoned DeBellis to write the death certificate. That sealed Hope's death. I hung up in tears. Peter and Laura came to me and we clung together in the still room, arms holding, heads touching.

I wanted to be alone with Hope, a kind of ceremony to embrace and solemnize the moment. I sat in a chair gazing across the familiar room at Hope's form shaping the white sheet — feet, legs, hands on breast, nose — as the garden had shaped the snow that morning. Our life history passed before me, sensations not images, fluid — what we had shared, liked, wanted, been to each other. Oh, Hopie. Now it was finished — the full story of Hopie Brooks — her existence severed by a mole on the back. Now all Hope's uncertainties were answered, even the ultimate question — the existence of God and heaven. Right now Josie must be saying to her, "Here's what was wrong with your deathbed scene." My chest ached with sorrow — and incredulity. Poor, poor Josie. Poor, poor Hopie.

Too restless to sit still, I gave my place to Peter Davis and went downstairs for a cup of tea but soon could not bear to be separated from Hope and returned. I felt myself following a fine line of ceremony between the maudlin and the macabre, and decided this should be my last solitary moment with Hope. I stood by the bed and projected upward love and gratitude. But I recoiled from lifting the sheet for a final look or kiss or touch. The figure on the bed was Hope but it was also a corpse.

I heard Whitney arriving in the front hall, and I reached her first to deliver the blow quickly: "Hopie just died." Whitney gasped and wept and through her tears said, "I prayed this morning that my sister would not suffer one more day." The chores of death — anticipated for so long they seemed to be dreamlike reenactments — were grooves that carried me forward and gave me a purpose, gave me a reason not to see and feel and dwell on anything. I telephoned Ed Kern to activate the undertaker he had retained. I telephoned John Groth and Gertrude and my mother in California. I telephoned Lanie in Dublin and told her the girls and I would be arriving the next night, driven by Peter Davis and Laura. I asked Whitney and Laura if they would dress Hope, and gave them a favorite Marimekko. I took the statue of the Blessed Mother from Hope's bureau, wrapped it in a dish towel and placed it in her beloved, battered saucepan — icons for the coffin. I folded the floor-length, green velvet gown, which Whitney had said looked like an old doll's dress, and which I now picked as the dress in which Hope should be buried. I placed everything in a shopping bag, ready for the undertaker, my minuscule version of King Tut. I telephoned Liz Hauser and said immediately, "It's all over."

"Oh, Dick," she said — a soft cry warming me with the knowledge that her sorrow was in part for me. Liz told me later that as we talked, she was at a window looking past bare trees, skeletal against the sky, to a small pond where the four children skated, dark figures silhouetted against the lightly falling snow. In her ears my details of Hope's death mingled with their shouts of fun. I told Liz I would pick up the girls the next day and she must say nothing to them, and then my voice broke and I cried out in turn, "Oh, Liz   "

In New York the house began to fill — Gertrude, disbelieving, stoic, sad that Hope did not see the bedspread she was making for Meredith — Ed Kern — Peter Hansen — John Groth, who asked to be alone with Hope. He kissed her "a sort of goodbye, hello, I'm still with you" — and was shocked by the chill of her lips. It was dark when DeBellis arrived to write the death certificate, a mission he considered beyond his duty as a doctor, but done now out of special feeling for Hope. "You don't often extend yourself to the point where you're vulnerable," he told me later.

I asked, "Do you want to see her?"

"I suppose I should," he said. He brusquely flipped back the sheet, his face expressionless. "When it's over," he told me later, "there's a revulsion, a sense of waste, of futility. You've lost; the disease has won. You go into automatic — this is just a body, nothing matters a damn now."

Then he gave me a touchingly concerned lecture, telling me in essence that now my problem of survival was not just psychological, it was also physical. "For the next year you will be in a dangerous period. Your defenses are lowered. During mourning you are statistically ten times more susceptible to illness, serious illness, than the normal population. Pay attention to trivial symptoms. Don't say to yourself, 'Oh, I'm just tired or sad or something.' Call me. I'll take care of you myself or recommend somebody."

While the undertaker's men removed Hope's body on a stretcher, I waited downstairs and allowed Whitney to officiate. I heard the front door slam behind Hope, as the screen door in

Dublin had slammed behind my father's body. When Whitney returned, I asked, "Is she gone?"

"Yes."

My heart contracted. Expecting to feel relieved, I was only distraught. With Hope's body in the house, her death was somehow still in process, our disconnection not complete. I felt a rush of thankfulness that Hope had died at home, in a sense an old-fashioned death allowing her dearest people their small rituals of farewell, saving us from goodbyes in the official, bustling void of a hospital. My thoughts went to Meredith and Helena, now my remaining physical link to Hope. Tomorrow I would look into their faces and tell them their mother is dead. Till then, in their unknowing minds, she was still alive. Upstairs Gertrude changed the bedsheets marked with Hope's blood.

Peter Davis spent the night on the sofa. Getting into the bed where Hope had died that afternoon was my first hard step toward recovery. Lying there I imagined that I could open my eyes and find Hope in place beside me, and I found that mysteriously comforting. The next day there were more tasks to keep me in motion. But only a half a step ahead of pursuing grief, I was constantly overtaken by tears: asking Peter to telephone an obituary to the *Times* — "the headline *must* say 'Artist' "; going through our telephone book in Hope's handwriting to apportion names to be called; entering Hope's studio — the "Swimmer" prints hanging from the line — to get the children's Christmas presents; finding her gift to me — a watercolor set for her embryo artist.

The children's clothes had to be packed for Dublin and I started helplessly into Meredith's drawers, wondering which of those miniature-looking shirts she liked, which pants she would want. I could hear her voice saying, "Oh, Daddy, not those," and I felt my abysmal and intrinsic separation from the female world of my two girls.

I made a circuit of errands by car with Peter Davis and Ed Kern. One stop was the undertaker. While they went inside to complete the arrangements, I waited, looking at the funeral urns in the unctuous facade and thinking, in spite of myself, of Hope's so-private person lying inside. Peter and Ed stated their business to a man behind a desk. Answering irritably, not caring whether one of them might be the bereaved husband, he said, "All I know is we got a body on our hands and we don't know who it belongs to or who's paying us."

It was early evening when Peter, Laura, and I reached Liz Hauser's house in Syosset. I asked them to stay in the car. Steeling my mind against the dread that had been building all day, remembering Peter and his boys, I moved rapidly up the long steps to the house, feeling that if I slowed my momentum even slightly, I would stop, frozen. Liz met me at the door, her face drawn with concern. I asked abruptly, "Where are they?"

"In the kitchen."

Meredith and Helena sat at the square table with Liz's two boys, eating tomato soup. I said, "Mere and Henny, I want to talk to you." They looked startled and followed instantly as Liz led us upstairs to her large bedroom and left us alone, sitting on the edge of the bed, Helena in the middle. The children were solemn, frightened. The thought flashed, "They know what I'm going to say"—and I said it with the same headlong swiftness that had carried me into the house. "Kids, Mommy died yesterday. She didn't suffer. She was asleep."

As though I had stabbed them—and indeed I had—their faces seemed to explode into wild screeches. They wailed, "It's not fair. It's not fair." We hung onto each other, streaming with tears. I tried to envelop them, pour myself into them—while frightened that the pain I had detonated was deeper than I could ever reach. Suddenly the moment was past endurance. "I want to go outside," announced Meredith. "Yes," said Helena.

Downstairs they rummaged frantically into their boots and then as though we could actually leave our agony behind in the house, we plunged into the darkness, the cold a welcome jolt against our faces. The children, side by side, headed up the rough driveway through the woods, walking fast, frantically, each step a stamp of anger in the snow. I stayed next to them, miserable but also comforted by the sense of the three of us finally together and alone.

Meredith said, furiously, "It's not fair. Why should *she* die. Why couldn't it have been somebody else, some bum."

"One of those loud guys on the subway," added Helena.

I could help them the most, I felt, by being one of them in any feelings they had, so I agreed, yes, it was unfair——but I knew that they also meant it was unfair to *them*. Gradually their frenzy was expended and we turned around, moving slowly now, conscious of our surroundings, the quiet, the night paled by the snow. I said, "Kids, it's going to be very hard without Mommy, but we will be together and we will help each other and we will be all right."

"Where are we going to live?" asked Helena, probably remembering that Peter Davis had moved after Josie's death. I had been warned by Marcia Lasswell, my psychologist friend, to keep the girls' lives the same, to keep them among friends and familiar surroundings, and not to compound the violent change they had just suffered. I told them, "We're staying right in our own home, and Gertrude and Laura will be with us."

"Good," said Helena, and then, "Where is Mommy now?"

"At the undertaker's."

Meredith asked, "When will she be buried?"

"After Christmas."

"Where are we going to have Christmas?"

"In Dublin with Harry's family."

"Good," said Meredith.

Helena said, "I don't want to have Christmas. It won't be Christmas without Mommy."

At the house the girls ran to Laura and clung to her. The rite of Hope's passage was winding down to final ceremonies. I took Liz aside and delivered Hope's thank-you woodcut print. She wept. Peter delivered to Helena the box containing Josie's two childhood bears, and repeated the message from his son

Timmy: "You gave them to me when my Mom died and now your Mom is dead and you need them." Helena took the cover off and looked at the two figures a long time.

I brought Helena the clay angel she had made for her mother for Christmas—so sweet, somehow so exactly representing her relationship with Hope—and said, "Do you want this buried with Mommy? Liz can arrange it."

She considered the question, carefully. "Yes," she said.

I asked Meredith whether she had anything. She thought hard, and shook her head. I told her, "It's okay, nothing of mine seemed just right." While the rest of us talked briefly in the living room, Meredith began roughhousing in the kitchen with Liz's two boys, Ned and Christopher, hurling herself back into normality, her nerves uncoiling like springs. Helena, sent to say we were leaving, stood in the doorway, angry at Meredith for not showing the proper grief. When Helena would not join the tumult, six-year-old Christopher said, "Oh, I guess she's not over her mother dying yet."

Meredith socked him.

Pulling away in the car—Peter at the wheel, Laura and the two girls in back—I felt intense relief. Now there would be a pause, a period of insensibility as speed and darkness disconnected me from the earth, from the past and the future. I was traveling away from Hope's illness and death toward a place where her absence would not be a background to every single minute. I was symbolically embarking on my journey through mourning—and I was glad to get started.

The back seat folded down to make a platform and the children, drugged by shock, lay there with Laura, trying to fill their emptiness with two kittens she had brought—"something warm and alive to hug." Helena's head rested on Big Teddy. From time to time I reached back and touched them. I felt a comradery. My needs were as infantile as theirs. Their grief was as grown-up as mine. When we stopped briefly for food, Peter asked Helena, "Can I do anything to make you more comfortable?"

"No," she said. "I just feel real bad."

In Dublin the Harry Meryman family sat waiting in the small living room. Already my grief was full upon me, an all-pervading sense of weight, an oppression as dense and gray as fog. My central gloom isolated me, putting a space between me and the world. Mourning, I soon learned, is the struggle to set aside that weight even briefly and fill that space even temporarily. Meredith and Helena came in first, looked around as though at a group of strangers, and ran to their sixteen-year-old cousin Charlotte, and clung to her, silent, as though within her arms they were safe from anybody tempted to approach and sympathize. I thought that their pain, like mine, was almost sacred, and they feared anything that might rattle their protective numbness.

Meredith slept with Charlotte. Settling her, I wanted to put my arms around that sinewy body and bury my head next to her head and somehow connect my grief with hers. But I sensed she wanted no melodrama, just the reassurance of a regular good night from the same old dad. I kissed that infinitely soft cheek and said, "I love you so much, Mere," and felt a delicate answering kiss.

"I love you too, Daddy."

Helena slept in Hope's twin bed next to me. She asked for a back rub, and as I kneaded the solid little body, her voice came from the pillow, "What's Mommy going to be buried in?"

"Her old doll dress."

There was a silence and then Helena said, "I remember when I had a birthday party in kindergarten and Mom made cupcakes with chocolate icing and on one she put a Big Teddy and this stupid kid said, 'I want the one with the *thing* on it.'"

After another silence I said, "Do you think you can go to sleep now?"

"Maybe." She turned to receive my kiss on her lips. Soon, as I lay with eyes closed, trying to immobilize my mind, Helena climbed into bed beside me. I held her in the dark until I was sure she was asleep, and then moved over to Hope's bed and felt mysteriously comforted.

The next morning Peter Davis flew home to New York. Laura stayed on with us. Late in the morning the two families trooped out to a woods across the next-door field to cut a Christmas tree for Dublin, our separate tracks patterning the unbroken snow. I was elated by any signs of normality—by the girls that day galumphing through the woods, hallooing, "Here's a perfect tree." I was even pleased by the reemergence of their obnoxious rivalry—Meredith saying she wanted a tiny tree all her own, one that Helena couldn't decorate, and Helena demanding one also—while I futilely explained the spirit of Christmas.

In the afternoon the children went to nearby Keene for Christmas shopping while I stayed home alone to tackle a racking decision. Hope's burial was to be in the late morning of December twenty-sixth in Pennsylvania. The presumption was that I would be there by the grave with the girls. Convention, tradition, loyalty, love, reputation—the probable wishes of Hope herself—required it. The burial rite, primordial, old as man, is still society's set piece for farewell and final catharsis. I had seen Hope through her illness; I owed it to myself to complete the symmetry and see her to the grave itself.

Yet all of me recoiled from making that trip to Pennsylvania. I knew it would be entirely harrowing, a reentry into that tunnel from which I had only just escaped. I pictured the departure on Christmas day, the night in New York in the house still redolent with Hope's death, my inevitable breakdown beside the grave, the intense sympathy focused on the children, the potential for further shock. The girls seemed far too fragile for that long journey to a box containing their mother's body. If I went alone, I would be leaving them at their peak moment of insecurity and need. Let the friends who had not nursed Hope month after month, who were not physically and emotionally exhausted —let them take over now and surround Hope.

In truth, that ceremony meant little to me. I had grown up in a nonreligious family that considered such services almost irrelevant — public emotional ordeals inevitably superficial. My father was cremated, and at his request we had no funeral, staged no memorial service. I had had my own death ceremony with Hope, supremely personal and tender. The children had observed the ritual decline of their mother toward death. My concern was for the living, not a symbol in a coffin. Hope was alive in my memories and feelings, and I was repulsed by the prospect of putting my most intimate pain on display beside the grave.

That afternoon and into the evening I was repeatedly on the telephone to friends, call after call, compulsively rummaging through my dilemma, my thicket of obligations, my tangle of pros and cons. Ostensibly I wanted everybody's honest opinion, but when anybody agreed with my reasons for coming to Pennsylvania, I instantly countered with opposite considerations. I vacillated wildly, deciding to go to the burial ("I want to see Hopie through to the very end"), then reversing ("The children need me"), then changing again ("I *do* care what people think"). At the same time I was telephoning friends in California and Hope's brother and sisters, reviewing the details of her death again and again, hanging up in tears. At last that evening I returned red-eyed to the family gathering. "I'm so tired of crying," I said.

With support from Laura and Lanie, I decided that the task of recovery, of life, was paramount, that the children and I were now more important than Hope. At the moment of Hope's burial the children could attend a special Communion at her church in Harrisville. On our return to New York there would be a memorial service, and, later, we would travel to Hope's grave for a short ceremony with a priest.

Today I regret the sacrifice of that final homage to Hope with its sense of completion. There are, after all, reasons for ceremony and ritual during the depths of grief. I wonder how much of my decision was a flight from climactic pain, from a dramatization of my own mortality. When Little Whitney died, I dissuaded Hope from attending her baby's burial, arguing that she should spare herself such a degree of anguish. Harry and Lanie represented us. Afterward, Hope never forgave me, nor did I forgive myself.

But today I am not the same person I was in Dublin. I am not used up, unstable, nerves worn raw. I no longer see my children in pain. That day I did what I had to do. I followed my instincts — one of my rules for survival.

On Christmas morning the tree was like an afterthought on a hill of packages. Anybody of even slight acquaintance had inundated the children with gifts, and Meredith and Helena, at first lackluster, brightened at opening presents. Harry's teenage son Henry received a tape recorder and the girls went giddily about the room interviewing us and we were silly and laughing. The day began to feel like Christmas and the sense of pathos, so powerful in us all, eased off. Then Meredith picked from the pile a wrapped pogo stick. Before she could open it, I called her over and whispered, "This is Mom's present to you. She picked it out herself."

Meredith ripped off the paper and saw what it was. She screamed, "I want my Mommy back!" — a cry torn from some deepest hiding place of grief. She hurled herself sobbing into my arms, her face buried against my neck, and I lifted her onto my knees. Poignantly aware of her smallness, her tenderness, caressing the knobby little back, I whispered into the silky hair, "I know, Mere. I know. I want her back, too. We all want her back."

Having traumatized the entire room, Meredith in a half hour was blithely tearing open another round of packages — which is the resilient way of children and of Meredith in particular. Her emotions have always reminded me of the dust devils one sees in the western plains, tiny twisters whirling erratically across the land sucking up and flinging out sticks and dirt, and finally subsiding into thin air. But in her tempestuous — and sweeet —

nature some storms were intolerable and she bottled them up like angry genies deep inside her. Much later Meredith told me, "When we got to Dublin, I just said to myself, 'Okay, this is it; nothing's going to be wrong,' and I just never would think about Mommy. And then one night I cried cuz I did think about Mommy."

I have wondered whether those first weeks, while the hurt was still so open, were a time when I failed Meredith. Ideally I should have been helping her surface and work through her feelings. But I was intent on holding everybody—including myself—together. I wanted Meredith calm, not stirred up, and I have never, before or since, known her to be so serene for so long.

In retrospect, the three of us had become, in a way, celebrities —special, fragile people who must be treated with total solicitude. We had a kind of power. For prickly Meredith, usually in and out of trouble, that was delightful. She may also have been enjoying and exaggerating the reversal taking place. Helena, venting her feelings in all directions, demanding attention, had become impossible. Nothing satisfied her. The food was cooked wrong, the plate was dirty. The socks were scrunched in the boots, the shirt itchy. If we wanted to sled, she wanted to toboggan. If I told her to wash her hands, they were already clean. There were awful scenes — Helena on the floor screaming and weeping with rage as I towed her by one arm away to her bedroom purgatory.

At the same time, Helena was breaking my heart with the dimensions of her sorrow. Almost every day she would lead me up to the bedroom and sit me down beside her on the bed and we would talk. She told me how unhappy she was and said, "I want to cry but everybody else is crying so much I'm embarrassed to cry." She told me, "I keep thinking after I die, things'll go back the way they should be," and she told me her dreams — "Mommy came back to life; I wanted to hug her and she kept saying, 'No, no, you can't hug me.'" And then Helena did cry and I held her and patted her, and she wailed through

· *166* ·

her tears, "I can't stand it." I cried, and felt her little hand patting me on the shoulder.

During one of our séances upstairs Helena showed me a drawing she had made. In the middle was a cross. On the left side was a girl, Helena, with "Grrr . . ." coming out of her mouth. On the right side another girl, also Helena, stood with one tear coming out of her eye, and on her finger a string was tied, so she would always remember. On the cross was the inscription "HOPE Meryman Died in a year that was too soon."

Meredith pestered me till I bought her a diary. She, too, I think, was instinctively searching for a way to concretize our catastrophe. Later I looked at what she wrote: "This Christmas my Mom died. I got a lot of good presents." I smiled—so like the here-and-now world of a child. But I was also very moved; Meredith could only bear the most fleeting touch on that nerve.

In the late morning of December twenty-sixth, visualizing Hope's casket born across that familiar graveyard, I drove through deep snow and glorious sun with Laura, Meredith, and Helena to nearby Harrisville, a bypassed, pristine, nineteenth-century town with a tiny white clapboard church. The priest there had agreed to give us a brief, private service of prayers and Communion.

Inside St. Denis's—a place Hope loved with its stained-glass windows, pale wood, white walls—the gentle, fussy priest beckoned us forward. In the empty church Laura and I sat on the first bench and Meredith and Helena knelt at the rail before the altar. Watching their backs, narrow and square, the rippled soles of their snow boots turned up, one brown head tipped back to receive the wafer, then one blond head—I was stirred by their vulnerability, by the difficulties ahead of them, by the intensity of my commitment. Was Hope in the ground yet, the last step of the way? I thought how much she had wanted to watch her two girls grow up. I felt a sadness beyond tears.

But the brief ceremony—the Bible passages read in a singsong lisp—did not bring me any communion with Hope through her religion. All of us — the priest, too, in a way — were onlookers, listening to distant words from a stranger. Grief is immeasurably intimate. Its tremors reach the most private recesses. Its pain feels unique, as though I was the first man who ever lost a wife, and Meredith and Helena were the first children who ever lost a mother. Only someone who had been part of our loss could be personal enough to touch deeply our emotions.

By accident, after we left the church, we did find the fitting way to mark the day. As usual we went next door to the grocery to buy treats — licorice strings and red-hots — and a New York *Times*. In the car I opened the paper to the obituary page. It was there, exactly as she wanted, a headline: "Hope Meryman Dies at 44, An Artist and Illustrator." I exploded into tears. I tried to read the obituary aloud to Meredith and Helena. I could not, and Laura tried and broke down, and then the children were sobbing. It was a shared rush of pain, and we felt better for it. Laura distributed paper napkins and we blew our noses.

I turned toward Meredith and Helena, wanting to say a sort of grace at the beginning of our future alone together. I told them, "While we are sitting here, Mommy is being buried where she wanted to be — next to Little Whitney. For quite a while now we're going to hurt when we think of her, but it's important to keep remembering her and talking about her because that helps get rid of the unhappy feelings. It may not seem so now, but the day *will* come when we'll be happy again and have fun and remember Mommy with a nice kind of sadness that doesn't make us hurt inside. And feeling happy doesn't mean we love Mommy any less."

Driving home, passing through the lower part of Harrisville, I said offhandedly, "There's the purple police car Hopie hated." Her name, so fraught with anguish, spoken for the first time casually to the children, stuck in my throat. I realized how easily avoidance and silence can become the habit. I forced out the words, determined to set an example, to make Hope an easy part of our family talk.

Helena piped up, "When Mommy saw it, she said, 'Vicious.'"

Meredith, to the tune of "Rudolph the Red-nosed Reindeer," began singing, "Patty the purple police car, had a very funny color . . ."

That evening I telephoned Whitney to hear about Hope's burial. Her word for it was "Fellini-esque." A torrential, driving rain fell, and the pallbearers, carrying the heavy casket through the cemetery, slipped and skidded in the mud. A small canopy covered the grave, and as the priest read the service of the dead, water dripped through a hole onto his head, splashing his book. "He was a remedial reader stumbling over words and mispronouncing them," Whitney said. "Hopie would have enjoyed that part of it." Whitney also talked about the infinite sadness in the face of John Groth and her own horror at Hopie going into the earth. Whitney said, "I wanted to jump down in there and wrap her in a warm blanket." As the casket was lowered, she threw upon it two roses, one for Meredith, one for Helena.

I stood alone in my bedroom weeping again. I wondered, "Will I *ever* run dry of tears?" Now Hope was buried, truly gone. But I was only beginning the task of putting her to rest within myself.

Ten

Once Hope was buried, I could collapse into the numbness that marks the first phase of mourning. Because I was anesthetized by shock, nothing had palpable existence for me except the children and the Dublin house and the New Hampshire countryside. I was faking my way through the days, playing along by ear, riding the rhythms around me. There was, however, a subtle euphoria in this half-life — like the release and extravagance of a vacation. I distracted myself with the children, sledding, tobogganing, and skiing. The three of us needed physical challenges that demanded strength and concentration, and replaced restlessness with muscular fatigue — intense, minute-to-minute realities that were unconnected to Hope, to the big reality of her death.

But the fundamental weight of grief is unshakable. I was careful about anything, including alcohol and mention of Hope's death, that would weaken control of my emotions. The children, too, seemed to avoid whatever might rub on fragile feelings — steering clear of their Aunt Lanie as though worried she might play the substitute mother. In this stunned, brittle state, the three of us asked for what we wanted — without asking. The children came unbidden to my lap, to Charlotte's and Laura's, and received our calm hugs and ran away reassured. Reading our needs, hiding the thoughts that underpinned everything, the entire household maintained a festive mood, in itself a message of comfort and affection. But the bereaved do want recognition of their special status and their loss. Old family friends, Janet and Raleigh Hansl, arrived from Washington, D.C., and Janet caught me alone and said, "Dick, I must tell you how we feel."

I cut her off, saying, "You don't have to tell me. I know." But I required that signal from her.

Meredith found Janet alone and said, "Did you know my mother died?"

"Yes, Mere, I do know it," Janet said.

Meredith, satisfied, turned quickly away.

Though I kept a space of privacy between me and others, I hungered for the intimate, tender support system so easily available to the children. A widower needs a wholly receiving audience for his endless ramblings of fear and sorrow. As much as a child he needs physical contact to comfort his tears and counteract his aloneness. The subtraction of his wife alters his identity, and he needs his self-esteem restored. He needs to sense an escape route out of anxiety and pain. He needs somebody entirely focused on him. The bereaved who have such a person do recover faster.

Married friends and relatives are usually absorbed in their own full lives and heavy concerns. A single woman will give that needed time and intensity, and it is easy to see why many widowers make new connections quickly. In fact, half of all widowers remarry within eighteen months. For me Elizabeth Hauser was heaven-sent. She was simultaneously a link to the past and bridge to the future. Having been part of my agony for months, she exactly understood my feelings. I called her daily from Dublin, reaching, clutching, pouring out my quandaries and incoherent emotions, and I invariably asked anxiously, "You are coming up, aren't you?"

We discussed her decision at length. Liz cared about conventional mores, about the decency of a single woman materializing now at my side. But she intensely identified the anguish of my bereavement with the trauma of her divorce. By nature impetuous and almost compulsively helpful, she could not resist my need and her empathy. Also, she had been profoundly involved with both Hope and me, and was, I think, caught up in the momentum, perhaps even the romance, of my drama.

I knew that the sudden surfacing of Liz was inappropriate. The behavior of the bereaved is prescribed: a subdued demeanor, a quiet life, a seemly interval of seclusion. But actually, the interval since Hope's death seemed vast to me. The visit did not feel premature. Time elapses differently for the bereaved. It creeps. Every minute had been so fraught, so filled with emotions, events and high drama, that each day had passed like a week.

Moreover, in the first days and months of mourning, there was an animal sense of self-preservation that brushed aside propriety and permitted whatever gave relief. In my dazed condition, disconnected from sober realities — somewhat crazy from shock — I told myself that I had earned the right to be selfish, that after giving for so long, the time had come to take. I did not truly care what people thought. I did not care if I was exploiting and manipulating Liz. I did not care about the problems I might be setting up in the future. I did not care about caution and good sense. I wanted to get well.

I guiltily did a selling job on Harry and Lanie, extolling Liz's friendship for Hope, her long history of help to Hope, her closeness to the children, her warm and comforting qualities. I also had to tell the children. During mourning, the ancient contest of will between parent and child is even more equal, the parent is depleted and the bereaved child wields the power of pathos.

Meredith said, "Fine" with clear, almost disinterested eyes, but I knew she was luxuriating in the full attention of Laura, Charlotte, and Harry's older daughter, Louise. Helena, however, was clinging to me—taking me away for her closed-door talks, riding the sled and the ski lift with me, sitting beside me at meals, climbing into bed with me at night—already putting me into Hope's place. She had now transferred to me the double hand squeeze that meant "I love you," and she would do it surreptitiously—each time breaking my heart. When I told her about Liz, she said angrily, "Why does *she* have to come?"

"Because I'm like you," I said. "I'm very unhappy. And it would be nice for me to have somebody here to talk to who has been a good friend to me and Mommy."

"We talk."

"That's true. I would be ten times sadder without you and Mere. But adults need adults, and I want to keep on being your daddy who takes care of you—and that won't change because Liz is here." I thought to myself, half apologetically, that if Helena planned to take me over, perhaps it was just as well if a Liz Hauser entered now.

On New Year's Day, leaving the children in the lavish care of the three older girls, I drove to the Keene airport to meet Liz. I was very nervous. Stricken once again by my boyhood insecurities with women, I was frightened that I was entrapping myself in a rash commitment, but the fear only magnified a romantic sense of inevitability. In the muddle of my emotions, my mind felt no more in charge of this turn of my life than in control of Hope's death.

Liz appeared in the entrance gate, tall, slender, a fur parka framing a silver and turquoise Zuñi necklace, dark hair, dramatic, olive-skinned face, eyes very bright. The sympathetic voice on the telephone was now a woman separate from Hope's illness. I felt that I hardly knew her. I was stiff and self-conscious as we talked blandly about her trip. In the car I reached for her, feeling that I was throwing myself through a barrier of inhibition. I held her very hard and we kissed and raw emotion erupted inside me and I groaned—a miniature cataclysm, a first momentous severance from Hope. It was a reach for a person able to mitigate my needs *now*. I said, "Oh, Liz, I'm so glad you're here."

At the house in Dublin the entire group was assembled before dinner in the living room, waiting for that awkward, comic moment which must happen to every widower — the arrival of a new and unknown woman. From my apologetic description of this adored friend of Hope's, they expected a comfortable, commodious auntie, buxom and bubbly — a Gotham earth mother. Now before their gaze stood an Indian queen.

The mood was festive, even cheerfully raucous, and I soon began to feel lighter, less alone. I was satisfying that impulse to return to the old status quo and reenter the normal world. But there was nothing normal about those days. I was on a shock high, careening along quite free of reality, winging Liz along with me. That night, as usual, I slept fitfully and woke at dawn. The sky was clear, the air still. I gently opened Liz's door and sat on the edge of her bed. She woke and looked up at me, startled but glad. I bent down and kissed her and buried my face in the pillow, my cheek next to hers. Her arms came around me, and I was filled with a simultaneous calm and excitement. There were no overtones of passion. So complex was this connection that the limit of my desire was to hold and be held. "Right now before anybody is up," I said, "let's go for a walk on the lake."

Warm in snow boots and parkas, we slipped from the house. I was reminded fleetingly of that long-ago departure for Spain, though the vast compartment of Hope was shut away and I existed only in this small moment. A few hundred yards down a forest-bordered road was Dublin Lake, a prairie of unbroken snow. Rising up on the far side was Mount Monadnock, a single, glorious peak of granite and gleaming ice. Gripping each other's arm, we forged out into that vast white space. I was intoxicated — by a feeling of mastery as this woman clutched me; by a sensation of newness as though we were pre-teens trying our first, tentative, thrilling intimacy; by the exhilaration of cold and brilliant sun; by the familiar landscape awesome and romantic under the snow.

Weaving through our excitement, and supercharging it, were the currents of anguish and pity and the strangeness of Liz here in this way. I began talking compulsively about Hope, saying it was important for me and the children that I be honest about her, that I not glorify her into a dream deity that no future woman could match. I told Liz, "It wasn't easy living with Hope." As I went on to describe her temper, my loss overwhelmed me and I began to cry. Liz held me and then we moved on, spirited again as I pointed out houses on the hills and told their histories. Then, in the middle of the lake, centered in that vast, frozen void, we stopped and kissed and I remember the startling warmth of Liz's face. Isolated from everything—in a sense from ourselves—we were riding an illusionary crescendo. Romance is a route out of grief, but this form of romance was cool filaments wrapping and soothing the fearful heat of grief.

Liz, without embarrassment, merged well with the family—helping in the kitchen, whooping with excitement as she sledded down our steep, favorite coasting road. On the third of January the Harry Merymans and the Hansls departed. That afternoon we joined another family sledding on their icy driveway. After a while Liz and I slipped off down a snow-smothered side road, the pine bows like green shadows under obese white branches. We discussed the future of our relationship. An unromantic side of me knew that this high-key flirtation was an accident of circumstances, a bubble in a vacuum. I knew it was craziness. But I also knew that in some middle distance between love and biology I did admire and cherish Liz. I thought I would be a fool to let her get away because of good sense. Nor was Liz eager to be cautious. The naked intensity of my need and the romance of the situation were almost irresistible. Was it too soon? Was it foolish? Were we disloyal to Hope? Were we causing anybody pain? We persuaded ourselves that the blanket answer was no. I said, "As long as I feel comfortable inside, I don't care what people think." Then I talked about my new sense of the preciousness of time, the hours and hours that Hope had given away, my resolve to take hold of my life and make every moment worthwhile. I voiced my new credo and my conscience-soothing warning to Liz—"I've lived so long for everybody else, now I'm going to live a little for myself."

Looking back on that conversation, which justified so much to come, I am more aware than ever that the shock of bereavement shattered my entire foundation, knocking apart my accumulated good sense and perspective and throwing me back into an overgrown boyhood. Mourning becomes a maturing process, a passage once again through the classic ages of man—a reexperiencing of the fears of childhood, the follies of adolescence, and then, after one or two years, there is a return to adulthood. It is, in truth, a second chance to grow up, to achieve a new degree of insight and wisdom.

On our last day, the fourth of January, before we returned to New York, Meredith and Helena and I went sledding again —our first outing alone together since Hope's death. We made several runs, the girls taking turns with me on the large sled, their small eight- and ten-year-old weights thumping down on me on the bumps, their legs held between mine, their gasps in my ear. Then at the bottom after the last run, delaying the long climb back up to the car, the girls began pelting me with snowballs as I lay on my sled. I grabbed their legs and pulled them down and we wrestled as they tried to rub snow in my face and called out as though I were Gulliver, "Hold his legs," "Watch out, he's got an arm free."

Finally, fatherlike, I began shouting, "Okay, that's enough. That's it. Uncle." And then we sat for a minute, panting, laughing, faces red and wet. I felt within the triumvirate of the children and me a gentle loosening from the past. We lay in the snow looking up at the gray sky and listening for the once-in-a-while winter bird. I had lost a person who satisfied my need to love, but I could focus my affections on the children without reserve. Snow had begun falling again, gently. I remembered the backyard on the morning Hope died.

When we returned to the house, Liz met me with a welcoming smile. I unexpectedly recoiled. The reality of the children had pulled me down from my emotional jag. I was back in touch with Hope, and suddenly Liz seemed like an invasion. In midafternoon — it was January fourth — we drove to New York, dropped Laura at her apartment, and headed toward our house. I was filled with foreboding. Now I would be resuming the extended ritual of Hope's death where it had been interrupted eleven days ago. In the same way that I had settled into a life of illness and doctors and fear, I would now be learning the ropes of mourning — finding out how to father these two girls, how to answer my needs, how to cope with memories and grief, how to keep the household running smoothly. The luxury of numbness and escape would no longer be possible.

As I drove, I mentally ticked off the household departments to see if I was covered. Laura had agreed to continue her three-days-a-week schedule from three o'clock to seven, and Gertrude worked two days, eleven to six. Breakfasts I would handle, and the girls would come home after school to Gertrude or Laura, who would cook dinner. Doctor's and dentist's appointments — they would be handled by both Laura and Gertrude. Groceries, minor errands — Laura. Sewing and laundry — Gertrude. Light cleaning and pickup — all of us. Heavy cleaning — a one-day-a-week cleaning lady, found for me by Whitney. Gertrude would provide loving continuity, and Laura, gaiety and warmth. I assigned myself the weekends, counting on physical help and practical advice from Liz Hauser and Whitney. Yes, everything seemed to be taken care of to set up a widower household. Perhaps I could get to work seriously on my book.

In the back of the car, lying on the bedlike platform, the girls stared out the windows, absorbed in the Christmas displays along Fifth Avenue. Red and blue and green lights flashed onto their faces. They seemed utterly wrapped up in the here and now, that wonderful capacity of children, and I envied Meredith and Helena their inability to project into the future, to foresee our return to a home without their mother. Meredith rolled onto her back and held close to her face one of the kittens Laura had brought. She said, "When I grow up, I'm going to have lots of kittens and puppies."

Helena said, "You'd better marry a half-dog, half-cat."

At the house I opened the door under the front steps and we carried the bags through Helena's room. Liz worked as hard as I, hurrying in and out, her face intent. I was impressed and grateful. But I was contending with the past. Now for the first time I felt disloyal. I was glad of Liz but wanted her gone. I wanted to immerse myself in the unpacking and in getting the girls to bed. I wanted privacy, sharing perhaps a little of Helena's feelings. The day before, while we were sledding, she said, "I like it when there's just the three of us. Then I can imagine that Mom is here."

Taking the car to the garage, I dropped Liz off at her apartment a few minutes away, and our parting was subdued. Back at the house, getting the girls into bed, Meredith snuggled down under her comforter, hugged Bearie, and serenely accepted her good-night kiss. "I love you Daddy." Helena, looking herself like one of "the gang," was almost crowded out of bed by bears. I sensed undercurrents of comfort and reassurance and realized how wrong it would be to move out of that house. Hope's death, dramatizing the precariousness of life, had been terrifying to all of us — and we needed the safety that comes from the continuity of home and possessions and routines.

When at last I stood alone in our bedroom, beset by loneliness and memories, I realized that the continuity of Hope in the house was crucial for all three of us. There would be ghosts there for a long time — feelings, words, the mental pictures which reflexively rush back, real as movies. But we must live with and through them until the pain was leached away. I could see Hope stuffing tissue paper into her shoes; Hope on the bed teaching two-year-old Meredith to talk, smiling, pointing, "Mouth, foot, eye, Daddy"; Hope sprawled motionless on the bed, her staring eye turning up into her head. I felt that familiar sick feeling in my stomach. But I knew that Hope must stay present and unrepressed. Only then could memories become relaxed and life could move ahead.

On the hook in the bathroom hung her ragged blue-plaid dressing gown. I left it there.

The next day, getting the children off to school, I practiced a particularly poignant form of remembrance. As a guide to managing the morning, I adopted Hope's habits—tidying a little as I walked through the girls' bedrooms, throwing laundry down the stairs and starting it early so it would be in the dryer while I cleaned the kitchen. That morning I biked both children to school. I decided not to coach their teachers; I had no specific suggestions and in these situations was inclined to let nature take its course.

In the afternoon, having promised Helena that every day I would be working in the studio just like Mommy—I sat there trying to write and insulate my thoughts from the room behind me, permeated with Hope's simultaneous presence and absence. At three-thirty the front-door buzzer sounded and I answered it and went out onto the landing as Hope always had. The sturdy figure of Helena came pounding eagerly up the stairs. I felt as though I were Hope, and experienced her pleasure. Helena, all business, followed the daily routine—getting out her paper and pencils and lying in the middle of the floor as she proudly labored over a drawing of Indians dancing around a campfire.

We talked and Helena said, "I remember once I picked up one of Mommy's special tools and started to make a woodcut and I broke the tool and cut myself. She got really mad and told you and you spanked me. But I could still see she loved me on her face and that it was really all right." Helena ran into trouble in her drawing and trustingly asked me for help. I could advise but could not show, and I felt Helena's frustration and disappointment—and the enormity of the void left behind in her life. My futility dramatized for me the humbling, sad fact that I could never be any part of Hope for the children, could never be more than a very good father.

· *179* ·

Helena went downstairs where Gertrude was presiding and I went to my office to work till seven, which became my routine. That evening as I read aloud to the girls before saying good night, the buzzer rang and it was Liz. Overdosed with the past, I was glad of this injection of the present. She joined us in Helena's tiny room while I finished a chapter of *The Princess and Curdy*. There is during mourning a constant temptation toward self-dramatization, and I was pleased by the image I must be projecting — the forlorn widower heroically, tenderly, caring for his bereft family. To my satisfaction, Liz looked moved and impressed. I began elaborating the tones and rhythms of my voice for even greater eloquence and effect.

"Come on, Dad," Helena said, "don't read so slowly. You sound like a priest." Liz laughed.

While she waited upstairs, I tucked in the two girls and asked with false casualness how the day had been at school. I wanted to treat everything as normal and now was the time for such questions. Meredith said, noncommittally, "Fine."

Helena said, "We were playing dodge ball and this boy was yelling at me, 'Your mother sucks.' Another girl told him, 'That's really mean cuz her mother died' and the boy kept right on saying it. And at the end of the period when he was running to go in I threw the ball at him. It hit him right on the head, and I said to myself, 'Bullseye.' It made him cry and I went and hid in the girls' bathroom. I felt really good. I told Mommy about it and in my mind I saw her smile."

Meredith, listening from her room next door, called out, "That kid lives with his father and almost never sees his mother."

I asked if anything had happened in class. Helena told me the teacher had hugged her. "For a second, I didn't know why," Helena said, "and then I didn't feel like being hugged." Both the girls' teachers, I learned, had asked them whether they wanted an announcement made to their classes so everybody would know and nobody would say the wrong thing. Helena had said she didn't care, and while she was out of the room, the teacher told the class that Helena's mother had died of cancer. Then Helena regretted it — "Mommy was sort of secret." Meredith answered "No" to her teacher and explained to me, "I didn't want sympathy, people coming around saying, 'Oh, I'm so sorry.'"

Though I drank in attention from the people closest to me, I, too, found sympathy from relative strangers difficult to handle. In those early days back in New York, I kept to the house, dreading the first meetings with acquaintances in the neighborhood and the curiosity in their eyes. They expected a reaction from me, which in some subtle and strange way felt like an invasion of my privacy. When they spoke in ritual formulas, that bothered me, though I wanted sympathy. And while I was constantly afraid of breaking down, I found my own answering clichés insulting to the deepness of my feelings. As long as the mourning period lasted, I was curiously upset by the almost universal inability to rise to the enormous occasion of death. Inevitably, people asked how I was. Nobody wanted to hear the long truth, so I developed stock answers, saying, "It's as though I have no skin" or "I feel like I've been sprayed through a nozzle." Sometimes I said, "Hope grew roots into every corner of me, and it's as though they were pulled out all at once." Sometimes I simply said, "I'm a mess."

My condition was the most vital question in my life. I was intensely focused on myself, which I suspect is typical of newly bereaved widowers. Hope and her illness had been the center of my worry — monitoring her condition, coping with crises, making her wishes possible. Now, though the children were a constant concern, I was the stricken one. The vacuum left by Hope's death was filled by worry about myself — taking my emotional temperature, finding ways to treat my anguish. That is human nature. But also my survival was crucial to the girls' survival. If I could not manage my own mourning, I could not help with theirs and be a source of reassuring strength.

Our return from Dublin to New York — two weeks, two

centuries, after Hope's death — marked the end of phase one, the period of numbness, and the start of the second and most painful phase of mourning, when most of the recovery takes place. Phase two lasted roughly a year and a half, but it was during the five days before the memorial service on January tenth that Hope's death came home to me and the classic agonies of mourning were at their most virulent. All the emotions dammed up during the illness broke through. My reactions were wildly exaggerated. Guilt flooded in. I ate poorly, lost weight, was exhausted to the marrow of my bones — almost an illness in itself. I felt there was little joy for me anywhere and saw seeds of calamity in everything. During those days a friend of Hope's and mine, Ann Blodgett, invited me and the children for dinner and she remembers me as "stunned," "blown out." Joan Rivers and her husband, Edgar, came to see us, and they remember me wandering restlessly, aimlessly, like a visitor in my own home. Tears waited constantly just behind my eyes.

I had a consuming need to be held. The absence of arms around me was sometimes a physical sensation. Liz stopped by daily, and one afternoon we sat side by side on the edge of my bed while I poured out despair at my inability to write my book. I drew her back on the bed and lay beside her and she did take me in her arms, holding me against the length of her body. In a purging torrent of relief and anguish, I wept uncontrollably — and she kissed me on the forehead as if I were a small boy.

In the early weeks of mourning, no matter how hard you lean toward the future, everything conspires to mire you in your tragedy. I could postpone a few painful duties. I did not pack away Hope's clothes; I left intact the semisacred turf of her studio. But there was Hope's savings account to empty, the long process of the will and taxes, the undertaker's bill to pay — "Toatl [sic] charges for treatment of remanis [sic]." Checks in Hope's name were endorsed "Estate of Hope B. Meryman." At the school's request I wrote a notice for its paper and could not bring myself to type anything but the euphemism "passed away."

Meredith bawled me out: "Mom's *dead* and you should have said it." And there were the letters of condolence, which I had allowed to accumulate. For that hurdle I turned again to Liz Hauser for support. To stimulate my courage, I made drinks. It was a bizarre scene. With the emotions of Hope's illness and death flooding back through me, I read each letter aloud. At those full of clichés, I was childishly incensed; at those full of feeling tenderness, I wept in gratitude and held on to Liz until the comforting escalated and I escaped into passionate kissing. And then we returned to the letters and the fits and the crying.

The memorial service on January tenth had loomed disturbing and daunting, but I wanted it exceedingly. It was what Hope would have desired too—a final, public demonstration of devotion. The children would sense the stature of their mother. Symmetry and ceremony required a final and completing statement. Making it exactly right would be an act of love toward Hope. But I doubted that for me it could be either climactic or comforting, and I have since learned that this is true of many widowers. I imagined myself weeping throughout the service, all eyes upon me, and at the end being led from the church, incapacitated.

On the tenth I walked with the girls, Harry, Lanie, Laura, and Liz to St. Joseph's Church, the church Hope had chosen for Meredith's and Helena's First Communion. The girls, startlingly feminine in their dresses, chased each other giggling along the sidewalk. Wishing them lightheartedness above everything, I was glad they were not attaching great solemnity or seriousness to the day. The church seemed nearly full, and I was relieved. As we made our entrance, I was intensely aware of the tableau—the single father and his motherless daughters—and I discovered that there is an odd lift, a form of support, which comes with being the center of attention, a sort of star.

After the Catholic funeral Mass, Peter Davis moved to a lectern and read a poem by an Italian monk, Fra Giovanni, which Hope had once picked to illustrate for a tiny edition she bound herself. The poem spoke directly to grief:

"No Peace lies in the future
which is not hidden in this present instant.
Take Peace.
The gloom of the world is but a shadow;
Behind it, yet within our reach, is joy.
Take Joy . . ."

Next John Groth spoke, passing on the pleasure he had always taken in Hope. He said that nobody in his life had been such an inspiration. "Everyone in this church," John said, "had their lives brightened and enriched by Hope, who always had time for everybody. And when we will talk of her, she will live."

At the end I walked quickly down the aisle, startled by the sensation of reexperiencing my wedding, that happy flight away from the altar with Hope. Outside, I hurried home alone, unwilling to linger as though courting condolences. Soon the guests began arriving at the house for the reception, and I was in a dazed state of stimulation. I stood in the living room spontaneously hugging men and women alike — "Thank you for coming. It means a tremendous amount."

After the reception Whitney and Peter Hansen gave a dinner at their apartment for the extended family. I was now on a rampant high of relief. I had not been disappointed by the ceremonies or myself. And the deference accorded the widower as chief mourner is adrenaline for his exhausted ago. Then, standing in a group opposite Liz Hauser, who was drinking a martini from a delicately thin champagne glass, I looked across at her and was suffused with appreciation and affection. She received my message. The rush of her response reached her hand and the glass shattered.

In those first weeks in New York the children were also starting their own version of the second phase, perhaps even more complicated than mine. I believe that resolving bereavement is harder for children than for adults. Children have not yet learned to live through separations. Their concept of death—its reality and its permanence—is rudimentary. They may not know how to reach out for help, particularly to a self-absorbed parent coping with grief. Their mourning takes place among events they cannot control. Like adults, they are assailed by anger, fear, denial, guilt, but lack sophisticated protective mechanisms and the objectivity to identify and treat emotions. They are controlled by immature, sometimes primitive reflexes.

During that time I dipped into a few books on children and bereavement, found little of use, but learned that children may believe that somehow they caused the parent's death. Often they are terrified that the surviving parent will also die and they will be left alone. They may be furious at one parent for dying and the other for letting it happen. They may pretend the death did not happen and that the parent will return. Sometimes ordinary behavior alters: the child regresses into thumb-sucking, stops eating, misbehaves, or, confusing sleep with death, is wakeful at night. I myself found that unless there are dramatic symptoms, it is easy to believe a child's outward pragmatism and normality, and to neglect the dry tears and private wonderings. I was astonished one night when Helena asked, "Would Mommy still be alive if she'd been in the hospital?"

I think my children were fortunate. Though Hope and I did not systematically prepare them for her death—perhaps because we ourselves had not come to terms with it—Meredith and Helena witnessed her decline and her own preparation to the very last day. Her death must have been undeniable and comprehensible, a last step in a natural progression. Afterwards, the girls had every proof of love and security. My work was flexible and nearby, and I could coincide with their lives and be on call. The flurry of attention at Hope's death did not fall away to nothing. The children's support system was in place beforehand and continued, unchanging.

Because of their different natures, the two girls chose opposite but prevalent mourning routes. Night after night Helena lay in the dark having conversations with her mother. "It's like she's in heaven and she's talking to me," Helena told me, "but I can't see her because her body isn't alive. Sometimes I cry, and Mommy used to kiss my cheek and my forehead when she'd comfort me, and I can feel that inside me."

Henny did her talking when I put her to bed. Later, almost nightly, she appeared as a dim shape in the darkness, clutching Big Teddy. "I can't get to sleep," she said as she climbed into bed and settled in her mother's place. When I came home late I sometimes found a note on my pillow — *"Important Message* I feel very punk Very!!! Punk!!! Love Henny." And on one particular note there was a drawing of herself in a chair, tears streaming down her face.

She asked me why her mother had died, and I told her there was no reason, just terrible, terrible bad luck for Hopie, for all of us. And Helena told me, "I was hoping, thinking Mom would be all right, and I'd cry at night that she'd get better, but inside of me I knew she wasn't going to get better."

One night she asked me, "Daddy, if you die, where would I live? With Harry and Lanie?"

"Probably," I told her. "Don't you want to?"

"No," Helena said. "I want to live with John Groth. Then I could hang out at the Art Students League."

Meredith's behavior was typical of the children who keep their grief buried. Unlike Helena, she was struggling, I think, with a sense of ambivalence toward her mother — the hardest of all feelings to resolve. Habitually, Meredith walked away from situations she could not handle, simply turning off, burying herself in television or hurling herself into the immediacy of the moment. Only in extremities of rage or anguish — the ways she asked for help — did she voice her deep feelings. So while Helena stayed at my elbow, Meredith stayed aloof, almost never speaking of her mother. When I invited her to come up at night instead of Helena, she refused. Though I sought her out, drawing her into conversations, playing games, giving her affection and attention, she no doubt believed that the father who had once been her special parent had been usurped.

I am still not sure how to deal with a mourning child who detaches herself from grief and, subtly, from the other mourners. Since dramatic symptoms and overt requests were lacking, I felt it would be brutal to probe Meredith about death and her mother, attacking her defenses. Nor did I wish to embarrass her, making her ashamed of acting differently from Helena and me, so I told Meredith that one does not have to cry, that there are many different ways of being sad.

But at the same time I instinctively, insensitively, equated talk with action. When Meredith no longer rose in the middle of dinner to do three cartwheels, I mistakenly attributed that to better discipline, not depression. Because of the complexities of her relationship with Hope, I did her the injustice of assuming that her sense of loss was less than Helena's. I did not have enough time and strength for everyone, including myself, so involuntarily I gave the squeaky wheel the grease, and Helena received much of the fatherly therapy.

One symptom of the children's mourning literally screamed at me. In those first weeks back in New York they became bratty and sassy. Putting Helena to bed, I dropped her pajamas by mistake, and asked her to pick them up. She said, "You pick 'em up." I said, "No, bending over hurts my back." She said, "You drop 'em, you pick 'em up." "Henny," I said menacingly. "*Daddy*," she answered rebelliously. So I started counting, "One, two, three . . ."

Both Laura and Gertrude confirmed the problem, which was in my lap as the primary enforcer. No employee, no matter how devoted, can have the clout and the commitment to overcome the passive resistance of a child. At first I diagnosed the girls as merely pampered. At home I had let rules go by the board in an orgy of softheartedness. Television was rampant. Bedtimes and bedmakings were ignored. If a request was at all reasonable, I rarely said no. And since our return to New York we had been the objects of a flurry of attention. Several mothers, acquaintances of Hope's, would ring the front-door buzzer and thrust into my hands dishes they had made for us, and I became a connoisseur of cheese-and-macaroni casseroles and meat loaf — our sustenance on weekends. Other friends, partly to give me a little relief, gave Meredith and Helena extravagant outings.

On reflection, I realized that overindulgence was not the main reason for the girls' bad behavior. At this time of acute insecurity, when they were disturbed and their world was out of control, I was offering them a swamp of freedom. Misbehavior was their subconscious way of demanding firmness and stability. Much later Helena said to me, "You always need somebody to fight with, and I used to have Mere and Mom for that. I only began to fight with you after Mom was sick and after she died. But it wasn't because I was all that angry. I guess I just needed to fight with somebody because I was upset."

I decided to crack down, and return the family to real life. I called a house meeting, which included Laura, and told the girls that having their mother die did *not* make them into privileged people entitled to special treatment.

Helena said, "At first I liked it when people took us out. But I didn't see it was because Mommy died, and then I knew they were only doing it because they were pitying us, and I don't like that."

Meredith said, "I don't see what's wrong with people taking us places and buying us things."

I explained very seriously that it was wrong to use Mommy's death to get anything. It was bad for them because it made them expect to be pampered and life is not like that.

Tuned out, Meredith said, "The good things about your mother dying is that everyone gives you casseroles."

On the fifteenth of January the mourners who had missed Hope's burial — the children and I, Laura, Liz (who had been sick in bed that day), Peter Davis — drove to Chester Heights. At the church I went in search of the priest, who shrugged on his surplice and led us briskly over the uneven ground to the narrow hummock of raw earth and rocks next to Little Whitney's headstone — "Whitney Therese Meryman." Meredith went over to it and read the inscription, her face inscrutable. I could see Helena noticing in the bushes a large pile of fresh dirt, the tailings from Hope's grave. We stood in uneasy reverence while the priest read prayers and passages from the Bible. The children looked numb and uncomfortable. The priest finished. Meredith and Helena self-consciously placed on the grave the flowers Liz had brought. The priest escorted me back toward the car, volubly impressing on me the long history of the church and the parish. At the edge of the cemetery I thanked him and passed over a white envelope containing money.

At last I could take my moment of communion, looking back to that place where Hope and I had soberly stood so many times. I heard Meredith say, "Look." Across the pale winter sunset flew a dark and wheeling flock of birds.

At home that night the girls and I discussed what to inscribe on Hope's gravestone. Helena suggested, "Why not a miniature picture of one of her prints because gravestones have pictures on them."

Meredith said, "No, just the title of a print — and then write, "A Beautiful Woman."

I said, "Well, I've been fooling around with something like 'Loved in Life, Loved in After-Life.'"

"That's corny," said Helena.

"Yes, that's really corny," said Meredith. "How about, 'Thank you for being a friend'? Or write, 'Hope Meryman,' and then, 'The story of our love has no end.' Mom's favorite song was the riddle song. That is so good, Daddy. I want that."

"I think it's corny," I answered.

"Daddy," said Meredith, "you don't have a bit of poetry in you."

Helena said, "How about something like, 'We loved her like a baby loves milk and the milk hasn't turned sour yet' or something."

"That's stupid," said Meredith.

"Maybe Hopie would be happiest if we just used her name and dates. That's what she wanted put on Little Whitney's stone."

"Yes," Meredith said. "Let's do that."

We did.

Eleven

Throughout that first winter, simply functioning each day was a full-time job. Reassembling myself was like putting together a child's toy without directions — picking up a piece, looking at it, and laying it down for another. It is precisely this chaos, however, that makes recovery possible. Only by blundering endlessly through the maze of your emotions and needs can you eventually escape them.

I had good hours, a good afternoon, when the sense of weight would lift and I could concentrate my mind outside myself. But just when I thought I might be emerging from the tunnel, from my sense of loss, I would relapse, and the weight would press down again. Sometimes these mood changes were a diurnal rise and fall, sometimes an unexpected zinger revved up the pain again. One day at home the telephone rang — a cousin of Hope's who had been out of contact for a few years. We chatted for a minute and then he said, "If Hopie's there, I'd like to speak to her." He did not know! During the split second of his question, there was a dizzying time warp, and Hope was back from the dead moving about the house, perhaps in the studio, and on my tongue were the familiar words, "Just a second, I'll get her."

I wallowed in worry like a becalmed ship—as I later learned, a classic symptom of mourning. Meredith often asked to ride her skateboard to school, intending to travel in the street on the smooth tar. I would say no, and tell her that the one chance in a thousand *does* happen—a single crazy driver and she would be a grease spot. I would say, "Remember Josie." To myself I said, "Remember Hopie." I had been robbed forever of the sublime assumption that disaster happens only to others and never to me or mine. When Helena had a nosebleed, I saw Hope's bloody smile and panicked that Helena was bleeding to death. When I had an unexplained ache I was sure it was a tumor. Then, when the ache disappeared I would joke to myself—but only half joke—that I had returned from the jaws of death.

Clearing my mind for sleep at night seemed only to make way for streams of self-doubt. I questioned whether I could write my book well enough, whether I would ever do another book, whether my magazine by-line would be remembered, and if I got magazine assignments, whether I could do them quickly enough to earn a living. Even with Liz Hauser in my life, I reexperienced those early doubts about myself and women. I doubted my capacity to be a good single parent. I began questioning whether this treadmill of mourning and sadness and self-doubt would ever ease.

Even the optimistic incidents—the silver clouds—had dark linings. One evening Helena appeared—very pleased with herself, as though it were a joke—wearing Hope's robe stolen from St. Vincent's Hospital. She wore it often and added hospital pajamas with "Columbia-Presbyterian" printed on the back. She found long red hairs caught on a wool sweater of Hope's, and with a delight wholly unmixed with sadness, exclaimed, "Oh, here's a goody"—and picked them off and saved them in an envelope. The healthiness, the resilience, in Helena's feelings—perhaps because she had no conflicting emotions about her mother—were an inspiration by example. But those mementos brought the familiar clench of my innards, and I relived in a composite instant, like sheet lightning, the anxiety of the past two years.

I could easily have used Helena and Meredith as shoulders to weep on, and without Liz Hauser I might have been tempted. But that would have eliminated me as their major source of strength and security. I even wondered whether the sight of me in tears would be an unsettling sign of weakness. I decided that crying told them how much I grieved for Hope, told them that tears were all right so they could shed their own, told them I was human. And God knows I was human when it came to single parenthood and caring for Meredith and Helena.

I liked the mornings, the special sense of ritual and family life enduring. I kissed the children awake and rubbed their heads and commiserated with their throes of waking. Helena always wiggled even deeper under the blankets, insisting, "My eyes are awake." Meredith said, "I hate school. It's boring" — but got up immediately to walk to school with a friend. I fried her morning egg and assembled their bag lunches. "If you're thinking of making me an egg-salad sandwich," Helena said, "don't think of it." I had *my* daily lines — my call to Helena, "Brush your teeth," and to Meredith, "Wear a hat."

I liked my sense of coping, of doing the housekeeping well. But after the children were gone to school, I did not like the picky, unexpected details that ate up my worktime. Morning after morning there was a forgotten lunch or textbook to be rushed to school, a repairman to be summoned or awaited. There were telephone calls about after-school invitations. If the other father answered the telephone, as out of touch as I used to be, I would say, "Maybe I should speak to Theresa's social secretary." Her mother would come on to negotiate the pickup and delivery — "I'd love to bring Helena home, but . . ." — and I would glimpse her exquisitely timed world as she juggled as many facets as I did.

Sometimes there were teacher's conferences to attend. Facing Meredith's teacher, I would sit scrunched in a child's schoolroom chair, my knees knocking the table edge, while she delivered her critique with a look of combined sympathy, apology, and helplessness. I had always been the prime architect of the children's education, but now I had no companion pair of shoulders to bear the teacher's litany: "Intelligent child with good mind but dashes off homework and is not self-motivated" . . . "Attitude offhand and distant". . . "With encouragement and support could develop study habits."

I would leave the school for the lonely walk home feeling overwhelmed. How could I, coming home at seven or eight, instill pride and turn around her study patterns? How could I expect any Laura, so much more a sister-friend than a mother power, to revolutionize Meredith's mind set? I knew that in child-raising, the least-efficient and least-businesslike of all processes, the shaping was done drop by drop, like water on sandstone, admonitions and admirations endlessly repeated. But now the primary influence was a father isolated by work exactly when Meredith needed me the most. I wondered about working mothers and how they did it and what price was paid by the children.

Yet I did not want to arrive home nightly as the big enforcer. That should not be my role. I was the girls' security, their continuity, their fount of approval and encouragement. When I walked in each evening, tired from a day of writing, I was immediately met by their silent cries of hear me, see me, touch me.

They would tell me their big news of the day ("I didn't get a ball in dodge ball") and their pronouncements ("The trouble with everybody over thirty is that they all die off"). They would demand some new this or that—a proof that I loved them that much. When I told Helena that she was asking me to spend a hundred dollars on ski boots she would outgrow in a year, she said, "That's the breaks, Dad." Having been angelic all afternoon, they would now start wrangling—interrupting me and each other to make accusations and get arbitrations. They would want to roughhouse—play "bucky bronco," riding me like a horse on the big bed till they made a bee-buzzing sound and stung me on the shoulder and then I would "go crazy" and buck them off. And I could see in their eyes their need for this physical contact, this touching.

Before Hope's illness, when Meredith needed something—a wish granted, a mood served, a problem solved—she could pick between two parents. If I made her angry, Hope was there, uncontaminated, to console and interpret. If Hope's attention was on Helena, I was available. If I was at work, Hope was a source of affection. If Meredith wore me out, Hope was there to spell me. And vice versa. And likewise for Helena.

With only one parent left, the rivalry between the two girls went into overdrive. When I began restoring order in the home and Meredith's special status at school wore thin, she returned to her old prickly self. Like many insecure children, she sometimes buttressed her self-image with assertiveness— demanding her TV program or the window seat in the car, giving peremptory orders to Helena—"Don't cough in my room." Helena, the subtle manipulator, easily retaliated by enraging Meredith, whose only real weapons were screamed denunciations and painful pinches, which brought down my wrath on Meredith.

One night the girls had been picking at each other interminably, and during dinner Meredith screamed at Helena, "Shut up!" With my nerves drawn thin, my temper snapped. Crashing my hand down on the table, I bellowed at Meredith, "God damn it! Stop it!" I can still see her small oval face flinching. She whirled from the table, raced into her room, and slammed the door. Helena said, "Well, we could cut a hole in her door and mail her dinner to her."

I felt awful. I had not helped Meredith. I had yelled exactly as she did and had attacked her. I went to her door and knocked. Silence. "Meredith." Silence. I went in. She lay outstretched on her bed sobbing into her pillow. Total misery. I sat on the bed and put my hand on her shaking body. She shrugged herself away from me. I sat quietly there for a long time, and then, saying, "Poor Mere," I broke the barriers by picking her thin length bodily from the bed and sitting her on my lap. She let me hold her, weeping against my shoulder. I rubbed my hand round and round on her hard little back, wishing I could flood her permanently with calm and not knowing how and feeling intensely my aloneness. "Poor Mere."

I was in the single-parent situation of wielding the heavy discipline one moment and a second later comforting the agony I had caused. The single father giveth hell; the single father taketh it away. And such is the acceptingness of children, that they never seemed to find this strange. "What's the matter, Mere?" I said.

In a desperate, defensive voice she said loudly into my shoulder, "I get so mad at you, and I really hate that. Helena screams twice as loud as me, but when she has a feeling you're coming, she gets quiet, and I'm always the one who looks mad, and it's like she was just defending herself, which makes you think I'm always the one at fault. And you act like I just stabbed Henny in the stomach, and I try to explain, and you don't understand and just get more mad at me. Mom never picked sides. She just sent us both to our rooms."

"Maybe I should do that, too," I said. "But you used to complain that she wasn't fair. You know, Mere, I care so much about you and Henny that it upsets me terribly when one of you is hurt — especially when you hurt each other." I kissed her wet cheek and continued, "I do so want to do the right thing, and I'm not always sure what it is. But always remember that I really love you."

"I know you do, Daddy."

Then Helena, in her own way and time, usually weighed in with her version of the war. One evening she sang me the rock song she had composed. It was entitled "Have You Ever Been Put Down":

> *Have you ever been put down*
> *Oh, so bad you feel the tears coming?*

You feel like the unfair part
of life has been picking on you.
Someone told me not to sing.
She tells you your voice sounds like a frog.
Oh, so unfair. She puts me downnn.

Sympathizing, agonizing for each child, hating even the possibility of the family divided into two armed camps, I felt like a shell-scarred no-man's-land between them. And I was equally embattled when the two of them suddenly forgot their enmity and conspired against me — for example, to delay their bedtime. When Hope and I shared discipline, my big voice — we called it the H-bomb — was held in reserve. Now the H-bomb was a firecracker from overuse. These days I was the sayer of both the big no's and all the pesky little ones that came out as commands: pick up your clothes off the floor, do your homework, wear a sweater, turn off the television, take your plate to the kitchen, go to bed. My resolve and intensity were worn out by the constant back and forth between being affectionate and being what Meredith called "mean." I was also worn down by the girls' energy and charm. A mere single father was literally child's play to them.

While I sat on Meredith's bed yawning and futilely calling out, "Come on, you guys, it's getting late," Meredith, meticulous as a Leonardo, would slowly brush her hair and slowly wash the bottoms of her feet. Threats — "You know you're not too old to spank. One, two, three . . ." — got Mere into her room; warnings of "no good-night kiss" got her into bed. One night, shrieking with delight, she held a pillow across her "beehind" and defied me. Laughing, I played the game, spanking her harmlessly, and soon both girls were screeching around the house, wiggling their pillow-protected bottoms at me like dwarf chorines.

When I did get them into bed, Helena needed ten minutes to arrange "the gang" — her twelve bears, all different because, explained Helena, "If they weren't different, they'd be everybody else's." If I rested my weight on one, Helena would say sharply, "Dad, be considerate." Big Teddy's position was always under Helena's blond head, and as I bent to kiss her, his lopsided face, sewn by Hope, looked up at me. At the last second Helena would dart her hand over her lips, snuggle down, and try to start a conversation. At last I would announce, letting exasperation come into my voice, "Okay, now, kids, this is really it," and as I turned out the lights, "One more peep out of you guys, and there'll be big trouble."

"Peep," said Meredith in the darkness.

Alone in my bedroom — finally — I would often sit on the end of the bed and feel the silence palpable around me, like ointment on my nerves. Forced to match a child's Gatling-gun attention span, my brain was limp. And every hour seemed to contain the decision: whom should I put first, the girls or myself? Usually in those early months, I chose Meredith and Helena. Like an unliberated housewife, I felt my place was in the home.

If that had meant consigning myself entirely to a kid's world, I might not have been so sacrificing. There was, however, Liz Hauser. She was willing to come to me at the house, and she would stop by at odd moments in a gust of high spirits — on her way to work in the morning or for an hour at dinner. Sometimes she stayed into the evening, and alone, later, Liz and I laughed and punned together, a wonderful, mindless silliness. I remember studying her face from a foot away for a long time and saying, "You're very beautiful," and then a moment later, "but your nose is crooked."

"So I have to be perfect?" she said in mock indignation. "I'm leaving. Taxi. Taxi. Somebody call me a taxi."

"You're a taxi," I said, and we convulsed at that ancient joke, and I imitated Liz laughing, and we laughed at laughing.

Sometimes, just before Liz left, I went to bed, and Liz pulled up the blankets and tucked me in, and I luxuriated in being babied. Sometimes I rolled over, and she rubbed my shoulders and neck and head; sometimes I pulled her down on me and we kissed; sometimes we lay side by side in the darkness, hardly touching, aware that Helena might appear at any moment with Big Teddy to join me in bed.

In the thin, city dark we would talk—woman friend as therapist—free Freud. Added now to my familiar recital of fears and guilts was single parenthood—the fundamental disorder of the family when no one person is present and in charge every day. Liz would say to me, "It's going to work out. Look how much you have going for you." And I would think to myself, "What does she know."

Though I was resolutely the center of my cosmos, Liz was allowed to talk about her difficulties—the disorder of *her* life, emotionally fragmented between her art research foundation, her continuing social life, my household, her sons, whose joint custody she shared with their father. One night I realized she was crying. "What's wrong?" I asked.

"Nothing. Really. Nothing."

"What's *wrong*? Tell me."

"Sometimes I miss Ned and Christopher so terribly."

I was too involved with myself to feel anybody else's pain, and I heard Liz with detached regret, mainly concerned that she might cut me out of her marathon days. Sometimes we decided that the relationship was moving too fast and we should see each other less. Soon my loneliness flooded back. I would telephone Liz and archly say, "Aren't you coming over this evening?" And Liz would stop by because she, too, had to survive and fill her own needs and gamble on the future.

Occasionally we went to the theater and to a dinner party. Peter Davis gave both the last party Hope and I attended and the first I went to with Liz. The comparisons were sharp, part of the shock treatment of small jolts very gradually separating me from the past. That earlier evening, with Hope, she as usual had been the center of attention while I, unwilling to compete, sat back. At the party with Liz I sometimes seized the floor, and began to realize how often Hope the talker and charmer had been interposed between me and others. To my astonishment, I saw that I had lived like a light in her shadow. I remembered those nights when Hope, after holding forth, would say to me on the way home, "Why were you so quiet? Didn't you have a good time?"

Liz Hauser, by nature attentive and appreciative, had been saying to me in many different ways, "You're wonderful." I felt myself opening into a new spontaneity and shrugging away old restraints and inhibitions. When Liz and I left Peter's apartment that night, I felt I was taking the party with me.

A sympathetic woman is probably a widower's primary way to recover his social and sexual self-esteem. The person he becomes for her, the sides of him she brings out, help shape his new image of himself. The degree of his admiration for her — his feeling that he has attracted a valuable woman — creates a new sense of self-worth.

A widower's appetite for such reassurance is almost unlimited. My self-esteem and sense of identity were shattered. For twenty-three years I had been an intrinsic part of a unit — Hope and Dick. My ego had been boosted by the mere fact that such a woman was my wife. The affection and admiration aimed at Hope had ricocheted onto me. I had been dependent on Hope, on her respect and love, and we consulted about every decision, for better or for worse, in argument and in accord. Hope, in turn, was dependent on me, which had buttressed my sense of value and importance. Her death cut away structural members of my edifice of self.

My self-esteem was under assault in another, even more profound way. I was not experiencing the common signs and sensations which indicate virility. I felt dead inside. My encounters with Liz, though passionate from a wild mix of emotions, had been essentially sexless. I did not then know that a period of impotency is normal for widowers, that sexual desire is dulled by a sense of infidelity, by depression, by long sublimation of those needs, that sexual anxieties travel circularly to the mind and back, feeding on themselves and bombarding the self-confidence. I was frightened that my condition might become to some degree permanent.

By mid-February I was better, and Liz and I planned a weekend alone in the Dublin house, empty while my mother was in California for the winter. We tacitly knew what would happen. It seemed the next step in a natural progression. There seemed no reason to wait; the risks had already been taken. We had both, after all, been married for years. Part of me, however, saw it as a test that could end in crushing embarrassment, while another part of me was palpitating with a bottled-up, almost illicit thrill. I was going to fulfill those fantasies which extended from Hope's illness back to boyhood.

Assuming that the world was keeping track of me and would disapprove, I told everybody I was going skiing — minutely true — and asked Laura to take care of the girls. When I left after elaborate goodbyes downstairs, Helena followed me to the front hall. She stood up on the seat of the antique coatrack and put her short arms around my neck and pressed her cheek against mine — like a *very* tall child, like an eight-year-old wife. I said, "I'm going to miss you, Henny."

She answered, "But you won't be missing a daddy. That's missing a lot — a daddy, money, a punching bag — a lot of good stuff." Then, after a pause, she added, "Don't go."

I felt in her, in both the children, the terror that something now would happen to me. "I'll be back in two days, Henny."

"Maybe," she said.

Fighting the impulse to become the girls' shadow and ruin all of us, I disengaged myself with more kisses and fled, a kite tail of guilt streaming out behind me.

That Saturday morning, standing with Liz in the kitchen in Dublin, encapsulated by the snowdrifts outside, I had felt a sense of intermission between past and future complexities as though we were between planes, coming from somewhere, going somewhere else. I took Liz in my arms and kissed her in a way that was wholly different and promissory — and gave myself up to the feel of her body both soft and hard against me. Then, suddenly, the moment was intolerable. To break the mood, I snapped her bra strap, which was my old, affectionate, irreverent salute to Hope. Guilt rose in my throat like bile.

All day the past stayed just behind my shoulder. I resurrected two pairs of boyhood skis, and we tramped cross-country, through pine groves and around an untouched snow pond —and sometimes Liz pushed ahead of me, and I followed in her tracks, admiring such gusto and strength. And she would turn back to me with tears of pleasure in her eyes and say, "It's *so* beautiful!" And I would think how Hope, who hated cold, would not have come on such a weekend and how her highest excitements were the most deeply contained—as though God might take the moment away. I was seizing on all the opposites in Liz to justify the alliance.

After dinner at the kitchen table, we finished the bottle of wine by the light of a single candle. The large white wood-and-plaster Victorian kitchen, intimate since my childhood, was now weird with black and wobbly shadows. Still recovering from her divorce a few years before, Liz was also in transition in her life, and we talked about our wishes for the future. I said that perhaps with her help I could liberate the unself-conscious person I had always felt inside me, like a thin man inside a fat one. I said, "If this terrible thing had to happen, at least some good should come out of it."

Liz told me she had broken up her marriage to refind her true self. She had been brought up by Swiss parents in the Swiss communities of New York and Westchester, and at twenty-three, utterly innocent, had married the wrong man. She stayed married ten years, increasingly desperate and in despair at her sense of atrophy and emptiness. She said, "I want to be in tune with the person I once was a long time ago—and with you I feel I am that person."

That night, like virginal children, we made love. It was the familiar turned eerie—like the kitchen in candlelight. In essence I was making love to Hope on somebody else's body, moving my hands in their accustomed ways but over unknown flesh, my mind abstracted, wandering, noticing irrelevant details, particular differences. And yet this very strangeness — weighted by the past, by the significance of this act, by the sense of our affinity — made the moment both exciting and exalted.

I felt grateful to Liz and to the fates and not a little triumphant. But I felt incapable of true and undistracted tenderness toward Liz. My relationship with her did not seem real. Reality was back before Hope's death, and this flirtation, like a parlor game, would end when it was time to return to real life — to Hope.

As we lay quietly holding each other, Liz said, reflectively, "What would have happened, I wonder, if I hadn't existed?"

I answered, "I guess I would have found somebody else."

She pulled away. "Oh, *no!* You wouldn't have. Don't say that!"

Laughing, I drew her back to me. "You're right. I would have looked until I found you."

The mourning process, which is beyond the bereaved's control, requires a great deal of patience. In my case, months were needed simply to absorb totally the fact of Hope's death — that this awful game would not end and Hope would not return. Only after I took serious charge of the household, and after my weekend with Liz, did I begin to feel truly single.

There is no more potent dramatization of one's singleness than sole responsibility for the control of a house and two children inside it. I would wake on a Saturday morning with the sensation that everything was in physical and emotional disarray, and with the belief that all repairs must come from me. On my mind was the constant list of chores: fix leaky radiators, pay bills, take coins out of washer, fix latches on kitchen cabinets, put washers in taps, plug cold-air leaks, et cetera, et cetera. But on the other hand I felt compelled to be present for the girls and provide them with constant proof that my commitment to them was limitless, that I was their rock. I worried that they felt abandoned — by Hope, by the natural mothers who had put them up for adoption—and I wondered whether they would always carry a sense of original hurt—like original sin.

My predicament was summed up for me one weekend when I was high on the fire escape on the back of the house, cutting back the wisteria vines. Helena appeared below, saying, "Meredith needs you." I rushed down the steps and ladder and into Meredith's room. She lay on the floor sobbing and holding her head. She had fallen off her skateboard and knocked her head, slightly as it turned out. When I knelt beside her, making soothing sounds, composing myself into a portrait of concern, her sobs turned to wails. "I called and you didn't come. You don't care about me."

Sometimes I saw the children as terrible burdens, consuming my life energies and time. But I was jittery when no project was ready to occupy them, and distract and ward off possible melancholy. And, the more you work to modulate and placate children's grief, the more they sense your accessibility. You are giving them real power, and they instinctively use it. They would take me from jobs to play Monopoly, to play basketball in the backyard, to play netless tennis on the street. As we had with Hope, we biked to Battery Park. With a tail wind blowing us along the abandoned, elevated West Side Highway, we looked down into the city, feeling as high as the pigeons, and Helena, lounging back in her seat, the personification of aplomb, rode "no hands." In the park, overlooking the harbor, the Statue of Liberty, the ferryboats, we played follow the leader, wheeling our bikes along winding paths, around monuments, through coveys of strollers.

Sometimes for sledding and skating we went uptown to Central Park and met Whitney and Peter Hansen with Brooks and Hope Hansen (named after Hopie). We stayed for dinner —a pleasure but also a poignancy that underlined our threeness and my singleness. I felt strange. I was not a relative but almost. Neither was I a friend but almost. I walked through the apartment sadly looking at Hope's paintings on the wall—the pavilion-bedecked beach in Spain where we had stopped for coffee that sunny morning. I returned to the kitchen and Whitney — my co-nurse of Hope — her ways and talk an embodiment of Hope. I loved being there; I wanted to hug Whitney. I wanted to cry; I wanted to run out of there.

On the telephone Whitney became a sort of umbilical mother, talking to us regularly. When I got in trouble at the stove — cooking dinner on a Saturday night after the casseroles gave out — it was her I called. While Hope was ill, I had mastered kid food: hot dogs, hamburgers, frozen beans and peas, baked potatoes (always puncture), bottled applesauce. Within my repertoire I was a virtuoso, able to fry a hot dog for Meredith at the same time as hamburgers for Helena and me. But spaghetti with meat sauce was uncharted wilderness. When I first tackled that, I stood for half an hour at the spaghetti-sauce section of the supermarket, carefully reading the labels of all the brands. I did not want to make a mistake. On the kitchen telephone I got Whitney's instructions: break up the hamburger and brown it; then pour in the sauce and bring to a boil. Yes, I thought I could manage that. I was absolutely thrilled one night when Helena, after polishing off a greasy hamburger drowned in ketchup, said, "I like your cooking."

Mothers have made themselves the folk doctors of the American family, and Whitney was my emergency room. Meredith, apparently sick with routine flu, spent a day under Gertrude's capable care. But I took over at six, and by eight, when I went in to read aloud to her, she was rolling her head from side to side and kicking the blankets down, calling out, "Daddy, please, I'm so hot." Her temperature was 105. Soon she began to stutter — "D-D-Daddy, p-p-please s-s-stop this." I was frantic. Typhoid and meningitis sounded in my head. I telephoned Whitney. Almost casually she explained that children regularly have very high temperatures, and I should bring it down by putting her in a tub of cold water and ice cubes. I undressed Meredith and carried her burning body to the tub, her two hot little arms encircling my neck. Without a whimper, totally trusting, she submerged. Whitney's remedy worked. Back in bed, Meredith said, "Thank you, Daddy." I felt terrific.

One night we camped out in the dining room with ebullient Laura. Helena pitched her treasured Teddy Bear Tent, a Christmas present Hope had decorated with large bears cut from felt and pasted over the printed Indians. We brought out the girls' mattresses and cooked hot dogs in a frying pan set on a 150-watt pot light. Afterwards we sat around this Con Ed campfire and I told a ghost story.

On weekends alone at home, the three of us continued our standard routines, outwardly unaffected by the empty space of Hope — a good sign of early adjustment. On Saturday evenings we religiously gathered on the huge bed for the "progrees," Meredith's baby word for the TV sequence of Mary Tyler Moore, Bob Newhart, and Carol Burnett. While the girls argued over the best place next to the set, I found myself lying in Hope's old spot.

Somewhat irreligiously we went to church as usual on Sundays. I had vowed to maintain scrupulously the girls' Roman Catholic upbringing. But after the initial spurt my intensity thinned, partly because I was growing away from Hope, partly because of my disillusionment when her faith did not seem to be her mighty fortress. Presently, I began getting resistance from Meredith — "Do we *have* to go? It's so boring."

I explained: "Mere, it is the very smallest thing we can do to honor Mommy's memory. But, more important, religion is the main force in the world for ethics and morality, and I would not be doing my job if I allowed you to grow up without that influence." So we would walk the eight blocks to our customary church, a cavernous place fallen on dingy times. Meredith was usually a little ahead, and Helena held my hand until a red iron fire alarm divided us — "bread and butter." In our pew during the service — "I believe in one God, the Father Almighty, maker of heaven and earth . . ." — I was a policeman trying to suppress two ruffians. When Helena stood up on the kneeling bar to be level with Meredith and make faces, I ferociously pointed my finger at her, mouthing, "Zap!" When Meredith lounged back as the Host was elevated, I whispered fiercely, "This is a reverent moment. Get into the attitude of prayer, please, and pray for Mommy, for me, and most of all for yourself." When Helena wrinkled her nose at the people in front of us and giggled into my ear, "I smell yellow smelly rhino belly," I tried to frown. When the two small figures went alone and knelt at the rail for Communion, Hope's image—well and smiling, sick and tottering—was strong beside them.

After the Mass, the children rushed to the one ritual they enjoyed—lighting candles for Hope and Josie in front of the Virgin. I fretted that they were fooling around and lighting too many, and they always said, "We *are* not." Then I made them stand quietly and say a prayer for Hope and Josie—and broke it off before my tears came.

Outside we proceeded for a treat to a delicatessen, a God-given, after-church right as immutable as the pursuit of happiness and as ritualistic as my decree: "No, you cannot have both a candy bar *and* a soda. Choose one." We would walk home along Hudson Street, dipping into the antique stores, fingering silk scarves from the twenties, trying on jackets, laughing at Buddhas with clocks in their bellies, while Meredith's quick little hands darted recklessly out to open every drawer in the secretary, and the proprietor called out, "Please do not touch."

During the week, I took one or two nights for myself, usually going out with Liz Hauser. Without really thinking about it, I had begun reliving my pre-Hope bachelor days, perhaps finding in those somewhat collegiate pleasures a satisfying sense of both continuity and carelessness. I sat with Liz at bars, and we got tight and flirted and talked extravagantly. We read aloud the poetry of my adolescence: Frost, Eliot, E. E. Cummings. I resurrected some New Orleans–jazz records, my passion in college, and I remember standing in Liz's apartment, eyes closed, letting the formalized melancholy of the blues — and my youth — wash through me.

Occasionally we went for weekends to Syosset when Liz had her boys. I remember driving out, listening to Meredith, kneeling to the rear on the front seat, talk to the other three lying on the back-seat platform. Seemingly oblivious to our ears, they were comparing notes on single fathers.

Helena said, "Dads always think fathers know best."

"Yeah," Meredith said, "When Dad dresses us, he sits there and says, 'You should put on this and this and this,' and it's always like green and orange, a big clash."

Christopher said, "That's what I hate — when your father makes you get something and you don't really like it."

Ned said, "Dad makes us work around the house."

"It's the same with our dad," Helena said. "He says, 'Everybody has to do their little bit.' Do you know how many errands I did yesterday?"

"Who cares," Ned said.

"Fathers are strict," Christopher said. "It's rules, rules, rules."

"I don't stick to ours," Meredith said, "but Helena does cuz she's Miss Merry Muffit."

"Shut up," said Helena.

Meredith said, "I could yell at Mommy, and she wouldn't do a thing. I yell at Liz, too, but not at Dad. I'd get whacked."

"Don't yell at my Mommy," Ned said. "If you do, you'll be in big trouble."

Helena said, "With just a father, you get all the attention. If there are two parents, they're upstairs talking and stuff, and you don't know what's going on."

"Or they're going out," Ned added.

"But, with one parent, you can't play four-way tennis," Christopher said.

Ned said, "When you rip something, a father is no good at sewing."

"Our dad cooks differently than my mom used to," Meredith

said. "You wake up on a weekend, and you have a three-day bellyache."

"My father cooks anything," Ned said.

Meredith answered, "You've got a gourmet father. All we've got is one man."

By March, though still subject to unpredictable emotions, rushes of tears, numbness, attacks of pensiveness and loneliness, I was feeling on balance better, with more of a grip on life and self. With Liz's help, I felt able to tackle the task of sorting, weeding, and filing Hope's art work. I was astounded at the size and artistic breadth of her accomplishment. I was sad that she had had doubts about it. Now, too, with help from Whitney and Liz, I was able to sort and pack away Hope's clothes, still there in her armoire and bureau. To contain the poignancy, the three of us joked about the amazing changes in styles, about Hope's obsession with Marimekko dresses. "If Hope had been cremated," Whitney said, "we could have scattered her ashes at Design Research."

A few days later I drove to Washington, D.C., on business, taking a quantity of Hope's clothes to my sister-in-law to use or distribute. All this time an equal quantity of Josie's clothes had been in my basement, awaiting delivery to her sister-in-law in Washington, Holly Mankiewicz. With an ache in my chest, I tied the large, matching, rectangular boxes side by side on the rack on top of the car. The twin catastrophes of Hope and Josie had come down to two cardboard coffins on an old green Ford.

Twelve

The first easing of grief is like frost going out of the ground. It happens almost invisibly until suddenly symptoms of recovery break through to the surface. Feeling these stirrings in myself, I watched the girls for signs of change, but Meredith remained congealed and Helena's attacks of "the blues" and her memory daydreams continued unabated.

As I grew a bit stronger and braver, I sometimes dwelt on thoughts of Hope. One night I dreamed about her in brilliant color coming out the back door at Dublin, and I thought, "So that's what she looked like." Then, a friend who dated back to my courtship of Hope in Los Angeles, Frank Pierson, came east with his fiancée, Dori Derfner. Liz Hauser and I had them to dinner. Triggered by a person who did not know Hope, I found myself talking compulsively about her art, her books, her courage, the might-have-beens. I can remember Frank's and Dori's friendly, fixed smiles, the sympathetic nods of their heads, their glances at Liz to see how she was taking it. Liz sat concealing her self-consciousness, adding a word about Hope from time to time to prove she did not mind. Swept along by a wonderful feeling of release and satisfaction, I thought, "I don't care if they're embarrassed. This is therapy." All that spring of 1976, looking into stiffly polite faces, I overtalked about Hope.

At the same time I was thinking more about the future, admitting that there would be one, that it could be good. I began to be less dependent on Liz's company and encouragement, as though I had climbed up over the edge of the world and were standing there in the open, blinking, looking around. I was taking in the possibilities of a universe that had no connection with Hope — new friends, new women, a new life. Perhaps it was the season of such thoughts. About then Helena, obviously after deep reflection, told me, "When you get married, I want it to be somebody brand-new, who never knew Mommy."

In early April my tenant vacated, and I took the job of sanding and refinishing the apartment floors. I was at work, filthy, sweaty, when the door buzzer sounded. Standing a little nervously at the stoop was Elizabeth Atherton, the poet who had been brought to the house the previous fall by our Dublin friend. She said she was in the neighborhood and on an impulse had stopped by to see how I was. I was glad to see her; she had made an impression on me. I brought her into the living room, and we asked each other about our new lives. She was established now in her SoHo loft, focused for the first time entirely on her poetry and excited with her life. I said that I was tremendously grateful Hope had died at home, that I was better now and writing; but, I added, "Mourning is like walking through molasses with your shoes sticking at every step."

Elizabeth Atherton was as I remembered her: in her forties, pretty with pink cheeks and light-brown hair a little out of control, stimulating, dazzlingly verbal, with a clear voice and a spirited mind. When a week later she asked me to a dinner party at her loft, I accepted — and experienced the shock of my first step outside the cotton cocoon of family, devoted friends, and special treatment.

I discovered that in a wholly new world of strangers I was like a cardboard cutout, with no depth of shared experience and knowledge and affection — no social equity. I sat silent, and when I did speak, the unfamiliar faces of the other guests, turning toward me in sudden silence, were frightening. At dinner they played a punning game based on famous names. I was paralyzed. Then, long after the game was past I startled even myself by blurting out, "While Virginia Woolfs, Edvard Munches."

But I was now launched on that time in the second phase when you are ready to begin the foundation of your future. I sensed that the key to the process was discovering the essential me, looking at my past to decide what was primary, what should be kept or discarded. And I had to discover what kind of woman I wanted to fill out—and thereby shape—my life.

Elizabeth Atherton soon became a force to this end, rattling my assumptions, shaking my perspectives, breaking open my past, and forcing on me fundamental choices that defined my vision of the future—the reappraisal which the bereaved sometimes seeks with a psychologist or psychiatrist. At her core was a compulsion to analyze, and whatever I did was given psychological significance—like the evening I came out of the subway and walked away from the restaurant where we were meeting (I had forgotten where it was), and then *ran* back to it and to her (I was late).

She started out, however, as a second romantic fling. This was my time, I thought, to be a bachelor and play the field. I wanted to test my powers on this smart, pretty woman, and prove again that I was attractive and desirable—a need that stretched deep into my past. I felt I was entitled to a time of irresponsibility.

As I once told Elizabeth, "Widowers are bad news."

When I invited her to lunch, I realized how drastic a break with my past she represented. She had written two privately published books of poetry, had undergone analysis, and had steeped herself in that literature. She was, as she put it, "trying to be honest with myself and be open to people and free from the 'oughts' and 'shoulds' we swallowed whole when we were children." She said, "Roots and the comfort of your old grooves are a handicap."

I was strongly drawn to this woman who was so different from any I had known — from Hope, all sweetness and covered-up intensity; from Liz Hauser, all instincts and uncomplicated enthusiasm. Elizabeth Atherton was a tonic, exciting and alive, her questing mind spinning off energy and ideas and language like a Fourth of July pinwheel. She turned a Maine fisherman's catch of three hundred mackerel into the image of "a balsam dropped over the side of the boat, each twig loaded with a tiny frenzy of bait, and then pulled back into the boat — a Christmas tree trimmed with silver mackerel." When she talked about her poetry, she said, "A poem begins when a thread appears as though from a closed ball. I pull the thread out very slowly and carefully, so it can all appear before I analyze it, which immediately breaks the thread."

One evening I took her to dinner and she took me to the opera, and in the restaurant I talked about my grief and she seemed to understand exactly. "Crying is a river," she said, "which carries away the pain and if you put the tears under a microscope, you would find tiny little pieces of fear, regret, guilt, sorrow." I felt the gears of our thoughts and our laughter connecting and spinning us onward, and she remembered later, "Our minds burrowed into each other, never coming to a gate which did not yield." During the opera I put my hand over hers on the arm of the seat, and on the way home told her that my daughters did not want me to marry anybody who had known Hope or been part of my past life. Looking back, she said afterwards, "I knew it was *much* too quick to be having such warm feelings. It was as though we were already beginning to have a love affair, and there was nothing I could do about it."

Meredith and Helena were also intrigued by Elizabeth Atherton, attracted by her talent for listening to them as equals, by the free child that lived in her. We played hide-and-seek in her loft, and she and the girls hid from me like mice under a huge down comforter — and when I found them I crawled under it, tickling them all. We went together to a portable amusement park squeezed into a church parking lot, and on the way had a footrace. The four of us went to the Statue of Liberty, and on the ferryboat I permanently shocked Elizabeth by blackly joking, "Maybe Mere and Henny will fall overboard and my problems will be solved."

On a spring Sunday I drove with the girls to Elizabeth's house in Garrison, New York, and while I did some work, the three lay together in a huge hammock. The girls began to test her. Watching Elizabeth's face, Helena told a child's dirty joke about a girl and three boys named Tom, Dick, and Harry, all the more delicious because it included my name and my brother's. Meredith told the sex lore received from our tenant's thirteen-year-old daughter, as though checking to see if it was true. And then some barrier broke. Meredith began pouring out to this sympathetic adult her little girl's fears that her breasts would suddenly appear full-grown, and that her period would come and there would be nobody to go to and she didn't want to go to Daddy.

A few hours later, acting out the dizzying permutations in the daughter-father relationship, Meredith was playing the ageless flirt. The four of us climbed through the adjacent woods to a high pond. On the way back Meredith taunted me and I chased her till she flung herself, at bay, on a huge flat rock. I put my hands on each side of her laughing face and, baring my teeth monster-like, came down toward her neck. At the last second I kissed her forehead. I loved those moments with Meredith while there was still no barrier between us, her femininity not yet drawn like a secret into herself.

Sending the girls off to explore a stream, Elizabeth and I settled down on her porch to talk. Soon they returned and wheedled me into fixing a swing they had found. Reluctant, dutiful, I stood up, joking about being my daughters' slave. When the swing was safe, they begged me to push them and I did, returning to Elizabeth with a sense of virtue. I had proved again that they could count on me. She immediately punctured my self-satisfaction. "You are like their puppet," she said. "The minute the girls say anything, you *jump*—as if I didn't exist. They need to learn that the adult world has its own validity and they are not the center of the world all the time." She reminded me of a day on the street when I interrupted our talk to catch a ball tossed by Helena and it had become a game and the conversation was abandoned. I thought to myself, "You really do not understand." But I was attracted by her even more. I knew that her comments came from an essential kindness, that they were her way of helping. And I wanted challenges that might jostle and expand me. I wanted to turn Hope's tragedy into an opportunity. I wanted to rebuild with alterations. I did *not* want to drift into a future formed by happenstance.

A few days later Elizabeth told me she had visualized a doorway and placed in it, one by one, each single man she knew. "When you appeared," she recounted, a trace of astonishment in her voice, "I realized I loved Dick Meryman. This is a human being I *love*." My reaction was to feel like the irresistible male—a high-octane fantasy. With conviction and tenderness I told her that we were unique together. She put her arms around me and said, "I can't believe this is real." I held her in return, saying, "But it is."

Now I was involved with two women—in actual fact with three. Liz Hauser knew I was seeing another woman. Elizabeth Atherton knew only that a friend of Hope's was helping me and the children. Liz continued to come regularly to the house, consoling, companioning, mingling my past and present. I was happily comfortable with her, taking her among my friends, even teaching her to ski. She was a kind of wife. Elizabeth, arriving fresh and whole over the horizon, was freedom personified. I treated her like a mistress, charging myself up for her, keeping her away from my friends and thereby keeping myself away from the pressure of their judgment. So I kept the two Elizabeths in hermetic compartments, just below my consciousness. But the presence of Hope was all pervasive. And there were also Meredith and Helena, my two additional

· *215* ·

females, absorbing my sympathies and my time, inhibiting like Hope any attachment to a new woman. How I worked out these powerful and opposing pulls would be a measure of my survival.

It was a paradox of my mourning cure that the more I faced the future, the more my past became obsessively alive. Recollection, once stimulated, reached beyond Hope and our marriage back into childhood. This became, month after month, a long and self-inflicted progress report on my life, a study of the past for guides to the future. And in June I plunged myself and the girls into the past, an important step in our mourning process. We returned for the first time alone to Hope's roots, to the scene of my courtship and our annual visits, and to the place I had spent every other summer as a boy. We stayed two weeks in California in my mother's empty beach cottage near the Brooks ranch and Hope's brother Bobby and sister Ky. The trip was also my first extended period of solo childcare. To solve the problem of two rambunctious girls out of school, I hoped to get free time to work by surrounding us with their cousins and helpful aunts. But more important, I wanted impressions of Hope, echoed by her brother and sisters, kept green in the girls' minds.

Before we left I had an intimation of the triangular war of nerves that lay ahead. Laura announced to me that Meredith and Helena needed dresses for the trip and for parties and dances that summer in Dublin. Everything was too small. I protested, "What about the dresses they wore to the memorial service? They looked terrific."

She told me, "Dick, it's all they have and they need more. Accept it. Your daughters are growing up. You've got two *girls*."

"How can I be sure?" I joked. "All they ever wear are pants and T-shirts. I thought they were the sons I always wanted."

We planned a shopping trip on the next Saturday, but at the last minute Laura could not go and I had *promised*. So I found myself alone with Meredith and Helena in the preteen shop of Macy's, surrounded by an archipelago of circular racks and seemingly thousands of dresses. Helena, like me, stood bewildered. I bravely started looking and I held one up to her. I liked it — appropriately short, a little lace at the throat, puffed sleeves.

She said, her voice dripping with disgust, "Come on, Dad, that's a *party* dress. You know, patent-leather pumps."

Abashed, I tried to recover with humor. "Pumps? That's what people wear for water on the knee." Helena's disgust deepened. I said defensively, "You used to think my jokes were funny."

"I'm older now," she answered, "and less tolerant."

"Okay, wise apple, find yourself a dress," I said, and turned my attention to Meredith, who had come out of the changing room in a slinky jersey number. She was now striking a pose in front of a mirror, hand on hip, *very* pleased with herself and undeterred by the knobby, narrow expanse of chest exposed in the low neckline, by hips marked only with two bumps of bone, and by the scarlet Adidas on her feet.

"Mere, it's too old for you," I said.

"No, Daddy, I really, really want it. Please, please, please. I'll wear it; you'll see. It's what I need for the dances this summer."

Hoping to cut off the discussion and spare us a scene, I caused one. I said, "You look like skinny Minnie."

"I do *not!*" she wailed.

We made an irritable progression through the teen department and the sport department. I remember Helena in a dress that made her look like a fireplug, and a thin saleslady with hair the color and rigidity of steel saying, "You look beautiful, honey" — and Helena, stricken, too polite to say anything to her, looking at me, silently pleading for help. I remember bringing my own offerings — plain dresses, frilly dresses, short, long, bright, dull — and receiving choruses of rejection. "Are you serious?" "That's dumb." When I held up one dress, Meredith said, "Sears Roebuck, page fifty-two." I remember my feet hurting and a wave of exhaustion and sinking down into a chair and turning off. Of course, that was when they found what they wanted — two simple cotton sundresses with ties at the shoulders and a tiny flower pattern. "Fine," I said, ready by then to accept even beads and boas.

In California I worked almost every morning, often leaving very early for interviews in Los Angeles for my Mankiewicz book. Normally I would not have left a ten-year-old (almost eleven) and an eight-year-old alone. But I found it impossible to find temporary help. The mothers I knew offered names of a few girls, but they either had summer jobs or required time-consuming pickup and return. Professional child care, hired through an agency, meant middle-aged or elderly women charging prohibitive rates. I decided that this trip was a good time for self-reliance.

The children got their own breakfasts, and under the threat of a stern ". . . or else," made their beds. Meredith efficiently put our dirty clothes through the washer and hung them out with Helena's reluctant help. Sometimes Ky or Bobby's wife, Kathy, took them away for the morning; sometimes they entertained themselves. I usually returned in time to eat lunch and to bawl them out for the messy house. I was guiltily aware of how indifferent the girls could be to the most elementary responsibilities — like closing the refrigerator door — and how skillful they were at clouding the issue, diverting blame, and wearing me down with arguing.

The third time I found the refrigerator open — after two warnings — I told Meredith I was going to punish her. She said angrily, "But, Daddy, I stood there this morning and shut it, and it opened again. I can't help it if that stupid, idiotic . . ."

I said, "It doesn't open by itself. You've got to stand there and shut it carefully. Understand that, Henny?"

"I didn't get anything," Helena said.

"Yes, you did," I said triumphantly. "Orange juice."

"Yeah, but that was before you had toast." I gave up.

I had looked forward to the trip as a time of intermission and relief, no miring machinery of daily life, no schoolwork, and especially no new women — a time for the best of single parenthood, when I could be, undiluted, the girls' father. I saw the time as an affirmation of the three of us as a family unit, whole and together. That did happen, more or less, but my sentimental fantasy had not reckoned with the gut dynamics of our three-cornered, father-daughter relationship.

After lunch, when the tide was low, we sometimes walked out on the wet rocks at the foot of the beach. I showed the girls how to stick their fingers into the sea anemones in the tiny tidal pools, and they said, "Yucky," and raced from one to another, and watched the little red crabs skitter behind pebbles and make a stand, claws at the ready, miniature menace.

Helena kept her soft hand in mine as we explored the pools, but Meredith stayed eight to ten feet away, cutting herself off, only coming close to see a new discovery. When I tried to free myself and go to her, Helena instantly said, "Daddy, hold my hand." Then I did escape and went to Meredith's rock and we pretended to push each other into the water, giggling, clutching each other. Suddenly Helena was on the rock, pushing Meredith away and saying to me, "C'mon." Meredith competed for a few seconds, then moved away. With Helena clutching me again, I went toward Meredith, but she kept her distance. Instinctively, perhaps genetically, Helena knew how to get affection, even fight for it. It is a skill, a technique like any other, like playing tennis. Poor Meredith, her distancing from us, a cry for help, usually hit the net.

We went to the Brooks ranch, and found Hope's mother in a wheelchair parked in a patch of sun on the rear patio. She now had cancer too and had deteriorated badly, her hair thin, her white face wasted. I said in a loud, cheery voice, "It's Dick, Hopie's husband, and these are Hopie's girls, Meredith and Helena." With forced, nervous smiles they came forward, and Mrs. Brooks touched each one and said in a tremulous voice with tears in her eyes, "They've grown so much I don't know them." Just before we left, in a voice so frail I had to bend close, she said, "I think of Hopie all the time. Whoever did that . . ."

On the way out I noticed Meredith in the living room studying

Hope's picture in the Connecticut College yearbook. "Even if I didn't know her," she said, "I'd think she was the most beautiful."

"Mommy was always the most beautiful woman everywhere," I said, "but she never thought of herself as beautiful." As we left I paused in the hall. The shaft of sun was moving imperceptibly across the floor as it had through all those years, and I looked back at Mrs. Brooks. From behind, with her scalp shiny through the wispy hair, she looked like Hopie.

Often we went to Ky's house for dinner and sometimes Bobby and Kathy were there. The evenings were laughing and fun and affectionate, but also it was like skating on transparent black ice and looking down to the bottom at the symbols of loss. I was back in the Hope part of my life. I liked it there. I wanted her alive. I did not want a new wife.

I knew that it was necessary and actually beneficial to come back and reawaken such feelings. Helena, with no such understanding, had to take her anguish straight. Even so, she began to show signs of recovery. Though still longing for her mother, she was now looking for a way out of her pain, and that put her in a *Catch 22* dilemma. If she got better, she would think less constantly about Hope. But that, she guiltily believed, would be a betrayal of her mother. One night, while I sat by the head of her bed, the surf pounding on the beach outside the louvered windows, Helena said, "Everything seems sort of black. Nothing matters. I hate it."

"I know. I cried a little in church on Sunday. But nothing's going to bring Mommy back, and we've got to go ahead and live our lives."

"You don't understand."

"Try to make me understand," I said, feeling Helena's awful sense of isolation.

"I don't know the words. I just don't always want to feel I have to be sad."

"Let me try. You feel that if you're not sad, it means you don't love Mommy."

"Sort of."

"Henny, Mommy will understand. She knows how much you'll always love her, and she *wants* you to be *happy,* not all worried. You can still make a wonderful life for yourself, even though you miss her. In mourning, time is the great healer and eventually loving thoughts for Mommy will be happy ones, not just sad ones, I promise. Now, how can we break your mood?"

"I know what I'd like."

"What?"

"A drink of beer. And Big Teddy would too."

This trip, also a return to my own roots before Hope, brought back the "oughts" and "shoulds" I had accepted in my own childhood. On the mesa above the beach was the low, Spanish-style house of my revered eighty-eight-year-old Uncle Bob, where throughout my boyhood the family spent alternate summers. We paid a call on him, the familiar collection of my father's paintings filling the walls in the house. Uncle Bob on crutches, beaming, dressed in layers of shirts and sweaters against the permanent chill of old age, was prepared to entertain the children. On his hand was a cloth puppet and he held it toward the picture on Helena's T-shirt. Opening and closing the puppet's mouth, he said in a high voice, "What's that?" The game was too young for the girls, but "Great-uncle Bob" was important to them; they appreciated him. Helena smiled and said, "It's a rock-and-roll record cover" — an icon of a faraway culture. Undismayed, he looked at Meredith and Helena and said, "What fine young girls."

He was a reminder of the strength and endurance that lay in his old-time "oughts" and "shoulds" — and of my responsibility to bring up Meredith and Helena as "fine young girls." Walking back, Meredith was ahead of me, her legs newly long like spring growth on her little girl's body. My heart ached with love and concern — the feeling of her at the threshold of a troubled or a splendid future. Some year soon Meredith's body would make its transition into womanhood. Who would be her guide through that dramatic change? How could I ever instruct her and Helena in femininity—how to dress, how to talk, how simply to be? Where would they find a model of the complex dynamics between a man and a woman? They were no longer witnessing the tender and the angry extremities of marriage, learning that love survives strife and is actually solidified by the right kind of confrontation—by being vulnerable to each other and taking the risks that keep a relationship alive.

I had fleetingly wondered about marrying again as soon as possible for the crassest reason—to get a woman and role model into the house for the children, and to get that decision behind me and my life organized. Many widowers do exactly that. But marriage before the children and I were purged of Hope would cut our mourning short and risk quadrupling every problem in my life. I knew I still had miles to go in the Ritual.

We left California in high spirits and moved on from New York to Dublin. It seemed an ideal place for single parenthood during the girls' summer vacation. A small swimming and tennis club, where the children needed no supervision, was the center of activity.

Laura, as scheduled, had moved to Maine in June, and before going to California I had hired a summer girl to divide her time between child care for me and housework and shopping for my eighty-year-old mother, who had asked for help. "I know what the expression 'mellowed with age' means," said my mother. "It means you just want to be able to stand on your feet." A medium-sized, white-haired, energetic woman of kindness, lively eyes, and wry jokes, she had committed her life to being a wife and mother, and had made a science out of practicality. Indomitable, she had had artificial sockets implanted in both hips, and when the doctor asked if she had been walking a half mile a day, she answered, "Yes—following people around and telling them what to do." In describing her once, Hope said, "She's a classic." At dinner, she would tell the girls stories about her past and my childhood. Occasionally she talked about their mother. "If anybody meets me at the pearly gates," she said, "it will be Hopie, who has dropped something of her own to do it." Watching my mother—such an echo of her brother, Uncle Bob—I realized that her "oughts" and "shoulds" had helped me through Hope's death. I thought how much I loved her, how grateful I was, how much of me I liked I owed to her.

The name of the girl I hired was Jane—soon in my mind "Poor Jane." She was a mother's helper for friends of friends in Maryland. When I interviewed her, she said she loved children so much she planned to be a teacher or run a nursery school. When I asked about skills—art, horseback riding, sewing—she flashed a radiant smile and admitted to being accomplished at all three. But we soon discovered she had oversold herself. She was a person who could not remember and follow directions, who never quite finished any chore, who vanished frequently on cigarette breaks. For the children, the contrast with Laura was devastating. Jane lacked the gift of fun, and the children gave her neither friendship nor obedience. While flunking her daily duties, Jane badgered me about grandiose projects—a huge treehouse with a roof, a dam over a tiny stream in the woods to make a pond. Instead of a helper, I had hired a third child.

But we could not have managed the summer without her. A single parent must have *somebody* to keep the machinery running, no matter how minimally. On the last lap of my book, I was working long hours, seven days a week, away from the house in a quiet room lent by a friend. When I left each morning, the primary authority departed. My mother, all her life equal to anything (she had even designed the beach house by herself), now suffered the anxieties of age and needed order and predictability. So each morning there was an elaborate session to give permissions and plan pickups and deliveries. But children of eight and ten live lives of constant emergency, and every day those telephone calls came to my mother: "I forgot my tennis racket, can Jane bring it down?" "I fell out of a sailboat and I need dry clothes." "I've been invited to Melora's house to ride the ponies and can Jane take me?"

I would return in the evening to be the focus of every need, to referee, to sympathize — to hear Helena tell me that Meredith was taking away her one friend, to hear my mother tell me that Jane had moved my bureau into Helena's room. I needed my already depleted energies to write, and they were being siphoned away. I felt trapped. There was nobody else to fill the roles of manager, counselor, disciplinarian, breadwinner, pal — and I still believed they all *had* to be filled, an attitude which bordered on self-indulgence. I was even trying to be a teacher. Meredith's school had encouraged me to tutor her in reading. It was agony for both of us. During a season in early July she told me through her tears, "Every time I see you, I think of the reading and I hate you. When somebody says 'father,' I think of it and I hate you. And I hate feeling that way." I gave up the tutoring. It is impossible for a single parent to fill every role; if he attempts it, nothing gets done adequately. I was poisoning my relationship with Meredith, the most important thing of all.

Occasionally I took a day off for a special event. One was the little local horse show, where I stood in terror as Meredith, like a mosquito on the back of a huge, snorting beast, flew through the air over towering jumps and won a blue ribbon. Another was her tenth birthday in mid-July. Some dozen girls, aged ten to thirteen, assembled at the corner of the porch. In the sunlight dappled by the vines it was a decorous tableau of imminent young ladies. Meredith gracefully opened her presents and graciously made her thanks. Then the true selves began leaking through the seams of their poise. Fathers are wonderful party givers; they let you eat nothing but cake, ice cream, and Coca-Cola — and at the large table on the porch the young ladies began gorging, giggling, laughing, screaming. There was a relay race carrying eggs in spoons, and Meredith's partner, Melora, dropped their egg so Meredith "smooshed" it in Melora's hair and Melora smooshed her back. Now came my special contribution — water pistols for all. The damsels became dervishes, stalking, ganging up, screaming — three of them soaking me while I cringed and laughed and fired back. As the pandemonium declined to gasping breathlessness, Meredith called out, "Let's go skinny-dipping." Everybody looked at me. I did not blush. "Last one in is a rotten egg!" I shouted, sitting down. Away they ran, fanning out across the field below the house.

Elizabeth Atherton was now, herself, away in California, and from time to time that summer Liz Hauser came up from New York for brief visits. I was very glad to see her, if only because she brought an interlude of stability to the household. But I was also embarrassed and panicky. So far, for my emotional convenience, I had approached my relationship with Liz as though she existed in a vacuum, affecting nobody, not even herself — as though she were some Venus, created especially for me from the foam of the sea, who would dematerialize when my need for romance and comfort was finished. However, before California, Whitney had said, her voice worried, "I think Liz is wonderful, but I want to be sure you're getting involved in something you really want." And Helena, the voice of reality, had said, "Sometimes I cry after you kiss me good night, but I can't come up because Liz is there." And then, while I was in California, Liz wrote me a series of tender letters and I was very pleased and moved, and answered in kind. But I was also saddened and scared.

I longed to go beyond tenderness to romantic love, full of fire. But I wondered whether after a marriage and a death, an all-consuming passion would ever be possible. *Certainly* not yet. So I was appalled that both Elizabeths had centered their hopes for love on so weak a reed as I. Knowing I had systematically made it happen, that I had used these two valuable women, I was besieged by guilt that summer. And perversely I still listened to other women friends who counseled me not to be squeamish, to play the field. One said, "It's true. Nobody ever died of a broken heart." Another joked, "If my husband died, I'd go right out and find a sailor, two if possible."

I negotiated a deal with my pliant conscience. My connection with Elizabeth Atherton was intense, but it was new and uncertain, with no debts amassed. My obligation to Elizabeth Hauser was enormous. Our involvement had been on many levels during a climactic and binding stretch of time. I owed her an accounting.

On a moonlit night in Dublin, we walked down to the lake and sat on the end of a jetty. In this idyllic, romantic setting we talked about our relationship. I told her I felt trapped, boxed in. I explained that I was now coming back to reality after a long period of emotional insanity. I said that love and commitment to one woman were not yet possible. I had to finish mourning and experience a full taste of bachelorhood. "If I don't," I said, "I'll never be able to settle down."

But I wanted it both ways—both Elizabeths. I told Liz, "I really care about you. Please bear with me." We talked about the risks, hers of getting hurt, mine of losing her, and we agreed that the most precious prizes require the biggest risks. I succeeded. I kept her on a string. As she put it later, "I stayed and I hated it."

Liz understood that she was being manipulated. She knew my capacity for sincerity was narrow and my truth was only true at that given moment. She was frightened that she had been hooked by my desperate need for help, that when I was recovered the relationship might be empty. But she was also afraid of missing what she felt was a chance for self-fulfillment. She recognized her own post-divorce mourning period in me, and knew where I would emerge in a year. Believing that there was a deep and genuine connection between us, she wanted that string in place. But as we left the lake, Liz stood looking wistfully out along the path of moonlight on the calm water. "Let's follow it till morning," she said.

Having calmed by conscience with Liz Hauser, I felt free to arrange a weekend in August with Elizabeth Atherton. She was now in Quebec and agreed on her way home to spend a day with me in Boston and two more in Dublin. We stayed together in the plastic paradise of a Boston Holiday Inn, and though we ate and toured, essentially it was an orgy of conversation, a deep connection with a person exquisitely tuned to me. We sat together on a bench in the eighteenth-century room of the Boston Museum of Fine Arts, pretending we were characters in a play set in that century, and as the twentieth-century people wandered, oblivious, through the gallery, we assigned them roles and took their parts in our improvised dialogue.

Boston was another of those chambers hollowed out of reality, and then we drove to Dublin and into the heart of my formative past. I gave her a tour of the house and showed off my father's paintings and told her what the place meant to me. But I remember best my laughter at some joke we shared — laughter released full out, unconfined, till I hurt, "as though," said Elizabeth, "a volcanic rock had split and from a subterranean depth gushed this living water."

When she met my mother the next morning, I was surprised that Elizabeth seemed palpably nervous and off balance, unable to find a self that fitted. She told me afterwards, "I think we were two women of the same nature — neither of us was going to be dominated. Eventually she respected me, but the minute we laid eyes on each other, we became worthy enemies." By agreement, I worked that day and built a fire for Elizabeth in the living room, where she spent much of the day with the book on Andrew Wyeth's painting, for which I had written the text. My mother stayed in her customary rounds of bedroom and kitchen. Only the next day did the two women find a common ground — their disapproval of me when after lunch I excused the children and cleared the table myself. Though Elizabeth then did make brief contact with my mother before departing that afternoon, I was left with a strong sense of somebody who considered my origins constricting and stunting, and alien territory.

I returned to New York that fall with the exhilarating knowledge that I had solved my father's-helper problem. After the Jane debacle, two options had emerged: an educated girl in her twenties, like Laura, who wanted only a winter of part-time work, or an older, semipermanent housekeeper of modest education and background.

I realized that a mature woman would consider herself a surrogate mother. There seemed little chance of finding an available woman with the requisite education, abilities, and attitudes. Nor did I think that a full-time servant in the house would be good for Meredith and Helena even if I could afford one. Salaries often exceeded two hundred dollars a week, plus room and board. The heavy housework could continue to be done by help coming in one day a week. Unique Gertrude, a virtual member of the family, was already handling the laundry and sewing, and cooking two dinners. A part-time girl, hired one school year at a time, would give me an annual chance to assess and perhaps change the agreement. And to fill the void left by Hope, I needed the intangibles of a surrogate big sister — vitality, spirit, sturdy nerves, the ability to help with homework, and youthful empathy. By using Hope's former studio, I would be able to offer board and room, which might be very attractive to a student on a limited budget.

I broadcast the job description throughout the mother-friend network and in August Joan Rivers offered me her *au pair*, Susan Dumois, a Californian who was leaving to live in New York and get a degree in education. Susan knew the children, liked them, and they her. She agreed to work half-time, like Laura from three to seven, for sixty dollars a week, and to live in the house. A pretty, very conscientious twenty-six-year-old with a gift for instant friendship, Susan was a curious mix of intense seriousness and whimsical gaiety, and I conceived of her as a reincarnated tooth fairy with intellectual aspirations. She fitted into Laura's place without a ripple. Soon she was initiating another camping sleepout in the dining room, this time with a blue brook running by — made of toilet paper.

In New York that fall of 1976, Helena's mood was what my father called an "in-and-out day" — the sun appeared and then was periodically shut off by ranks of clouds. Meredith seemed more relaxed, starting school with a better attitude, and Susan, going to college in the mornings, was ideal for homework. My emotions were becoming steadier, my light moments more frequent, my reactions more rational. But paradoxically, because I was moving ahead, I was confronted with a formidable and crucial hurdle in the Ritual, the culmination of my "obsessional review."

The mourning process is partly external. Its physical tasks became mile markers promising progress—"When that's done, I'll feel better." So the presence of Hope's untouched studio, the heart of her nest, hindered my recovery. With a massive effort of will I sat at her worktable going through bags and boxes of mementos—a library card from Chicago, notes from widows thanking her for condolence letters, ancient programs ("Sonja Henie, Unchallenged Queen of the Ice, in Her Hollywood Ice Revue"), an old note from Helena ("To mom I love you in fact I love you so much I could die mom"). There were two pressed flowers from our wedding and letters from Hope to me ("I love you more than I ever did at first") and an early poem from me to Hope (". . . though you have decorated my heart with love . . ."). And there were my later letters of conflict ("Somehow we must shovel the peaks of love into the valleys so that these awful angers can be covered up by love").

In sorting this flotsam diary, I had two revelations: how irrevocably intertwined Hope and I had been, and how we had longed for a more overt and romantic form of tenderness. Why had Hope and I withheld it from each other? I thought perhaps it had to do with dependence. Hope needed me to take care of her. But she blamed me for that subtle loss of independence. I was afraid of Hope's temper and feared she might stop loving me, so I needed to protect her, to solve her problems, to make her life run smoothly. That was my subtle form of dependency, which I resented. During her illness, when her dependence was valid, we were never closer.

My obsessional review had been coming in surges all that spring and summer. Now it peaked and I was inundated by "what-ifs," some of which had been hammering at me since Hope first fell sick. Did my behavior early in our marriage kill some central tenderness, create some permanent fear and resentment? Suppose I had lavished romantic affection on her, would Hope have responded? Left to herself, would Hope have shown her mole to a doctor in France? If she had, would she now be lying in that bed reading her newspaper, instead of lying in that box in Pennsylvania? Did I kill Hope?

Such awful questions can never be answered, only worn out. Brutal hindsight and ransacking your guilt, admitting that your marriage was not sublime, that your love and loved one were not perfect, are very painful. But mourning is a process of slow assimilation: examining over and over from every point of view all the aspects of the marriage and the illness, exorcising the self-hate, making peace with the memories, and finally, shutting down the past by exhausting it.

Knowing more than ever the possibilities of both happiness and misery, surrounded by failed marriages among my friends and acquaintances, I wanted what I had had with Hope and even more. I wanted to preserve the best and not repeat my mistakes. But does one wait, perhaps indefinitely, for a burning and undeniable love? Or does one think in terms of words like affection, compatibility, sympathy, admiration, equality, fun? Do these qualities add up to a truer love, which grows and deepens only after marriage? Or does married love still need an irrational catalyst, a sublime trigger?

A widower soon feels he is a hot item on the marriage market. I was told, "You are a widower at your own risk." My friend Ed Kern said to me, "You're catnip." The women a widower meets are often further down the road to recovery and looking for permanence, a nest, while I suspect that many a newly bereaved man is simply looking for sex — to see if he can succeed, to restore his ego, to satisfy his physical needs. But powerful sex can derail a quest for love, bringing a relationship into his life stillborn. It can destroy perspective, cause illusory intimacy, create a courtship context long before he is ready. It brings an element of possession — "my man," "my woman." Then expectations and intensity are heightened; on some level each one has invited the other to fall in love. In friends' minds and faces there is that silent question: "Are they going to get married?" The new vocabulary of fun and release begins to include those words "obligation" and "betrayal."

Whenever I neared that invisible line past which lay commitment, I pulled back, withheld my emotions. When this happened with Elizabeth Atherton, she found psychological explanations — that I had "gone dead," that I was unable to love because of "a neurotic fear of intimacy." She told me, "You have internalized a mother who forbade you to feel and love, and you have been taught that safety lies in control, and control has become so important it has starved your feeling self." She began urging me to go to an analyst or join an encounter group. I rejected the idea.

The essence of mourning is gradualism, taking each step when you are ready and not before. I was still a convalescent, my gait still uncertain. I was surviving this catastrophe and felt heroic and unwilling to be shaken again to the marrow of my psyche. But whether right or wrong in her analysis, Elizabeth did me a great service. Though I recoiled, she crystallized the necessity to seek the central *me* and cultivate him in my new life. She herself, fascinating and frightening, like a furnace door flung open, was too hot a blast of change. I felt rushed, crowded, invaded by analysis. I felt she would sand and polish me until I fitted into *her* mold, into her radically different world and approach to life. I would be back where I was with Hope, living in the shadow of another woman's identity and talk.

During the winter of 1977 — the second since Hope's death — I made my choice. I stayed with the "oughts" and "shoulds," which Elizabeth believed had repressed me, which I believed had strengthened and nourished me. To have snapped my continuity with my roots would have been for me a double death. Our connection was still strong and Elizabeth's generosity extraordinary. For many months she had been an informal and invaluable editor of my Mankiewicz chapters. I wanted that to be the basis of a transition into friendship, and, trying to make each other understand, we had agonizing meetings which left both of us sad with a sense of failure and loss. But I knew now that Liz Hauser was what I wanted: unreserved warmth, her own restorative brand of excitement, her extraordinary faithfulness, her harmony with me and my roots. Even when we fought, our sympathy was like a bleacher seat from which we tolerantly watched our anger.

I remember a chilly fall Sunday afternoon. I built a fire in the rarely used living room. In front of it on the rug the four of us played a game of Yahtzee, with Liz shrieking, "I did it, I did it" when she rolled four of a kind, and Meredith saying, "Write it on that line." Then I read the Sunday paper, and Helena fetched two bears — Max and Antique Teddy — who needed medical attention. They lay on the operating table — the wooden coffee table — while Liz gently replaced their entrails and sewed up their wounds. As each was finished, Nurse Helena gave him a drink of water, wrapped him in a towel, and laid him lovingly in the recovery room, a supermarket cardboard box. All the while, Meredith played rock records and danced, watching her image in the tall pier mirror. Joined with the music she was for a moment unself-conscious, liquidly loose.

Later Helena said, "This was a great day." The connections had felt right to me, too. I wondered if that was the way it all began again — with a sense of rightness.

Thirteen

The complete mourning ritual, according to my reading and questioning, lasts a year and a half to two years. And there are no clear demarcations between the stages of mourning. Meredith, Helena, and I needed a year before we began the slow, slow turn into the third phase that winter of 1976–1977. If the first two phases are the times of surgical removal, the third is the recovery period, when you finally learn to live without the dead. The times of ease grow longer, and the sudden relapses into acute distress are fewer. Memories become increasingly welcome, almost sweet, and the awful details of illness and death become more and more distant — blurred and smoothed like the ravaged face of an actress photographed through gauze.

The first anniversary of Hope's death — Christmastime — came as a kind of litmus test of our progress. The countdown days to December twenty-second and Christmas were happy. Helena ceremonially presented me with her annual list addressed to Santa: "a cemistrey kit, hokey younaform (with pads), a desk with drows on top, lethar gloves." I would come home to the sight of Susan presiding at the dining-room table heaped with red and blue and green felt and gold string, two brown heads and one blond one bent over decorated Kleenex boxes and paper pads. One evening we each, myself included, made a tray of cookies. We used the cardboard patterns Hope had made for herself — an angel, a bear, a horse — and Meredith patiently showed me how — "See, Dad, you can't pull the knife through because it tears the dough." We gaudily decorated our cookies with colored sugar and silver balls and red hearts, and I undertook to bake Meredith's and mine. I burned them, and while Susan and Helena rolled their eyes heavenward and sighed, "Men," Meredith was magnanimous. "It's all right," she said, hugging me. "You're only a father."

But, as the twenty-second approached, while Meredith remained undecipherable, Helena again got "the blues." As before, she was unresponsive, negative, and announced, "I feel punk." When we discussed where to have Christmas, Helena voted with the rest of us to join Harry's family in Dublin, saying, "Harry gets the tree, and that helps us not think about not having Christmas at home without Mommy."

In Dublin, aside from occasional clutchings in the heart, I still felt no particular depression. I decided against any sort of observance on the twenty-second. I did not want to train the girls in special wallowings in grief. To me the loss was the same every day of the year.

On the day itself, however, I awoke despondent. To the two girls I said simply, "You know this is the day Mommy died." Helena was silent. Meredith said matter-of-factly, "I know." We soon lost ourselves in winter play outdoors, and I was surprised to realize that the hour of Hope's death had passed unnoticed. When Peter Davis telephoned and apologized for bothering me "on this day when you have so much on your mind," I was troubled that he expected me to be deep in grief. Was I being disloyal to Hope?

I decided instead that my peace meant recovery. Having kept to the mourning ritual and relived in endless ways our time with Hope, this ultimate memory was almost an anticlimax. I have since read that many bereaved suffer a phenomenon called the "anniversary reaction." Every year on the day of death the grief returns with its full, original force, often evidence that the mourning was incomplete, short-circuited.

Even the most successful mourning leaves a residual pool of anguish deep at the center, and there will always be those sudden instants that lance through to your grief and release it. I received a Christmas card from Hope's dearest girlhood friend, Helena Leigh-Hunt, who now lived in Paris. At the line, "I think of Hopie all the time," I put my face in my hands and began to sob. Her namesake, my Helena, reached a chubby arm around my shoulders and hugged me—wordless comfort from a little girl, awkward, completely womanly.

After Christmas the patterns of the fall continued into the winter. I think Meredith, burdened by a sense of rejection, faced the most difficult and complex task of mourning. She continued to be switched off, immersed in escape through play, allowing me only occasional clues to her feelings. Once, describing a TV program in a social studies paper, she wrote, "*Eight Is Enough* is when somebody dies and everybody sticks together because they are afraid they will lose somebody else." She still shied away from mentions of her mother, and I longed to have her release emotions in talk. One day I tried to create an opening. "Do you ever think about Mommy?" I asked.

"Sometimes I get a lump in my throat," Meredith answered.

"If you want to come to me then, I'd love to comfort you," I said.

"No, I like to be alone."

Helena was less clingy but still appeared sometimes at my bedside in the dark. Once, awakened, I said with irritation, "Don't say you can't sleep!" and she answered, "Okay, I can*not* sleep." When I returned from a short trip, I found on my telephone-answering machine Helena's voice saying, "I know you're not there, but I can pretend you're there, and I want to tell you . . ." Her mourning was seriously complicated by Liz Hauser's frequent presence in the house. For Meredith, who always welcomed another source of attention, Liz was an asset. To Helena she was an upsetting problem. One night, as I settled Helena in bed, she said, "I never get to be with you. You're with Liz all the time. It's like she's trying to take Mommy's place."

I answered, "Henny, I'm always there for you, and any time you need me, just call. I'm lonely without Mommy, like you, and Liz is somebody I really enjoy, and I think she brings a lot of cheer into the house, which we all need. Someday I will get married again, and I promise you I'll never marry anybody you don't like. And maybe someday soon Liz can be—"

"It isn't someday time yet," interrupted Helena.

Although there are no boundaries between the mourning phases, the girls and I had independent experiences that I now see as breakthroughs, or more precisely breakouts, marking a leap from survival into recovery. It was late in January that Sheila Harris called me to her bedside at Memorial Hospital to talk about Hope and me and survival. During that night Sheila passed into a coma, and after a few days, as George Harris put it, "she slipped away from us." The funeral was in Princeton, New Jersey. Inside the traditional, dark-paneled Episcopalian chapel, I sat with my eyes on Sheila's closed casket. I pictured her stretched out inside it, and then the image changed to Hope in her old doll dress, her red wig, her blanked-out glasses, with the battered saucepan, Helena's clay angel, and the BVM—her statue of the Virgin. After the service I returned to the car and wept and wept, pouring out a final torrent of pain and grief through an unsuspected floodgate.

About that same time some final dam also broke within Meredith and Helena. In talking to Susan about Hope, they suddenly began reliving the experience of their mother's death. They said they were mad at me for sending them away to Syosset, for not telling them immediately that Mommy had died. "It wasn't fair," said Meredith, and recollecting those days she said, "I was scared, but I didn't know what I was scared of." Helena remembered: "I was trying to have a nice time, I *was* having a nice time ice skating, but I felt way down that something wasn't right and I didn't know what." Holding on to Susan, the two girls wept their tears — until Meredith suddenly said, "Let's bake some cookies."

Now they could talk to me about Hope and death. One day in the car they began asking me why Mommy was not cremated, and how do you scatter the ashes?

"Do you wear gloves?" asked Helena.

Meredith said, "I think you should have made a double grave for you and Mommy."

"Yes," said Helena, "she wouldn't want to be next to a stranger."

They began speculating on what dying was like, and I told them about the experiences of people who had been medically dead and returned to life. Then Meredith asked if Mom knew she was going to die. I told her, "Yes," and Helena said, "If you'd told us, it would be like every time we were around her, we'd be in tears." Meredith asked how I knew Mom was dead, and I described Hope's last hours in detail. Helena wanted to know whether Mommy died with her eyes open — "really wide or just regular."

And then Meredith told me, "Once I looked a long time at that picture of Mommy on Henny's desk, and I just started to cry, and each time I see it I get a little lump in my throat. But, when I think about her, I really rack my brain cuz, when I put her out of my mind, I forgot all the things that went on."

In that second winter of recovery, I still felt like some patented stop-all compound, plugging hourly leaks in the household routines. There was a tearful, emergency appeal from Meredith about a headband she had borrowed for the basketball game that afternoon, and then the band had been taken away from her for somebody else, and "All the girls are being mean to me." I bought one at a sports store and took her out to a comforting lunch and later at the game watched Meredith, after three minutes, discard the headband.

But my mind was easing, and I was able to work long hours rewriting my book for the third time. Gertrude and Susan had the house running more smoothly, and my spirits lifted with the children's. Helena and Susan, the serious sprite, developed a game they called Mac's Bar and Grill. Helena set up a table with liquor bottles — and ginger ale — and they took turns playing customers. Sometimes Meredith joined in, slinking over like Mata Hari, a scarf flung dramatically about her neck. Helena would call out coarsely to Susan, "Ova heah, Mac. Da lady wants some booze."

Though I knew intellectually that Susan would not abandon me before June, I suffered from the widower's gut terror that this solution to my problems might vanish, impossible to replace. I also wanted Susan to return to me the next year and the next. Every time she got a serious boyfriend, I would think, "My God, she's not going to marry him, is she?" and I would unromantically applaud when they broke up. So, knowing that half-time jobs tend to drift into three-quarter jobs, I was careful to keep track of hours, and I would ask her, "Is it working out to half time? Do you feel imposed upon?"

Fortunately the girls and I went out of town almost every weekend that winter. There was escapism in so much motion, but mainly there was a zest in rejoining the main current of life and distancing ourselves from death and grief. I remember my sense of gratitude the first time I walked past St. Vincent's Hospital and did not relive the anguish and suspense I knew inhabited that building. We visited Liz Hauser and her boys in Syosset or Harry in Maryland, but usually we drove with Liz north to the snow. There was tremendous release in skiing, in expending our energy in action, not emotion, in having companionship away from the cockpit of our difficulties. Sometimes rapport broke down when I tried to teach them to ski. Meredith said, "I want to do it my own way." Helena said, "I don't want to learn. I'd rather teach people to ski than learn."

Building my morale by rebuilding my body, I was more able now to relish the perquisites of single fatherhood. Busy men, I suspect, are not often close to their young daughters. They remain idealized figures, a little scary, so rare and exciting that, when they come home, as Helena once said about me, "it's like Christmas." Nowadays Meredith and Helena witnessed me being all too human, and they became to me entire little persons. I could watch with pleasure their teetering balance between dependency and self-assertion. Helena took a proprietary interest in my appearance, picking my neckties when I went out at night, standing on the bed behind me and combing my hair into weird styles. When I put on a new pair of light-blue summer pants, she said scathingly, "You look like those suburban jerks who wear coats with patches all over them." When I stayed in bed with a sore throat, she imperiously knotted a sock around my neck. When she herself was sick and I started to do the same, she pushed away my hand, saying, "You're not going to tie a silly sock around *my* neck."

I once asked Helena, "Are fathers easier to get your way with?" She said, "They're more casual," and she was right. The girls were growing up in a looser framework, and partly because of the male-female dynamic, partly because of our past, they were still indulged. I remember talking to Liz Hauser in the kitchen one evening after hearing a teacher's report on Meredith's lack of effort. I was incensed and full of dire threats to eliminate TV. That night, full of resolution, I went in to her and sat on the edge of the bed. But I saw the small face on the pillow, her delicacy, her fragility. I kissed her good night on those small, soft lips, which often brought back the feel of Little Whitney's. I said, "Good night, Mere. Hit the road to dreamland."

She said, "Okay, I'll put myself to sleep by following a road in my mind."

I said, "Suppose you come to a stop sign."

She laughed and said, "You're a funny daddy."

During that second year after Hope's death, normality moved back into our lives steadily and subtly—like fog. Meredith began to speak spontaneously about her mother, telling me, "Mommy and I used to read this catalogue together," or, "On this road I had to grab the steering wheel when Mommy let go of it to fix her hair." Sometimes now, like Helena, she came up to me in the night, but briefly, to touch base.

My own grief seemed to exit from my stomach, pass up and through my chest, and linger for a time in my head as a vague, self-pitying melancholy. Eventually that, too, was finally gone. As my life became more ordinary, I was no longer seeing all behavior in the context of mourning. Once Meredith fought with Helena over whose turn it was to set the table and then lay on her bed sobbing to me, "Tell Henny to run away, tell her to kill herself; if she did, I'd jump for joy." I thought of her appalling reaction as Meredith after a bad day at school, not as Meredith after losing her mother. When Helena complained bitterly about the way Meredith treated her, I no longer coddled her like a tender vessel of sorrow. I told her that she often provoked Meredith, and I said, "You shouldn't feel unusually abused; all siblings fight."

"Not Dick and Jane," said Helena.

When we had wonderful family times together, I no longer saw us as survivors temporarily evading grief, but I did have a sensation of breaking out into light and staying there longer and longer. And that is my impression of our second year of mourning. I remember us on a warm March day on a Vermont mountaintop skiing all in a line, turning in each other's tracks, exhilarated, linked together. I remember cooking hamburgers in the backyard in the spring and Meredith calling, "Watch me," and, balletlike, swinging her leg over a bouncing ball—"One, two, three O'Leary, O'Leary . . ." I remember an overnight camping trip that summer by a lake with Liz Hauser. Helena spent an hour arranging an elaborate, woodland toilet, and then I was led over to admire it. Meredith begged me for a ghost story after dinner, and I can still see the glee on her firelit face as "the little girl named Meredith reached out to touch the old man and her hand passed right through him." Then the four of us in the full moonlight canoed on the black water, so calm, so full of stars, it seemed a second sky.

Now, by the second year after Hope's death, Liz Hauser was deep in my affections and family. I remember the way my heart lifted when I said on the telephone, "See you tonight," and she answered, "Yes, isn't it exciting." I remember holding her in my arms and saying, "You are really with me, aren't you," and she answered, "I am. I am. But, of course, if you didn't kiss so nicely . . ." And there was the day she said, "You feel better, don't you. I can tell by the way *I* feel."

Helena still complained occasionally, "I don't want Liz around all the time," but then admitted, "When she's not here, I wonder, 'Where's Liz?'" Like Meredith, she did welcome Liz's warmth and energy and motherly services: helping to find the hairbrush, rinsing out the shirt needed the next morning, drilling her in spelling words. All winter Helena had not wanted a good-night kiss from Liz, who never pressured but waited. Then one day on a walk Helena's hand came up naturally into hers. One night at home, laughing together, Helena glued on Liz's forehead an address sticker reading, "c/o Richard Mery-man." That July Helena went with Whitney for two weeks in California, and afterwards Liz drove her up to Dublin from New York. They began to sing everything they said to each other, and on their arrival performed a song they had concocted — dancing a little soft-shoe step, arms linked, chanting, "A family, a great big family . . ."

But Helena that second summer was still partially in mourning, was still wearing out her concentration on Hope. Sometimes she sat dazed and dreamy-eyed, dwelling on her mother. "I smile at the corners of my mouth," she told me, "because I loved her so much and love her now." So Helena must have worried about attaching herself to Liz, fearing that Liz, too, might suddenly disappear. She must have suffered unhappy pangs of disloyalty, wrenching between affection for Liz and fidelity to her mother. She set high standards for me. When the beautiful girls in the TV perfume ads appeared on the screen, Helena, only half joking, rushed to cover my eyes.

I could see that a future wife must not move into a widower's life suddenly and assertively, impressing her personality and habits on the household. Her presence must come as an evolution. It takes many months of shared games, arguments, crises, and gradual accommodation before the new woman can be an unthreatening part of the family flow and not a boulder in midstream — the man torn between loyalty to her and loyalty to the resentful children, who see her forever as an interloper. I recognized Helena's back-and-forth ambivalence because I myself sometimes shared it. When Liz unknowingly drank from Hope's favorite coffee mug, I thought, "How dare she."

I still talked too much about Hope, still suffered a sort of hangover of the spirit, still could be pensive and tiresomely indecisive. When people perfunctorily asked me, "How are you?" I still emphasized the negative, perhaps subconsciously the tragic — "I can't get rid of this sense of a weight on my life." I told myself that finishing the Mankiewicz book would be my graduating catharsis, the period marking the end of the third phase. After a summer-long, seven-days-a-week dash, I delivered the manuscript to my agent and in his office was ecstatic, intoxicated, triumphant. Then, out on the sidewalk of Madison Avenue, tears streamed down my face. People stared. In my head Hope's voice said again, "I'll never be able to read your book."

The days that followed were filled with my last panic. The book, I realized, had been a cocoon protecting me from facing my professional future after Hope. Now my old nighttime terrors returned at noontime. How was I going to live? Would anybody remember me without *Life?* I wrote letters to several editors I knew, and to my overwhelming relief, *McCall's* assigned me an interview with Carol Burnett. A few days later I found myself in Hollywood sitting across from the woman who had made Hope laugh throughout the illness — on rented TVs in the hospital and at home with all of us sprawled across the bed — the woman I was accustomed to seeing past Hope's bandanna-covered head. Carol Burnett talked at length about her difficult childhood. I soon understood that she was the product of her philosophy of positivism. She said, "It's easy to blame outside circumstances and tell yourself, 'I can't do that; I have this to take care of; I'm under these pressures.' But you are responsible for you."

During a post-college adventure, I rode a freight car across the plains of the Dakotas, and occasionally, like a perfectly aimed silver dart, the bel canto call of a meadowlark would pierce through the rattle and bang of the train. I thought of that out there in Hollywood. Carol Burnett's words, though hardly silver darts, were nonetheless true, and they penetrated the cacophony of my last remaining self-pity and challenged my self-respect. I had reached the point where I was ready to hear them. The Ritual was ended. I had emancipated myself from Hope and my pain. I was set now to launch my future and to bring Meredith and Helena forward with me. I had reached that state described by Albert Camus: "Once we have accepted the fact of loss, we understand that the loved one obstructed a whole corner of the possible, pure now as a sky washed by rain. . . . Free, we seek anew."

Henceforth, when people asked how I was, I answered enthusiastically, "Fine! I'm terrific!"

In time I was.

Epilogue

In New York on Christmas Eve four years after Hope's death, Meredith, fourteen, lounged on my lap and Helena, twelve, sat on the wooden coffee table while we looked at the decorated tree. I told them that when they were little peanuts, they hung the ornaments only as high as they could reach — about four feet — until the tree wore a pretty skirt. "Mommy thought that was a kill," I said, using Hope's private word for funny.

Meredith said, "I remember Mommy once gave me a windup train that went around a track under the tree and played 'Jingle Bells,' and I was such a little jerk I thought it was really cool."

"This is the best tree we've ever had," I said.

"You say that every year," answered Helena.

I told her, "That's an important part of Christmas, doing exactly the same things over and over, year after year." And then I stopped, feeling the irony of my words. To the three of us the tree was a symbol of interruption, of the void left by Hope that would never be entirely filled. There would always be that cyst of grief which my words had just touched. I asked Helena if she still thought a great deal about Hope.

She said, "Sometimes I see a whole lot of things all at once in a sort of flash but not as much as I used to, and I feel guilty about it."

"Don't, Helena," I said. "You'll never forget Mommy and you'll always love her. Now it's right for all of us to think about the present and the future."

I knew, however, that we had not come unscathed through four years of illness and mourning. My nerves, I felt, were permanently tender, my impatience threshold low. My illusion of indestructibility, that bliss of ignorance, was gone; I would forever fear the unthinkable. And perhaps the exigencies of my own survival and single fatherhood had short-changed Meredith and Helena in the process of maturing. But with my mourning hysteria finished, with all of us settled into our new circumstances and happier, the more ordinary problems of life could be attacked and we could go forward.

Grateful for the leggy, teenage length of Meredith on my lap, squeezing her with my arms, I felt cheerful, optimistic. And I was not facing the future and its perplexities alone. Liz Hauser was now intrinsic to my life — a strength, a center for me and the children. In fact, I was at last ready to consider marriage.

John Groth had been there earlier while we decorated the tree, and now we were waiting for Liz, who had been having her Christmas Eve with her boys. She arrived, excited, calling out "Merry Christmas" and "This is *so* nice!" She had promised us a taste of her childhood Swiss tradition. With pleased concentration she began clipping holders to the tips of branches and loading them with little white candles. After Helena turned out the lights, Liz lit the candles one by one till there in front of us was the tree from every European Christmas story we had ever read — the glint of the tiny flames turning the balls to colored stars.

The tree was now a symbol of change, the most radical of all, a change of ritual. Yet I felt a wonderful peacefulness and pleasure. The spring in Meredith's body was softening. Helena's face was rapt, open, clear. I wished them many such moments of love and joy — and wondered, as I often did, about their lives that lay ahead.

But I believe that the pain of Hope's death had left us especially tender to the touch of joy, anger, love — and if feeling is living, we three will always be twice alive. That is the way I see survival now. It is not simply emerging from the long, dark tunnel unharmed and comfortable. It is finding the part of your tragedy that can be a blessing. It is enduring the entire experience to its dregs and then turning your loss into a rebirth, into Christmas. I said in the quiet of the room, "It's very beautiful."